The Autobiography of
John Stuart Mill

Edited by
A. O. J. Cockshut

Ryburn Publishing

Mill's *Autobiography* was first published in 1873
Ryburn Library Edition published in 1992
Ryburn Publishing Limited
Krumlin Halifax

ISBN 1 85331 026 3 *Imperial Bonded Leather
Limited Edition of 250 copies*

ISBN   1 85331 017 4 *Library Buckram*

ISBN   1 85331 032 8 *Sewn Paperback*

Composed by Ryburn Publishing Services
Bound in Edinburgh by Hunter & Foulis
Printed by Ryburn Book Production, Halifax, England

Contents

Introduction

Though autobiography is a form of art, and potentially of art equal to the highest, there are several reasons why Mill's tends to resist aesthetic judgement. First, it is a palimpsest, rather than a single work. It was constantly subject to alteration over a period of many years. His wife influenced the earliest version; and his step-daughter the final one. And he was always more concerned with the accurate presentation of facts than with the inner development and total meaning of his life. One vital quality of the true autobiographer, however, he had which many celebrated predecessors and successors lacked, perfect sincerity. In this he equals Newman, and far excels all those who tailor facts to fit the lights and shades of a satisfying self-portrait.

When the first version was being written in the spring of 1854, he was working against time, contemplating a very early death, writing in his journal things like this:

> The only change I find in myself from a near view of probable death is that it makes me instinctively conservative.

and

> I look upon it as a piece of excellent fortune to have the whole summer to die in.[1]

His marriage to Harriet Taylor was less than three years old. She read and marked his manuscript; in response to this he suppressed family details (so that in the final published version his mother, for instance, does not feature at all), and softened, though he did not remove, many self-deprecating phrases.

Writing to his wife on 10 February 1854, he says:

> But of what particularly concerns *our* life there is nothing yet written except the descriptions of you, and of your effect on me; which are at all events a permanent memorial of what I know you to be ... & and of what I owe to you *intellectually*.... But we have

to consider, which we can only do together, how much of our story it is advisable to tell, in order to make head against the representations of enemies.... If it was not to be published for 100 years I should say, tell all, simply and without reserve.[2]

Two points, to which I shall return, stand out here, that the book was conceived as a celebration of Harriet more than of himself, and that he was anxious about their good reputation for sexual purity in the years of association before marriage. Returning to the task as a widower in 1861, he was more detached, less severe on other people (dropping, for instance, a sharp character-sketch of Sarah Austin, and softening comments on Sterling), and perhaps less deeply interested in what he was writing. The last section, composed in 1869–70, seems at times almost perfunctory. Mill always seems older than his years, in youth because of precocity, in middle age because of ill-health, in later years because of the emotional bleakness consequent on his wife's death.

Mill's death in May 1873 was felt as the end of an era; he was associated with the far distant struggles of the 1820s and early '30s against the repressive legacy of the eighteenth century and the Napoleonic Wars, even though, of course, he had been in the public eye in the mid-'60s, as a Member of Parliament and campaigner for female suffrage. When the *Autobiography* appeared later the same year, many critics and reviewers took the opportunity to take stock of a past remote even for those old enough to remember it.

Curiosity about Mill's relation with Harriet Taylor, which had been intense from the 1830s to her death in 1858, was naturally revived. Some of Mill's closest friends wondered whether the whole project of telling their story, which had been so dear to Mill's heart, was not misconceived. Alexander Bain, a life-long friend and associate, wrote to Helen Taylor on 6 September 1873:

> I greatly doubt the propriety of your printing ... Harriet ... greater poet than Carlyle ... greater thinker than himself ... greater leader than his father. I venture to express the opinion that no such combination has ever been realized in the whole history of the human race.[3]

By writing this he was inaugurating a controversy which has continued to the present day. Mrs Grote thought Harriet stupid. Leslie Stephen, his natural bluntness of speech struggling perhaps with traditional ideas of chivalry, wrote:

It may be true that Mrs Mill was more of a poet than Carlyle, and more of a thinker than Mill himself; that she was like Shelley, but that Shelley was but a child.... It may, I say, be true, for one cannot prove a negative.... Yet it is a weakness, though an amiable weakness ... to try to dictate to the world an opinion which it cannot receive upon any single authority.[4]

He goes on, however, to suggest, that Mill may not have been exaggerating what Harriet did for Mill's lonely heart.

Many commentators, at the time and since, have suggested that she was an echo, who pleased Mill by returning his opinions in more shapely and softer form. Whether we agree with this or not, we must note that Mill was aware of this as a possible interpretation, and strenuously rejected it.

All the leading reviews gave the book full treatment in the winter of 1973–4. Henry Reeve, writing in the *Edinburgh*, showed that he was a sharer in that journal's long memory, going back to Macaulay's epic struggle against James Mill more than forty years before. His appeal, like Macaulay's, was to history, common sense and experience against theory:

A course of argument sustained with inimitable subtlety and art, landed him at last in conclusions which the common sense of a child would have rejected.[5]

He blames Mill for describing mediocre people, his own acolytes, as being of the highest eminence, but nevertheless pays the highest compliment of comparing the work to the achievements of St Augustine and Rousseau. He is one of several reviewers who seize on the important point that James Mill's revolt against Christianity was a revolt against Calvinism, a perverted form of it, and that he did not know or wish to know much of real Christianity.

Abraham Hayward in *Fraser's Magazine* was more severe:

... an attempt has been made to pass off as a model of philosophic candour a book which is undoubtedly defaced by a great deal of calm and concentrated though unconscious egotism ...[6]

He notes the absence of Mill's mother and siblings, and, in a rather extreme passage, compares the reproaches against his father (more implied than stated in the published version) to those of the monster to his creator in Mary Shelley's *Frankenstein*. He is sure that the utilitarian doctrines have been immensely harmful, and dwells with pleasure on Gladstone's withdrawal of his original agreement to subscribe to a memorial.

In the *Quarterly*, an old and doughty opponent of the *Westminster*, Bentham and James Mill, F.T. Palgrave, (the editor of the *Golden Treasury*), reminded his readers that James Mill has been demolished for ever by Macaulay; and shrewdly observed that:

> declamation and sentiment are often not fused with his logic, but ... suspended in it mechanically.[7]

His paradoxes were both pointed and elegant:

> The passionate lover of freedom and individuality – yet more than any man we know of similar power the creature of external circumstance ... truly lovable yet almost without the charm of love ... at the same time an iconoclast and an idolater.

J.M. Capes in the *Contemporary Review* tends to take away with one hand what he gives with the other; for, after saying that the book is one of the most important and instructive pieces of self-portraiture ever given to the world, and comparing Mill's achievement to Newman's, he complains that men and women are reduced to abstractions, while ideas appear to possess for Mill a superior reality. He sees Harriet as a substitute in Mill's heart for an absent God. He also neatly points out that Mill was mistaken in saying there was no Greek–English lexicon at the time when he was struggling on the floor of his father's study with a Greek–Latin dictionary which hardly helped him. It was characteristic of James Mill, he thinks, to ignore the Greek–English dictionary which did exist, because it had been composed for the purpose of translating the Bible.[8]

It was natural that John Morley in the *Fortnightly Review*, a much closer sympathizer with Mill's religious and political views than any of the others, should try to redress the balance. Mill's self-effacement before father, wife and step-daughter, absurd or incomprehensible to most other reviewers, is impressive to him; and he is inclined to rebuke other reviewers for their insensibility to the grandeur of Mill's theme and thought.[9]

It is interesting that the first readers, who had not yet had the opportunity of reading the posthumous *Three Essays on Religion*, all assumed that Mill's attitude to Christianity had been to the end wholly negative. Morley approved of this; while W.R. Browne, in a lecture for the Christian Evidence Society, maintained that Mill's argument against religion would be convincing 'on one assumption.... It is the assumption that man is not a free agent, that he is in the hands of God exactly as a machine is in the hands of its maker'. The anti-religious arguments these writers found in the *Autobiography* were really much more those of James Mill (and to a certain extent of Harriet) than his own. Only when the *Three Essays* were published was a more balanced view possible.[10]

We must turn to the complex question of the relation of Mill's autobiographical account with what we can learn of his life from other sources. The first difficult problem is his relation with his mother and siblings. For a view totally different from Mill's own, which nevertheless must have great authority, we turn to the evidence of his sister, Harriet. She wrote:

> My poor mother's married life must have been a frightfully hard one, from first to last: I hope and think that the eighteen following years [by which she survived her husband] always excepting the desertion of her eldest son, were years of satisfaction and enjoyment. Here was an instance of two persons, a husband and wife, living as far apart under the same roof, as the north pole from the south.... I have no recollection of John's ever teaching me Latin – the only thing my father professed to teach us, expecting us, however to know everything else and abusing us for our ignorance if we did not.[11]

Mary Taylor, grand-daughter of Harriet, and niece of Helen wrote:

> An unconquerable and deplorable resentment makes him [JSM] silent on his mother

and

> They [the family] recognize that he is cruel and insulting to them, and they suffer acutely, but their affection is as irrevocable as his resentment.[12]

We can place beside this evidence that of Roebuck, a very old friend. When he saw Harriet Taylor in 1834 (her husband, of course, still alive) enter a room hanging on Mill's arm:

> My affection for Mill was so warm and sincere that I was hurt by anything which brought ridicule upon him ... I determined, most unwisely to speak to him ...[13]

He remonstrated. Mill listened, but at their next meeting made it clear that their friendship was at an end.

Against this, we have one piece of welcome evidence that Mill did retain some feeling for the long-suffering mother, even if, perhaps, she never knew it. In a letter to his wife, 11 April 1854, when his mother was near her end, he wrote:

> I am sorry to say darling that I had two notes from Clara and Mary both saying that my mother is very ill …[14]

Taking all this together we may conclude: James Mill despised his wife, and was harsh and ill-tempered with her and his children. John was so much under his father's spell that he found it less painful to suppose that his mother was to blame for the injuries she suffered. Later, he was so obsessed with Harriet Taylor (possibly subconsciously aware that no-one in his senses could adulate her as he did) that he was implacable towards mother, sisters and old male friend if they could not sincerely echo his fatuous praises.

His mother's offences against Harriet Taylor were entirely imaginary; she did her very best to please her son in this as in every other matter. It is hard to say whether her omission from the final version, when she had been mentioned (though somewhat slightingly) in the early draft, is due to resentment, refuelled by her inability to please him over his marriage, or to a feeling that it was more decent and filial to omit her altogether than to give such a faint impression of her.

Mill's relation to his father is somewhat less enigmatic, though here, too, the *Autobiography*, taken alone, might be very misleading.

The salient point is that Mill could not admit to himself either his intellectual divergence from, or his inner moral criticism of, his father. On the first, about which a great deal might be written, we may be content with the definitive statement of John Plamenatz:

> There is not much left of Benthamite utilitarianism when John Stuart Mill has completed his defence of it. What is left is, strictly speaking, not utilitarianism at all …[15]

His inability to understand that this was so, his continued proclamation that he was a utilitarian, as he proceeded to demolish utilitarian arguments, must surely have been due to a deeper inability to come to terms with his father's image in his memory. In 1833, he professes to be unaware of Macaulay's dialectical victory over his father in the *Edinburgh Review*, complaining:

> Mr. Macauley [sic] – assuming, I suppose, the divine prerogative

of genius – only entered the contest, in order to carry away the argument he protected in a cloud of words.[16]

It would be hard to imagine a more misleading account of Macaulay's style of argument. Mill makes him sound like his eternal opposite, Carlyle. Equally significant is his failure to perceive, in his account of his recovery from the crisis of 1826, the obvious meaning of the subject of the work of Marmontel which he was reading: the death of his father.

This unawareness of the depths of his own feelings about his father is reflected also in the realm of ideas. Many of his opinions and judgements of value are in opposition to those of Bentham and his father. Take for instance his view of poetry:

> ... eloquence is *heard*, poetry is overheard. Eloquence supposes an audience; the peculiarity of poetry appears to us to lie in the poet's utter unconsciousness of a listener.[17]

Bentham and his father, immersed in their world of bustling practicalities, would have gaped in astonishment at such a sentimental doctrine. Mill's peculiarity here, which makes him especially easy to misinterpret, is that he is willing to wander to an unlimited distance away from Bentham's and his father's track, so long as he is not speaking or thinking of them. But when his attention returns to them (and in the *Autobiography* it is seldom far away) then an inner censor inhibits criticism, and tries to obviate disagreement.

All this makes Mill a most unusual figure among the leading writers of the nineteenth century – or perhaps of any time. Wordsworth, Shelley, Carlyle, Macaulay, Dickens (and the list could be lengthened indefinitely) have all a natural dominance, a sense of their own rightness, a conviction that they were born to instruct their contemporaries. Mill, equal in intellect, though perhaps not in genius, to any of these, alone underrates himself, and shelters behind those who seemed to him (though not to us) his obvious superiors. First his father is dominant, then Harriet Taylor, then Helen. Even more striking, perhaps, than his published tributes to these three are the signs of practical subservience, and deference to their supposed wisdom. One example may suffice, because so many could easily be given:

> About the matter of my mother's inheritance, of course as your feeling is so directly contrary, mine is wrong, and I give up entirely ...[18]

Now it is obvious that James Mill, Harriet and Helen were unalike, except in this one point of having dominance over Mill. We are dealing not, as he thought, with three persons of unparalleled genius, but with three who responded to Mill's need to worship and submit.

Here, perhaps, we approach the easily-missed strangeness of Mill's personality. He had a powerful intelligence, feelings of terrible strength, and very little imagination. He lacked even that humdrum kind of imagination that makes commonplace people realize that their concerns and affections are indifferent to other people. For most of us, a few people are uniquely important because of irreplaceable ties. There is nothing unusual in the influences (father, wife, step-daughter) that were decisive for Mill's emotional life. What is very unusual is his unawareness that in this he was comparable to millions of others. He wanted to *generalize* his affections. Instead of assuming, as most people tacitly do, that others have ties and feelings comparable to their own, he thought and wrote as if no-one else had ever had a father or wife or daughter. He experienced his strong affections, and his unusually strong powers of admiration as definitive judgements. The result was that he tried to assimilate three rather ordinary people (one of whom – his father – possessed some talent) to the great geniuses of the centuries. He was totally unaware of confusing his affections with his intellectual judgements. Moreover, he was unable to stand back for a moment from himself, and see how this confusion would appear to others; indeed, that to unsympathetic readers it would be highly comic. Most people, even though self-love, vanity and prejudice may distort their judgement more or less, have a rough idea of the way they appear to others. Mill – and this is the unique feature of his autobiography – had none at all. He lacked self-awareness; he treated his own sensations, just as personal to himself as those of everyone else, like pointer-readings in a laboratory, or images on a telescope. This highly emotional man discounted his feelings. So his feelings appeared in the disguise of detached judgements and abstract thoughts.

To find a structural relation between Mill's reaction to James, Harriet and Helen is by no means to deny differences. Against his father there seems to have been a deep resentment, emerging occasionally into partial consciousness (as when he says he never was a boy, and never played cricket) but yet remaining for the most part hidden. There is no sign of such feeling about Harriet and Helen. The feminine in Harriet's person invaded and overwhelmed a nature whose austerity, high principles and low-toned senses left defence-less. Helen took over a man numbed with loss.

His own subservience to these two women contrasts strangely with his constant assertion that women in general are utterly dominated by men. It is amusing to notice how Harriet Taylor managed to combine treating her remarkably easy-tempered and accommodating husband as entirely subordinate to herself and Mill, with assertions that married women are only chattels. The actual variety of feminine nature in the world and in literature seemed to escape them both. Reading what both wrote about women, no-one would dream of women like Clytemnestra, or Goneril, or Clarissa, or Emma, or Mrs Poyser.

All this means that we need to read Mill's book in two different ways, and sometimes adjust from one reading to another in a few sentences. On the one hand, it is the fullest, most informative and most accurate account of an intellectual milieu of abiding historical importance. On the other, it is a truthful but uncomprehending self-portrait of one of the strangest men that ever lived.

Notes to the Introduction

1. F.A. Hayek, *John Stuart Mill and Harriet Taylor*, (1951), pp.203–4
2. Hayek, op. cit., p.194
3. Mill-Taylor collection, vol. 14, item 5
4. Leslie Stephen, *Hours in a Library*, 3 vols, New Ed. (1892), Vol III, p.263
5. *Edinburgh Review*, January 1874
6. *Fraser's Magazine*, December 1873
7. *Quarterly Review*, January 1874
8. *Contemporary Review*, December 1873
9. *Fortnightly Review*, January 1874
10. See my *The Unbelievers*, (1964), pp.19–30 for an assessment of the religious content of *Three Essays*
11. Harriet Mill to Rev. J. Crompton, 26 October 1873. Hayek, op. cit., p.286
12. Hugh S.R. Elliot (ed.), *Letters of John Stuart Mill*, 2 vols, (1910), (I xxxix & xlvi)
13. Hayek, op.cit., p.80
14. Hayek, op.cit., p.206
15. John Plamenatz, *The English Utilitarians*, 2nd Ed. (1958), p.144
16. From an unsigned appendix to Edward Lytton Bulwer, *England and the English*, (1833). See *Collected Works*, Vol I (Toronto, 1981), p.594. The misspelling of Macaulay's name is perhaps significant
17. *Poetry and its Varieties*, (1859). Quoted from 'English Critical Essays of C19', Ed. Edmund Jones, p.406. This essay was a rewriting of a much earlier production
18. Letter to Harriet, 4 July 1854. Hayek, op.cit., p.210

The Autobiography of
John Stuart Mill

A page from the Rylands Transcript of Mill's autobiography, reproduced by courtesy of the Director and University Librarian, the John Rylands University Library of Manchester. Many of the errors and alterations in the first and subsequent printed editions originated with the transcript. This edition returns to the text from which the transcript was copied.

Explanatory notes (pp.223–252) are indicated by a dagger, thus †
and textual notes (pp.213–222) by a double dagger ‡
whilst Mill's own notes appear as numbered
footnotes to the body text

CHAPTER I

Childhood, and Early Education

It seems proper that I should prefix to the following biographical sketch, some mention of the reasons which have made me think it desirable that I should leave behind me such a memorial of so uneventful a life as mine. I do not for a moment imagine that any part of what I have to relate, can be interesting to the public as a narrative, or as being connected with myself. But I have thought that in an age in which education, and its improvement, are the subject of more, if not of profounder study than at any former period of English history, it may be useful that there should be some record of an education which was unusual and remarkable, and which, whatever else it may have done, has proved how much more than is commonly supposed may be taught, and well taught, in those early years which, in the common modes of what is called instruction, are little better than wasted. It has also seemed to me that in an age of transition in opinions, there may be somewhat both of interest and of benefit in noting the successive phases of any mind which was always pressing forward, equally ready to learn and to unlearn either from its own thoughts or from those of others. But a motive which weighs more with me than either of these, is a desire to make acknowledgment of the debts which my intellectual and moral development owes to other persons; some of them of recognised eminence, others less known than they deserve to be, and the one to whom most of all is due, one whom the world had no opportunity of knowing. The reader whom these things do not interest, has only himself to blame if he reads farther, and I do not desire any other indulgence from him than that of bearing in mind, that for him these pages were not written.

I was born in London, on the 20th of May 1806, and was the eldest son of James Mill, the author of *The History of British India.*† My father, the son of a petty tradesman and (I believe) small farmer, at Northwater Bridge, in the county of Angus, was, when a boy, recommended by his abilities to the notice of Sir John Stuart, of Fettercairn, one of the Barons of the Exchequer in Scotland, and was,

1

in consequence, sent to the University of Edinburgh at the expense of a fund established by Lady Jane Stuart (the wife of Sir John Stuart) and some other ladies for educating young men for the Scottish Church. He there went through the usual course of study, and was licensed as a Preacher, but never followed the profession; having satisfied himself that he could not believe the doctrines of that or any other Church. For a few years he was a private tutor in various families in Scotland, among others that of the Marquis of Tweeddale; but ended by taking up his residence in London, and devoting himself to authorship. Nor had he any other means of support until 1819, when he obtained an appointment in the India House.†

In this period of my father's life there are two things which it is impossible not to be struck with: one of them unfortunately a very common circumstance, the other a most uncommon one. The first is, that in his position, with no resource but the precarious one of writing in periodicals, he married and had a large family; conduct than which nothing could be more opposed, both as a matter of good sense and of duty, to the opinions which, at least at a later period of life, he strenuously upheld.‡ The other circumstance, is the extra-ordinary energy which was required to lead the life he led, with the disadvantages under which he laboured from the first, and with those which he brought upon himself by his marriage. It would have been no small thing, had he done no more than to support himself and his family during so many years by writing, without ever being in debt, or in any pecuniary difficulty; holding, as he did, opinions, both in politics and in religion, which were more odious to all persons of influence, and to the common run of prosperous Englishmen, in that generation than either before or since;† and being not only a man whom nothing would have induced to write against his convictions, but one who invariably threw into everything he wrote, as much of his convictions as he thought the circumstances would in any way permit: being, it must also be said, one who never did anything negligently; never undertook any task, literary or other, on which he did not conscientiously bestow all the labour necessary for per-forming it adequately. But he, with these burthens on him, planned, commenced, and completed, the *History of India*; and this in the course of about ten years, a shorter time than has been occupied (even by writers who had no other employment) in the production of almost any other historical work of equal bulk, and of anything approaching to the same amount of reading and research. And to this is to be added, that during the whole period, a considerable part of almost every day was employed in the instruction of his children: in the case of one of whom, myself, he exerted an amount of labour, care, and perseverance rarely, if ever, employed for a similar purpose, in endeavouring to give, according to his own conception, the highest order of intellectual education.

A man who, in his own practice, so vigorously acted up to the principle of losing no time, was likely to adhere to the same rule in the instruction of his pupil. I have no remembrance of the time when I began to learn Greek. I have been told that it was when I was three years old. My earliest recollection on the subject, is that of committing to memory what my father termed Vocables, being lists of common Greek words, with their signification in English, which he wrote out for me on cards. Of grammar, until some years later, I learnt no more than the inflexions of the nouns and verbs, but, after a course of vocables, proceeded at once to translation; and I faintly remember going through Æsop's *Fables*,[†] the first Greek book which I read. The *Anabasis*,[†] which I remember better, was the second. I learnt no Latin until my eighth year. At that time I had read, under my father's tuition, a number of Greek prose authors, among whom I remember the whole of Herodotus,[†] and of Xenophon's *Cyropædia*[†] and *Memorials of Socrates*;[†] some of the lives of the philosophers by Diogenes Laertius;[†] part of Lucian,[†] and Isocrates[†] *Ad Demonicum* and *Ad Nicoclem*. I also read, in 1813, the first six dialogues[†] (in the common arrangement) of Plato, from the *Euthyphron* to the *Theætetus* inclusive: which last dialogue, I venture to think, would have been better omitted, as it was totally impossible I should understand it. But my father, in all his teaching, demanded of me not only the utmost that I could do, but much that I could by no possibility have done. What he was himself willing to undergo for the sake of my instruction, may be judged from the fact, that I went through the whole process of preparing my Greek lessons in the same room and at the same table at which he was writing: and as in those days Greek and English lexicons were not,[†] and I could make no more use of a Greek and Latin lexicon than could be made without having yet begun to learn Latin, I was forced to have recourse to him for the meaning of every word which I did not know. This incessant interruption he, one of the most impatient of men, submitted to, and wrote under that interruption several volumes of his *History* and all else that he had to write during those years.

The only thing besides Greek, that I learnt as a lesson in this part of my childhood, was arithmetic: this also my father taught me: it was the task of the evenings, and I well remember its disagreeableness. But the lessons were only a part of the daily instruction I received. Much of it consisted in the books I read by myself, and my father's discourses to me, chiefly during our walks. From 1810 to the end of 1813 we were living in Newington Green,† then an almost rustic neighbourhood. My father's health required considerable and constant exercise, and he walked habitually before breakfast, generally in the green lanes towards Hornsey.† In these walks I always accompanied him, and with my earliest recollections of green fields and wild flowers, is mingled that of the account I gave him daily of what I had read the day before. To the best of my remembrance, this was a voluntary rather than a prescribed exercise. I made notes on slips of paper while reading, and from these, in the morning walks, I told the story to him; for the books were chiefly histories, of which I read in this manner a great number: Robertson's histories,† Hume,† Gibbon;† but my greatest delight, then and for long afterwards, was Watson's *Philip the Second* and *Third*.† The heroic defence of the Knights of Malta against the Turks, and of the revolted provinces of the Netherlands against Spain, excited in me an intense and lasting interest. Next to Watson, my favorite historical reading was Hooke's *History of Rome*.† Of Greece I had seen at that time no regular history, except school abridgments and the last two or three volumes of a translation of Rollin's *Ancient History*,† beginning with Philip of Macedon. But I read with great delight Langhorne's translation of Plutarch.† In English history, beyond the time at which Hume leaves off, I remember reading Burnet's *History of His Own Time*,† though I cared little for anything in it except the wars and battles; and the historical part of the *Annual Register*, from the beginning to about 1788, where the volumes my father borrowed for me from Mr. Bentham† left off. I felt a lively interest in Frederic of Prussia† during his difficulties, and in Paoli,† the Corsican patriot; but when I came to the American war,† I took my part, like a child as I was (until set right by my father) on the wrong side, because it was called the English side. In these frequent talks about the books I read, he used, as opportunity offered, to give me explanations and ideas respecting civilization, government, morality, mental cultivation, which he required me afterwards to restate to him in my own words. He also made me read, and give him a verbal account of, many books which would not have interested me sufficiently to induce me to read them of myself: among others, Millar's *Historical View of the English Government*,† a book of great merit for its time, and which he

4

highly valued; Mosheim's *Ecclesiastical History*,[†] McCrie's *Life of John Knox*,[†] and even Sewell's[†] and Rutty's[†] histories of the Quakers. He was fond of putting into my hands books which exhibited men of energy and resource in unusual circumstances, struggling against difficulties and overcoming them: of such works I remember Beaver's *African Memoranda*,[†] and Collins's account of the first settlement of New South Wales.[†] Two books which I never wearied of reading were Anson's *Voyage*,[†] so delightful to most young persons, and a collection (Hawkesworth's, I believe) of Voyages round the World,[†] in four volumes, beginning with Drake[†] and ending with Cook[†] and Bougainville.[†] Of children's books, any more than of playthings, I had scarcely any, except an occasional gift from a relation or acquaintance: among those I had, *Robinson Crusoe*[†] was preeminent, and continued to delight me through all my boyhood. It was no part however of my father's system to exclude books of amusement, though he allowed them very sparingly. Of such books he possessed at that time next to none, but he borrowed several for me; those which I remember are, the *Arabian Nights*,[†] Cazotte's *Arabian Tales*,[†] *Don Quixote*,[†] Miss Edgeworth's *Popular Tales*,[†] and a book of some reputation in its day, Brooke's *Fool of Quality*.[†]

In my eighth year I commenced learning Latin, in conjunction with a younger sister, to whom I taught it as I went on, and who afterwards repeated the lessons to my father: and from this time, other sisters and brothers being successively added as pupils, a considerable part of my day's work consisted of this preparatory teaching. It was a part which I greatly disliked; the more so, as I was held responsible for the lessons of my pupils, in almost as full a sense as for my own: I however derived from this discipline the great advantage, of learning more thoroughly and retaining more lastingly the things which I was set to teach: perhaps, too, the practice it afforded in explaining difficulties to others, may even at that age have been useful. In other respects, the experience of my boyhood is not favorable to the plan of teaching children by means of one another. The teaching, I am sure, is very inefficient as teaching, and I well know that the relation between teacher and taught is not a good moral discipline to either. I went in this manner through the Latin grammar, and a considerable part of Cornelius Nepos[†] and Caesar's *Commentaries*,[†] but afterwards added to the superintendance of these lessons, much longer ones of my own.

In the same year in which I began Latin, I made my first commencement in the Greek poets with the *Iliad*.[†] After I had made some progress in this, my father put Pope's translation[†] into my hands. It was the first English verse I had cared to read, and it became one of the books in which for many years I most delighted: I think I must have read it from twenty to thirty times through. I should not have thought it worth while to mention a taste apparently so natural to boyhood, if I had not, as I think, observed that the keen enjoyment of this brilliant specimen of narrative and versification is not so universal with boys, as I should have expected both *a priori* and from my individual experience. Soon after this time I commenced Euclid,[†] and somewhat later, algebra, still under my father's tuition.

From my eighth to my twelfth year, the Latin books which I remember reading were, the *Bucolics* of Virgil,[†] and the first six books of the *Æneid*;[†] all Horace, except the *Epodes*;[†] the *Fables* of Phædrus;[†] the first five books of Livy[†] (to which from my love of the subject I voluntarily added, in my hours of leisure, the remainder of the first decad); all Sallust;[†] a considerable part of Ovid's *Metamorphoses*;[†] some plays of Terence;[†] two or three books of Lucretius;[†] several of the Orations of Cicero,[†] and of his writings on oratory; also his letters to Atticus,[†] my father taking the trouble to translate to me from the French the historical explanations in Mongault's notes. In Greek I read the *Iliad* and *Odyssey*[†] through; one or two plays of Sophocles,[†] Euripides,[†] and Aristophanes,[†] though by these I profited little; all Thucydides;[†] the *Hellenics*[†] of Xenophon; a great part of Demosthenes,[†] Æschines, and Lysias;[†] Theocritus;[†] Anacreon;[†] part of the *Anthology*;[†] a little of Dionysius;[†] several books of Polybius;[†] and lastly, Aristotle's *Rhetoric*,[†] which, as the first expressly scientific treatise on any moral or psychological subject which I had read, and containing many of the best observations of the ancients on human nature and life, my father made me study with peculiar care, and throw the matter of it into synoptic tables. During the same years I learnt elementary geometry and algebra thoroughly, the differential calculus and other portions of the higher mathematics far from thoroughly: for my father, not having kept up this part of his early acquired knowledge, could not spare time to qualify himself for removing my difficulties, and left me to deal with them, with little other aid than that of books: while I was continually incurring his displeasure by my inability to solve difficult problems for which he did not see that I had not the necessary previous knowledge.

As to my private reading, I can only speak of what I remember. History continued to be my strongest predilection, and most of all ancient history. Mitford's *Greece*[†] I read continually.[‡] My father had

6

put me on my guard against the Tory prejudices of this writer, and his perversions of facts for the whitewashing of despots, and blackening of popular institutions. These points he discoursed on, exemplifying them from the Greek orators and historians, with such effect that in reading Mitford, my sympathies were always on the contrary side to those of the author, and I could, to some extent, have argued the point against him: yet this did not diminish the ever new pleasure with which I read the book. Roman history, both in my old favorite, Hooke, and in Ferguson,† continued to delight me. A book which, in spite of what is called the dryness of its stile, I took great pleasure in, was the *Ancient Universal History*: through the incessant reading of which, I had my head full of historical details concerning the obscurest ancient people, while about modern history, except detached passages such as the Dutch war of independence, I knew and cared comparatively little. A voluntary exercise to which throughout my boyhood I was much addicted, was what I called writing histories. I successively composed a Roman history, picked out of Hooke; an abridgment of the *Ancient Universal History*; a History of Holland, from my favorite Watson and from an anony-mous compilation; and in my eleventh and twelfth year I occupied myself with writing what I flattered myself was something serious. This was no less than a history of the Roman Government, compiled (with the assistance of Hooke) from Livy and Dionysius: of which I wrote as much as would have made an octavo volume, extending to the epoch of the Licinian Laws.† It was, in fact, an account of the struggles between the patricians and plebeians, which now engrossed all the interest in my mind which I had previously felt in the mere wars and conquests of the Romans. I discussed all the constitutional points as they arose: though quite ignorant of Niebuhr's† researches, I, by such lights as my father had given me, vindicated the Agrarian Laws† on the evidence of Livy, and upheld to the best of my ability the Roman democratic party. A few years later, in my contempt of my childish efforts, I destroyed all these papers, not then anticipating that I could ever feel any curiosity about my first attempts at writing and reasoning. My father encouraged me in this useful amusement, though, as I think judiciously, he never asked to see what I wrote; so that I did not feel that in writing it I was accountable to any one, nor had the chilling sensation of being under a critical eye.

But though these exercises in history were never a compulsory lesson, there was another kind of composition which was so, namely writing verses, and it was one of the most disagreeable of my tasks.

Greek or Latin verses I did not write, nor learnt the prosody of those languages. My father, thinking this not worth the time it required, contented himself with making me read aloud to him, and correcting false quantities. I never composed at all in Greek, even in prose, and but little in Latin: not that my father could be indifferent to the value of this practice, in giving a thorough knowledge of these languages, but because there really was not time for it. The verses I was required to write were English. When I first read Pope's Homer, I ambitiously attempted to compose something of the same kind, and achieved as much as one book of a continuation of the *Iliad*. There, probably, the spontaneous promptings of my poetical ambition would have stopped; but the exercise, begun from choice, was continued by command. Conformably to my father's usual practice of explaining to me, as far as possible, the reasons for what he required me to do, he gave me, for this, as I well remember, two reasons highly charac-teristic of him. One was, that some things could be expressed better and more forcibly in verse than in prose: this, he said, was a real advantage. The other was, that people in general attached more value to verse than it deserved, and the power of writing it was, on this account, worth acquiring. He generally left me to choose my own subjects, which, as far as I remember, were mostly addresses to some mythological personage or allegorical abstraction; but he made me translate into English verse many of Horace's shorter poems: I also remember his giving me Thomson's 'Winter'† to read, and afterwards making me attempt (without book) to write something myself on the same subject. The verses I wrote were of course the merest rubbish, nor did I ever attain any facility of versification, but the practice may have been useful in making it easier for me, at a later period, to acquire readiness of expression.[1] I had read, up to this time, very little English poetry. Shakespeare my father had put into my hands, chiefly for the sake of the historical plays, from which however I went on to the others. My father never was a great admirer of Shakespeare, the English idolatry of whom he used to attack with some severity. He cared little for any English poetry except Milton† (for whom he had

---

[1] In a subsequent stage of boyhood, when these exercises had ceased to be compulsory, like most youthful writers I wrote tragedies; under the inspiration not so much of Shakespeare as of Joanna Baillie,† whose *Constantine Paleologus*† in particular appeared to me one of the most glorious of human compositions. I still think it one of the best dramas of the last two centuries.

the highest admiration), Goldsmith,[†] Burns,[†] and Gray's 'Bard',[†] which he preferred to his *Elegy*: perhaps I may add Cowper[†] and Beattie.[†] He had some value for Spenser,[†] and I remember his reading to me (unlike his usual practice of making me read to him) the first book of *The Fairie Queene*;[†] but I took little pleasure in it. The poetry of the present century he saw scarcely any merit in, and I hardly became acquainted with any of it till I was grown up to manhood, except the metrical romances of Walter Scott,[†] which I read at his recommendation and was intensely delighted with; as I always was with animated narrative. Dryden's Poems[†] were among my father's books, and many of these he made me read, but I never cared for any of them except *Alexander's Feast*,[†] which, as well as many of the songs in Walter Scott, I used to sing internally, to a music of my own: to some of the latter indeed I went so far as to compose airs, which I still remember. Cowper's short poems I read with some pleasure, but never got far into the longer ones; and nothing in the two volumes interested me like the prose account of his three hares. In my thirteenth year I met with Campbell's[†] Poems, among which 'Lochiel,' 'Hohenlinden,' 'The Exile of Erin,' and some others, gave me sensations I had never before experienced from poetry. Here, too, I made nothing of the longer poems, except the striking opening of 'Gertrude of Wyoming,' which long kept its place in my feelings as the perfection of pathos.

During this part of my childhood, one of my greatest amusements was experimental science; in the theoretical, however, not the practical sense of the word; not trying experiments, a kind of discipline which I have often regretted not having had – nor even seeing, but merely reading about them. I never remember being so wrapt up in any book, as I was in Joyce's *Scientific Dialogues*;[†] and I was rather recalcitrant to my father's criticisms of the bad reasoning respecting the first principles of physics which abounds in the early part of that work. I devoured treatises on Chemistry, especially that of my father's early friend and schoolfellow, Dr. Thomson,[†] for years before I attended a lecture or saw an experiment.[‡]

From about the age of twelve, I entered into another and more advanced stage in my course of instruction; in which the main object was no longer the aids and appliances of thought, but the thoughts themselves. This commenced with Logic, in which I began at once with the *Organon*,[†] and read it to the Analytics inclusive, but profited little by the Posterior Analytics, which belong to a branch of specu-lation I was not yet ripe for. Contemporaneously with the *Organon*, my father made me read the whole or parts of several of the Latin treatises on the scholastic logic;[†] giving each day to him, in our walks, a minute account of what I had read, and answering his numerous and searching questions. After this, I went, in a similar manner, through the 'Computatio sive Logica' of Hobbes,[†] a work of a much higher order of thought than the books of the school logicians, and which he estimated very highly; in my own opinion beyond its merits, great as these are. It was his invariable practice, whatever studies he exacted from me, to make me as far as possible understand and feel the utility of them: and this he deemed peculiarly fitting in the case of the syllogistic logic, the usefulness of which had been impugned by so many writers of authority. I well remember how, and in what particular walk, in the neighbourhood of Bagshot Heath[†] (where we were on a visit to his old friend Mr. Wallace, then one of the Mathematical Professors at Sandhurst)[†] he first attempted by questions to make me think on the subject, and frame some conception of what constituted the utility of the syllogistic logic, and when I had failed in this, to make me understand it by explanations. The explanations did not make the matter at all clear to me at the time; but they were not therefore useless; they remained as a nucleus for my observations and reflections to crystallize upon; the import of his general remarks being interpreted to me, by the particular instances which came under my notice afterwards. My own consciousness and experience ultimately led me to appreciate quite as highly as he did, the value of an early practical familiarity with the school logic. I know of nothing, in my education, to which I think myself more indebted for whatever capacity of thinking I have attained. The first intellectual operation in which I arrived at any proficiency, was dissecting a bad argument, and finding in what part the fallacy lay: and though whatever capacity of this sort I attained, was due to the fact that it was an intellectual exercise in which I was most perseveringly drilled by my father, yet it is also true that the school logic, and the mental habits acquired in studying it, were among the principal instruments of this drilling. I am persuaded that nothing, in modern education, tends so much, when properly used, to form exact thinkers, who attach a precise meaning to words and propositions, and are not imposed on by vague, loose, or ambiguous terms. The boasted influence of mathematical studies is nothing to it; for in mathematical processes, none of the real difficulties of correct ratiocination occur. It is also a study peculiarly adapted to an early stage in the education of philosophical students, since it does not

10

presuppose the slow process of acquiring, by experience and reflection, valuable thoughts of their own. They may become capable of disentangling the intricacies of confused and self-contradictory thought, before their own thinking faculties are much advanced; a power which, for want of some such discipline, many otherwise able men altogether lack; and when they have to answer opponents, only endeavour, by such arguments as they can command, to support the opposite conclusion, scarcely even attempting to confute the reasonings of their antagonists; and therefore, at the utmost, leaving the question, as far as it depends on argument, a balanced one.

During this time, the Latin and Greek books which I continued to read with my father were chiefly such as were worth studying not for the language merely, but also for the thoughts. This included much of the orators, and especially Demosthenes, some of whose principal orations I read several times over, and wrote out, by way of exercise, a full analysis of them. My father's comments on these orations when I read them to him were very instructive to me. He not only drew my attention to the insight they afforded into Athenian institutions, and the principles of legislation and government which they often illustrated, but pointed out the skill and art of the orator – how everything important to his purpose was said at the exact moment when he had brought the minds of his audience into the state most fitted to receive it; how he made steal into their minds, gradually and by insinuation, thoughts which if expressed in a more direct manner would have roused their opposition. Most of these reflections were beyond my capacity of full comprehension at the time; but they left seed behind, which germinated in due season. At this time I also read the whole of Tacitus,[†] Juvenal,[†] and Quintilian.[†] The latter, owing to his obscure stile and to the scholastic details of which many parts of his treatise are made up, is little read and seldom sufficiently appreciated. His book is a kind of encyclopædia of the thoughts of the ancients on the whole field of education and culture; and I have retained through life many valuable ideas which I can distinctly trace to my reading of him, even at that early age. It was at this period that I read, for the first time, some of the most important dialogues of Plato, in particular the *Gorgias*,[†] the *Protagoras*,[†] and the *Republic*.[†] There is no author to whom my father thought himself more indebted for his own mental culture, than Plato, or whom he more frequently recommended to young students. I can bear similar testimony in regard to myself. The Socratic method,[†] of which the Platonic dialogues are the chief example, is unsurpassed as a discipline for correcting the errors, and clearing up the confusions incident to the *intellectus sibi permissus*,† the understanding which has made up all its bundles of associations under the guidance of popular phraseology. The close, searching *elenchus*† by which the man of vague generalities† is constrained either to express his meaning to himself in definite terms, or to confess that he does not know what he is talking about; the perpetual testing of all general statements by particular instances; the siege in form which is laid to the meaning of large abstract terms, by fixing upon some still larger class-name which includes that and more, and dividing down to the thing sought – marking out its limits and definition by a series of accurately drawn distinctions between it and each of the cognate objects which are successively parted off from it – all this, as an education for precise thinking, is inestimable, and all this, even at that age, took such hold of me that it became part of my own mind. I have felt ever since that the title of Platonist belongs by far better right to those who have been nourished in, and have endeavoured to practise Plato's mode of investigation, than to those who are distinguished only by the adoption of certain dogmatical conclusions, drawn mostly from the least intelligible of his works, and which the character of his mind and writings makes it uncertain whether he himself regarded as anything more than poetic fancies, or philosophic conjectures.

In going through Plato and Demosthenes, since I could now read these authors, as far as the language was concerned, with perfect ease, I was not required to construe them sentence by sentence, but to read them aloud to my father, answering questions when asked: but the particular attention which he paid to elocution (in which his own excellence was remarkable) made this reading aloud to him a most painful task. Of all things which he required me to do, there was none which I did so constantly ill, or in which he so perpetually lost his temper with me. He had thought much on the principles of the art of reading, especially the most neglected part of it, the inflexions of the voice, or *modulation* as writers on elocution call it (in contrast with *articulation* on the one side, and *expression* on the other), and had reduced it to rules, grounded on the logical analysis of a sentence. These rules he strongly impressed upon me, and took me severely to task for every violation of them: but I even then remarked (though I did not venture to make the remark to him) that though he reproached me when I read a sentence ill, and *told* me how I ought to have read it, he never, by reading it himself, *shewed* me how it ought to be read. A defect running through his otherwise admirable modes of instruction, as it did through all his modes of thought, was that of trusting too much to the intelligibleness of the abstract, when not embodied in the concrete. It was at a much later period of my youth, when practising elocution by myself, or with companions of my own age, that I for the first time understood the object of his rules, and saw the psychological grounds of them. At that time I and others followed out the subject into its ramifications and could have composed a very useful treatise, grounded on my father's principles. He himself left those principles and rules unwritten. I regret that when my mind was full of the subject, from systematic practice, I did not put them, and our improvements of them, into a formal shape.‡

A book which contributed largely to my education, in the best sense of the term, was my father's *History of India*. It was published in the beginning of 1818. During the year previous, while it was passing through the press, I used to read the proofsheets to him; or rather, I read the manuscript to him while he corrected the proofs. The number of new ideas which I received from this remarkable book, and the impulse and stimulus as well as guidance given to my thoughts by its criticisms and disquisitions on society and civilization in the Hindoo part, on institutions and the acts of governments in the English part, made my early familiarity with it eminently useful to my subsequent progress. And though I can perceive deficiencies in it now as compared with a perfect standard, I still think it, if not the most, one of the most instructive histories ever written, and one of the books from which most benefit may be derived by a mind in the course of making up its opinions.

The Preface, among the most characteristic of my father's writings, as well as the richest in materials of thought, gives a picture which may be entirely depended on, of the sentiments and expectations with which he wrote the *History*. Saturated as the book is with the opinions and modes of judgment of a democratic radicalism then regarded as extreme; and treating with a severity at that time most unusual the English Constitution, the English law, and all parties and classes who possessed any considerable influence in the country; he may have expected reputation, but certainly not advancement in life, from its publication; nor could he have supposed that it would raise up anything but enemies for him in powerful quarters: least of all could he have expected favour from the East India Company,† to whose commercial privileges he was unqualifiedly hostile, and on the acts of whose government he had made so many severe comments: though, in various parts of his book, he bore a testimony in their

13

favour, which he felt to be their just due, namely, that no government had on the whole given so much proof, to the extent of its lights, of good intention towards its subjects; and that if the acts of any other government had the light of publicity as completely let in upon them, they would, in all probability, still less bear scrutiny.

On learning, however, in the spring of 1819, about a year after the publication of the *History*, that the East India Directors desired to strengthen the part of their home establishment which was employed in carrying on the correspondence with India, my father declared himself a candidate for that employment, and, to the credit of the Directors, successfully. He was appointed one of the Assistants of the Examiner of India Correspondence; officers whose duty it was to prepare drafts of despatches to India, for consideration by the Directors, in the principal departments of administration. In this office, and in that of Examiner, which he subsequently attained, the influence which his talents, his reputation, and his decision of character gave him, with superiors who really desired the good government of India, enabled him to a great extent to throw into his drafts of despatches, and to carry through the ordeal of the Court of Directors and Board of Control, without having their force much weakened, his real opinions on Indian subjects. In his *History* he had set forth, for the first time, many of the true principles of Indian administration:† and his despatches, following his *History*, did more than had ever been done before to promote the improvement of India, and teach Indian officials to understand their business. If a selection of them were published, they would, I am convinced, place his character as a practical statesman fully on a level with his eminence as a speculative writer.

This new employment‡ of his time caused no relaxation in his attention to my education. It was in this same year, 1819, that he took me through a complete course of political economy. His loved and intimate friend, Ricardo,† had shortly before published the book which formed so great an epoch in political economy; a book which never would have been published or written, but for the entreaty and strong encouragement of my father; for Ricardo, the most modest of men, though firmly convinced of the truth of his doctrines, deemed himself so little capable of doing them justice in exposition and expression, that he shrank from the idea of publicity. The same friendly encouragement induced Ricardo, a year or two later, to become a member of the House of Commons; where during the few remaining years of his life, unhappily cut short in the full vigour of his intellect, he rendered so much service to his and my father's opinions both in political economy and on other subjects.

Though Ricardo's great work was already in print, no didactic treatise embodying its doctrines, in a manner fit for learners, had yet appeared. My father, therefore, commenced instructing me in the science by a sort of lectures, which he delivered to me in our walks. He expounded each day a portion of the subject, and I gave him next day a written account of it, which he made me rewrite over and over again until it was clear, precise, and tolerably complete. In this manner I went through the whole extent of the science; and the written outline of it which resulted from my daily *compte rendu*, served him afterwards as notes from which to write his *Elements of Political Economy*.† After this I read Ricardo, giving an account daily of what I read, and discussing, in the best manner I could, the collateral points which offered themselves in our progress. On Money, as the most intricate part of the subject, he made me read in the same manner Ricardo's admirable pamphlets, written during what was called the Bullion controversy. To these succeeded Adam Smith;† and in this reading it was one of my father's main objects to make me apply to Smith's more superficial view of political economy, the superior lights of Ricardo, and detect what was fallacious in Smith's arguments, or erroneous in any of his conclusions. Such a mode of instruction was excellently calculated to form a thinker; but it required to be worked by a thinker, as close and vigorous as my father. The path was a thorny one even to him, and I am sure it was so to me, notwithstanding the strong interest I took in the subject. He was often, and much beyond reason, provoked by my failures in cases where success could not have been expected; but in the main his method was right, and it succeeded. I do not believe that any scientific teaching ever was more thorough, or better fitted for training the faculties, than the mode in which logic and political economy were taught to me by my father. Striving, even in an exaggerated degree, to call forth the activity of my faculties, by making me find out everything for myself, he gave his explanations not before, but after, I had felt the full force of the difficulties; and not only gave me an accurate knowledge of these two great subjects, as far as they were then understood, but made me a thinker on both. I thought for myself almost from the first, and occasionally thought differently from him, though for a long time only on minor points, and making his opinion the ultimate standard. At a later period I even occasionally convinced him, and altered his opinion on some points of detail: which I state to his honour, not my own. It at once exemplifies his perfect candour, and the real worth of his method of teaching.

At this point concluded what can properly be called my lessons. When I was about fourteen I left England for more than a year; and after my return, though my studies went on under my father's general direction, he was no longer my schoolmaster. I shall therefore pause here, and turn back to matters of a more general nature connected with the part of my life and education included in the preceding reminiscences.

In the course of instruction which I have partially retraced, the point most superficially apparent is the great effort to give, during the years of childhood, an amount of knowledge in what are considered the higher branches of education, which is seldom acquired (if acquired at all) until the age of manhood. The result of the experiment shews the ease with which this may be done, and places in a strong light the wretched waste of so many precious years as are spent in acquiring the modicum of Latin and Greek commonly taught to schoolboys; a waste, which has led so many educational reformers to entertain the ill-judged proposal of discarding those languages altogether from general education.† If I had been by nature extremely quick of apprehension, or had possessed a very accurate and retentive memory, or were of a remarkably active and energetic character, the trial would not be conclusive; but in all these natural gifts I am rather below than above par.‡ What I could do, could assuredly be done by any boy or girl of average capacity and healthy physical constitution: and if I have accomplished anything, I owe it, among other fortunate circumstances, to the fact that through the early training bestowed on me by my father, I started, I may fairly say, with an advantage of a quarter of a century over my cotemporaries.†

There was one cardinal point in this training, of which I have already given some indication, and which, more than anything else, was the cause of whatever good it effected.‡ Most boys or youths who have had much knowledge drilled into them, have their mental capacities not strengthened, but overlaid by it. They are crammed with mere facts, and with the opinions or phrases of other people, and these are accepted as a substitute for the power to form opinions of their own. And thus, the sons of eminent fathers, who have spared no pains in their education, so often grow up mere parroters of what they have learnt, incapable of using their minds except in the furrows traced for them. Mine, however, was not an education of cram. My father never permitted anything which I learnt, to degenerate into a

16

mere exercise of memory. He strove to make the understanding not only go along with every step of the teaching, but, if possible, precede it. Anything which could be found out by thinking, I never was told, until I had exhausted my efforts to find it out for myself. As far as I can trust my remembrance, I acquitted myself very lamely in this department; my recollection of such matters is almost wholly of failures, hardly ever of success. It is true, the failures were often in things in which success in so early a stage of my progress, was almost impossible. I remember at some time in my thirteenth year, on my happening to use the word idea, he asked me what an idea was; and expressed some displeasure at my ineffectual efforts to define the word: I recollect also his indignation at my using the common expression that something was true in theory but required correction in practice; and how, after making me vainly strive to define the word theory, he explained its meaning, and shewed the fallacy of the vulgar form of speech which I had used; leaving me fully persuaded that in being unable to give a correct definition of Theory, and in speaking of it as something which might be at variance with practice, I had shewn unparalleled ignorance. In this he seems, and perhaps was, very unreasonable; but I think, only in being angry at my failure. A pupil from whom nothing is ever demanded which he cannot do, never does all he can.

One of the evils most liable to attend on any sort of early proficiency, and which often fatally blights its promise, my father most anxiously guarded against. This was self conceit. He kept me, with extreme vigilance, out of the way of hearing myself praised, or of being led to make self-flattering comparisons between myself and others. From his own intercourse with me I could derive none but a very humble opinion of myself; and the standard of comparison he always held up to me, was not what other people did, but what a man could and ought to do. He completely succeeded in preserving me from the sort of influences he so much dreaded. I was not at all aware that my attainments were anything unusual at my age. If I accidentally had my attention drawn to the fact that some other boy knew less than myself – which happened less often than might be imagined – I concluded, not that I knew much, but that he, for some reason or other, knew little, or that his knowledge was of a different kind from mine. My state of mind was not humility, but neither was it arrogance. I never thought of saying to myself, I am, or I can do, so and so. I neither estimated myself highly nor lowly: I did not estimate myself at all.‡ If I thought anything about myself, it was that

I was rather backward in my studies, since I always found myself so, in comparison with what my father expected from me. I assert this with confidence, though it was not the impression of various persons who saw me in my childhood. They, as I have since found, thought me greatly and disagreeably self-conceited; probably because I was disputatious, and did not scruple to give direct contradictions to things which I heard said. I suppose I acquired this bad habit from having been encouraged in an unusual degree to talk on matters beyond my age, and with grown persons, while I never had inculcated on me the usual respect for them. My father did not correct this ill breeding and impertinence, probably from not being aware of it, for I was always too much in awe of him to be otherwise than extremely subdued and quiet in his presence.‡ Yet with all this I had no notion of any superiority in myself; and well was it for me that I had not. I remember the very place in Hyde Park where, in my fourteenth year, on the eve of leaving my father's house for a long absence, he told me that I should find, as I got acquainted with new people, that I had been taught many things which youths of my age did not commonly know; and that many persons would be disposed to talk to me of this, and to compliment me upon it. What other things he said on this topic I remember very imperfectly; but he wound up by saying, that whatever I knew more than others, could not be ascribed to any merit in me, but to the very unusual advantage which had fallen to my lot, of having a father who was able to teach me, and willing to give the necessary trouble and time; that it was no matter of praise to me, if I knew more than those who had not had a similar advantage, but the deepest disgrace to me if I did not. I have a distinct remembrance, that the suggestion thus for the first time made to me, that I knew more than other youths who were considered well educated, was to me a piece of information, to which, as to all other things which my father told me, I gave implicit credence, but which did not at all impress me as a personal matter. I felt no disposition to glorify myself upon the circumstance that there were other persons who did not know what I knew; nor had I ever flattered myself that my acquirements, whatever they might be, were any merit of mine: but now when my attention was called to the subject, I felt that what my father had said respecting my peculiar advantages was exactly the truth and common sense of the matter, and it fixed my opinion and feeling from that time forward.

It is evident that this, among many other of the purposes of my father's scheme of education, could not have been accomplished if

hc had not carefully kept me from having any great amount of intercourse with other boys. He was earnestly bent upon my escaping not
only the ordinary corrupting influence which boys exercise over
boys, but the contagion of vulgar modes of thought and feeling; and
for this he was willing that I should pay the price of inferiority in the
accomplishments which schoolboys in all countries chiefly cultivate.
The deficiencies in my education were principally in the things
which boys learn from being turned out to shift for themselves, and
from being brought together in large numbers. From temperance
and much walking, I grew up healthy and hardy, though not
muscular; but I could do no feats of skill or physical strength, and
knew none of the ordinary bodily exercises. It was not that play, or
time for it, was refused me. Though no holidays were allowed, lest
the habit of work should be broken, and a taste for idleness acquired,
I had ample leisure in every day to amuse myself; but as I had no boy
companions, and the animal need of physical activity was satisfied by
walking, my amusements, which were mostly solitary, were in general
of a quiet, if not a bookish turn, and gave little stimulus to any other
kind even of mental activity than that which was already called forth
by my studies. I consequently remained long, and in a less degree
have always remained, inexpert in anything requiring manual
dexterity; my mind, as well as my hands, did its work very lamely
when it was applied, or ought to have been applied, to the practical
details which, as they are the chief interest of life to the majority of
men, are also the things in which whatever mental capacity they
have, chiefly shews itself. I was constantly meriting reproof by
inattention, inobservance, and general slackness of mind in matters
of daily life. My father was the extreme opposite in these particulars:
his senses and mental faculties were always on the alert; he carried
decision and energy of character in his whole manner, and into every
action of life: and this, as much as his talents, contributed to the
strong impression which he always made upon those with whom he
came into personal contact. But the children of energetic parents,
frequently grow up unenergetic, because they lean on their parents,
and the parents are energetic for them. The education which my
father gave me, was in itself much more fitted for training me to *know*
than to *do*. Not that he was unaware of my deficiencies; both as a boy
and as a youth I was incessantly smarting under his severe
admonitions on the subject. There was anything but insensibility or
tolerance on his part towards such shortcomings: but, while he saved
me from the demoralizing effects of school life, he made no effort to

provide me with any sufficient substitute for its practicalizing influences. Whatever qualities he himself, probably, had acquired without difficulty or special training, he seems to have supposed that I ought to acquire as easily. He had not, I think, bestowed the same amount of thought and attention on this, as on most other branches of education; and here, as well as in some other points of my tuition, he seems to have expected effects without causes.

CHAPTER II

Moral Influences in Early Youth.
My Father's Character and Opinions

❦

In my education, as in that of every one, the moral influences, which are so much more important than all others, are also the most complicated, and the most difficult to specify with any approach to completeness. Without attempting the hopeless task of detailing the circumstances by which, in this respect, my early character may have been shaped, I shall confine myself to a few leading points, which form an indispensable part of any true account of my education.

I was brought up from the first without any religious belief, in the ordinary acceptation of the term. My father, educated in the creed of Scotch presbyterianism, had by his own studies and reflexions been early led to reject not only the belief in revelation, but the foundations of what is commonly called Natural Religion. I have heard him say, that the turning point of his mind on the subject was reading Butler's *Analogy*.† That work, of which he always continued to speak with respect, kept him, as he said, for some considerable time, a believer in the divine authority of Christianity; by proving to him, that whatever are the difficulties in believing that the Old and New Testament proceed from, or record the acts of, a perfectly wise and good being, the same and still greater difficulties stand in the way of the belief, that a being of such a character can have been the Maker of the universe. He considered Butler's argument as conclusive against the only opponents for whom it was intended. Those who admit an omnipotent as well as perfectly just and benevolent maker and ruler of such a world as this, can say little against Christianity but what can, with at least equal force, be retorted against themselves. Finding, therefore, no halting place in Deism, he remained in a state of perplexity, until, doubtless after many struggles, he yielded to the conviction, that concerning the origin of things nothing whatever can be known. This is the only correct statement of his opinion; for dogmatic atheism he looked upon as absurd; as most of those,

21

whom the world has considered Atheists, have always done. These particulars are important, because they shew that my father's rejection of all that is called religious belief, was not, as many might suppose, primarily a matter of logic and evidence: the grounds of it were moral, still more than intellectual. He found it impossible to believe that a world so full of evil was the work of an Author combining infinite power with perfect goodness and righteousness. His intellect spurned the subtleties by which men attempt to blind themselves to this open contradiction. The Sabæan,† or Manichæan† theory of a Good and an Evil Principle, struggling against each other for the government of the universe, he would not have equally condemned; and I have heard him express surprise, that no one revived it in our time. He would have regarded it as a mere hypothesis; but he would have ascribed to it no depraving influence. As it was, his aversion to religion, in the sense usually attached to the term, was of the same kind with that of Lucretius:† he regarded it with the feelings due not to a mere mental delusion, but to a great moral evil. He looked upon it as the greatest enemy of morality: first, by setting up factitious excellences, – belief in creeds, devotional feelings, and ceremonies, not connected with the good of human kind, – and causing these to be accepted as substitutes for genuine virtues: but above all, by radically vitiating the standard of morals; making it consist in doing the will of a being, on whom it lavishes indeed all the phrases of adulation, but whom in sober truth it depicts as eminently hateful. I have a hundred times heard him say, that all ages and nations have represented their gods as wicked, in a constantly increasing progression; that mankind have gone on adding trait after trait till they reached the most perfect conception of wickedness which the human mind can devise, and have called this God, and prostrated themselves before it. This *ne plus ultra*† of wickedness he considered to be embodied in what is commonly presented to mankind as the creed of Christianity. Think (he used to say) of a being who would make a Hell – who would create the human race with the infallible foreknowledge, and therefore with the intention, that the great majority of them were to be consigned to horrible and everlasting torment. The time, I believe, is drawing near when this dreadful conception of an object of worship will be no longer identified with Christianity;† and when all persons, with any sense of moral good and evil, will look upon it with the same indignation with which my father regarded it. My father was as well aware as any one that Christians do not, in general, undergo the demoralizing consequences which

22

seem inherent in such a creed, in the manner or to the extent which might have been expected from it. The same slovenliness of thought, and subjection of the reason to fears, wishes, and affections, which enable them to accept a theory involving a contradiction in terms, prevents them from perceiving the logical consequences of the theory. Such is the facility with which mankind believe at one and the same time things inconsistent with one another, and so few are those who draw from what they receive as truths, any consequences but those recommended to them by their feelings, that multitudes have held the undoubting belief in an Omnipotent Author of Hell, and have nevertheless identified that being with the best conception they were able to form of perfect goodness. Their worship was not paid to the demon which such a Being as they imagined would really be, but to their own ideal of excellence. The evil is, that such a belief keeps the ideal wretchedly low; and opposes the most obstinate resistance to all thought which has a tendency to raise it higher. Believers shrink from every train of ideas which would lead the mind to a clear conception and an elevated standard of excellence, because they feel (even when they do not distinctly see) that such a standard would conflict with many of the dispensations of nature, and with much of what they are accustomed to consider as the Christian creed. And thus morality continues a matter of blind tradition, with no consistent principle, nor even any consistent feeling, to guide it.

It would have been wholly inconsistent with my father's ideas of duty, to allow me to acquire impressions contrary to his convictions and feelings respecting religion: and he impressed upon me from the first, that the manner in which the world came into existence was a subject on which nothing was known: that the question 'Who made me?' cannot be answered, because we have no experience or authentic information from which to answer it; and that any answer only throws the difficulty a step further back, since the question immediately presents itself, Who made God? He, at the same time, took care that I should be acquainted with what had been thought by mankind on these impenetrable problems. I have mentioned at how early an age he made me a reader of ecclesiastical history; and he taught me to take the strongest interest in the Reformation,† as the great and decisive contest against priestly tyranny for liberty of thought.

I am thus one of the very few examples, in this country, of one who has, not thrown off religious belief, but never had it: I grew up in a negative state with regard to it. I looked upon the modern exactly as I did upon the ancient religion, as something which in no way concerned me. It did not seem to me more strange that English people should believe what I did not, than that the men I read of in Herodotus should have done so. History had made the variety of opinions among mankind a fact familiar to me, and this was but a prolongation of that fact. This point in my early education had however incidentally one bad consequence deserving notice. In giving me an opinion contrary to that of the world, my father thought it necessary to give it as one which could not prudently be avowed to the world. This lesson of keeping my thoughts to myself, at that early age, was attended with some moral disadvantages; though my limited intercourse with strangers, especially such as were likely to speak to me on religion, prevented me from being placed in the alternative of avowal or hypocrisy. I remember two occasions in my boyhood, on which I felt myself in this alternative, and in both cases I avowed my disbelief and defended it. My opponents were boys, considerably older than myself: one of them I certainly staggered at the time, but the subject was never renewed between us: the other, who was surprised and somewhat shocked, did his best to convince me for some time, without effect.

The great advance in liberty of discussion, which is one of the most important differences between the present time and that of my childhood, has greatly altered the moralities of this question; and I think that few men of my father's intellect and public spirit, holding with such intensity of moral conviction as he did, unpopular opinions on religion, or on any other of the great subjects of thought, would now either practise or inculcate the withholding of them from the world, unless in the cases, becoming fewer every day, in which frankness on these subjects would either risk the loss of means of subsistence, or would amount to exclusion from some sphere of usefulness peculiarly suitable to the capacities of the individual. On religion in particular the time appears to me to have come, when it is the duty of all who being qualified in point of knowledge, have on mature consideration satisfied themselves that the current opinions are not only false but hurtful, to make their dissent known; at least, if they are among those whose station, or reputation, gives their opinion a chance of being attended to. Such an avowal would put an end, at once and for ever, to the vulgar prejudice, that what is called, very improperly, unbelief, is connected with any bad qualities either of mind or heart. The world would be astonished if it knew how great a proportion of its brightest ornaments – of those most distinguished even in popular estimation for wisdom and virtue – are complete sceptics in religion;

many of them refraining from avowal, less from personal considerations, than from a conscientious, though now in my opinion a
most mistaken apprehension lest by speaking out what would tend
to weaken existing beliefs, and by consequence (as they suppose)
existing restraints, they should do harm instead of good.

Of unbelievers (so called) as well as of believers, there are many
species, including almost every variety of moral type. But the best
among them, as no one who has had opportunities of really knowing
them will hesitate to affirm (believers rarely have that opportunity),
are more genuinely religious,[†] in the best sense of the word religion,
than those who exclusively arrogate to themselves the title. The
liberality of the age, or in other words the weakening of the obstinate
prejudice, which makes men unable to see what is before their eyes
because it is contrary to their expectations, has caused it to be very
commonly admitted that a Deist may be truly religious: but if religion
stands for any graces of character and not for mere dogma, the
assertion may equally be made of many whose belief is far short of
Deism. Though they may think the proof incomplete that the universe
is a work of design, and though they assuredly disbelieve that it can
have an Author and Governor who is absolute in power as well as
perfect in goodness, they have that which constitutes the principal
worth of all religions whatever, an ideal conception of a Perfect Being,
to which they habitually refer as the guide of their conscience; and this
ideal of Good is usually far nearer to perfection than the objective
Deity of those, who think themselves obliged to find absolute
goodness in the author of a world so crowded with suffering and so
deformed by injustice as ours.

My father's moral convictions, wholly dissevered from religion,
were very much of the character of those of the Greek philosophers;
and were delivered with the force and decision which characterized
all that came from him. Even at the very early age at which I read
with him the *Memorabilia*[†] of Xenophon, I imbibed from that work
and from his comments a deep respect for the character of Socrates;
who stood in my mind as a model of ideal excellence: and I well
remember how my father at that time impressed upon me the lesson
of the 'Choice of Hercules.'[†] At a somewhat later period the lofty
moral standard exhibited in the writings of Plato operated upon me
with great force. My father's moral inculcations were at all times
mainly those of the 'Socratici viri';[†] justice, temperance (to which he
gave a very extended application), veracity, perseverance, readiness
to encounter pain and especially labour; regard for the public good;

estimation of persons according to their merits, and of things according to their intrinsic usefulness; a life of exertion in contradiction to one of self-indulgent sloth. These and other moralities he conveyed in brief sentences, uttered as occasion arose, of grave exhortation, or stern reprobation and contempt.

But though direct moral teaching does much, indirect does more; and the effect my father produced on my character, did not depend solely on what he said or did with that direct object, but also, and still more, on what manner of man he was.

In his views of life he partook of the character of the Stoic,[†] the Epicurean,[†] and the Cynic,[†] not in the modern but the ancient sense of the word. In his personal qualities the Stoic predominated. His standard of morals was Epicurean, inasmuch as it was utilitarian, taking as the exclusive test of right and wrong, the tendency of actions to produce pleasure or pain. But he had (and this was the Cynic element) scarcely any belief in pleasure; at least in his later years, of which alone, on this point, I can speak confidently. He was not insensible to pleasures; but he deemed very few of them worth the price which, at least in the present state of society, must be paid for them. The greatest number of miscarriages in life, he considered to be attributable to the overvaluing of pleasures. Accordingly, temperance, in the large sense intended by the Greek philosophers – stopping short at the point of moderation in all indulgences – was with him, as with them, almost the central point of educational precept. His inculcations of this virtue fill a large place in my childish remembrances. He thought human life a poor thing at best,[‡] after the freshness of youth and of unsatisfied curiosity had gone by. This was a topic on which he did not often speak, especially, it may be supposed, in the presence of young persons: but when he did, it was with an air of settled and profound conviction. He would sometimes say, that if life were made what it might be, by good government and good education, it would be worth having: but he never spoke with anything like enthusiasm even of that possibility. He never varied in rating intellectual enjoyments above all others, even in value as pleasures, independently of their ulterior benefits. The pleasures of the benevolent affections he placed high in the scale; and used to say, that he had never known a happy old man, except those who were able to live over again in the pleasures of the young. For passionate emotions of all sorts, and for everything which has been said or written in exaltation of them, he professed the greatest contempt. He regarded them as a form of madness. 'The intense' was with him a bye-word of scornful disapprobation. He regarded as an aberration of the moral standard of modern times, compared with that of the ancients, the great stress laid upon feeling. Feelings, as such, he considered to be no proper subjects of praise or blame. Right and wrong, good and bad, he regarded as qualities solely of conduct – of acts and omissions; there being no feeling which may not lead, and does not frequently lead, either to good or to bad actions: conscience itself, the very desire to act right, often leading people to act wrong. Consistently carrying out the doctrine, that the object of praise and blame should be the discouragement of wrong conduct and the encouragement of right, he refused to let his praise or blame be influenced by the motive of the agent. He blamed as severely what he thought a bad action, when the motive was a feeling of duty, as if the agents had been consciously evil doers. He would not have accepted as a plea in mitigation for inquisitors, that they sincerely believed burning heretics to be an obligation of conscience. But though he did not allow honesty of purpose to soften his disapprobation of actions, it had its full effect on his estimation of characters. No one prized conscientiousness and rectitude of intention more highly, or was more incapable of valuing any person in whom he did not feel assurance of it. But he disliked people quite as much for any other deficiency, provided he thought it equally likely to make them act ill. He disliked, for instance, a fanatic in any bad cause, as much or more than one who adopted the same cause from self-interest, because he thought him even more likely to be practically mischievous.‡ And thus, his aversion to many intellectual errors, or what he regarded as such, partook, in a certain sense, of the character of a moral feeling. All this is merely saying that he, in a degree once common, but now very unusual, threw his feelings into his opinions; which truly it is difficult to understand how any one, who possesses much of both, can fail to do. None but those who do not care about opinions, will confound this with intolerance. Those who, having opinions which they hold to be immensely important, and the contraries to be prodigiously hurtful, have any deep regard for the general good, will necessarily dislike, as a class and in the abstract, those who think wrong what they think right, and right what they think wrong: though they need not therefore be, nor was my father, insensible to good qualities in an opponent, nor governed in their estimation of individuals by one general presumption, instead of by the whole of their character. I grant that an earnest person, being no more infallible than other men, is liable to dislike people on account of opinions which do not merit dislike; but if he neither himself does them any ill office, nor connives at its being done by others, he is not intolerant: and the forbearance, which flows from a conscientious sense of the importance to mankind of the equal freedom of all opinions, is the only tolerance which is commendable, or, to the highest moral order of minds, possible.‡

It will be admitted, that a man of the opinions, and the character, above described, was likely to leave a strong moral impression on any mind principally formed by him, and that his moral teaching was not likely to err on the side of laxity or indulgence. The element which was chiefly deficient in his moral relation to his children, was that of tenderness. I do not believe that this deficiency lay in his own nature. I believe him to have had much more feeling than he habitually shewed, and much greater capacities of feeling than were ever developed. He resembled most Englishmen in being ashamed of the signs of feeling, and, by the absence of demonstration, starving the feelings themselves. If we consider further that he was in the trying position of sole teacher, and add to this that his temper was constitutionally irritable, it is impossible not to feel true pity for a father who did, and strove to do, so much for his children, who would have so valued their affection, yet who must have been constantly feeling that fear of him was drying it up at its source. This was no longer the case, later in life and with his younger children. They loved him tenderly: and if I cannot say so much of myself, I was always loyally devoted to him. As regards my own education, I hesitate to pronounce whether I was more a loser or gainer by his severity. It was not such as to prevent me from having a happy childhood. And I do not believe, that boys can be induced to apply themselves with vigour, and what is so much more difficult, perseverance, to dry and irksome studies, by the sole force of persuasion and soft words. Much must be done, and much must be learnt, by children, for which rigid discipline, and known liability to punishment, are indispensable as means. It is, no doubt, a very laudable effort, in modern teaching, to render as much as possible of what the young are required to learn, easy and interesting to them. But when this principle is pushed to the length of not requiring them to learn anything *but* what has been made easy and interesting, one of the chief objects of education is sacrificed. I rejoice in the decline of the old brutal and tyrannical system of teaching, which however did succeed in enforcing habits of application; but the new, as it seems to me, is training up a race of men who will be incapable of doing anything which is disagreeable to them.† I do not, then, believe that fear, as an element in education, can be dispensed with; but I am sure that it ought not to be the main element; and when it predominates so much as to preclude love and confidence on the part of the child to those who should be the unreservedly trusted advisers of after years, and perhaps to seal up the fountains of frank and spontaneous communicativeness in the child's nature, it is an evil for which a large abatement must be made from the benefits, moral and intellectual, which may flow from any other part of the education.

During this first period of my life, the habitual frequenters of my father's house were limited to a very few persons, most of them little known to the world, but whom personal worth, and more or less of congeniality with at least his political opinions (not so frequently to be met with then as since) inclined him to cultivate; and his conversations with them I listened to with interest and instruction. My being an habitual inmate of my father's study made me acquainted with the dearest of his friends, David Ricardo, who by his benevolent countenance, and kindliness of manner, was very attractive to young persons, and who after I became a student of political economy, invited me to his house and to walk with him in order to converse on the subject. I was a more frequent visitor (from about 1817 or 1818) to Mr. Hume,[†] who, born in the same part of Scotland as my father, and having been, I rather think, a younger schoolfellow or college companion of his, had on returning from India renewed their youthful acquaintance, and who coming like many others greatly under the influence of my father's intellect and energy of character, was induced partly by that influence to go into Parliament, and there adopt the line of conduct which has given him an honorable place in the history of his country. Of Mr. Bentham I saw much more, owing to the close intimacy which existed between him and my father.[‡] I do not know how soon after my father's first arrival in England they became acquainted. But my father was the earliest Englishman of any great mark, who thoroughly understood, and in the main adopted, Bentham's general views of ethics, government, and law: and this was a natural foundation for sympathy between them, and made them familiar companions in a period of Bentham's life during which he admitted much fewer visitors than was the case subsequently. At this time Mr. Bentham passed some part of every year at Barrow Green House, in a beautiful part of the Surrey hills, a few miles from Godstone,[†] and there I each summer accompanied my father in a long visit. In 1813 Mr. Bentham, my father, and I made an excursion, which included Oxford, Bath and Bristol, Exeter, Plymouth, and Portsmouth. In this journey I saw many things which were instructive to me, and acquired my first taste for natural scenery, in the elementary form of fondness for a 'view.' In the succeeding winter we moved into a house very near Mr. Bentham's, which my father rented from him, in Queen Square, Westminster.[†] From 1814 to 1817 Mr. Bentham lived during half of each year at Ford Abbey, in Somersetshire (or rather in a part of Devonshire surrounded by Somersetshire), which intervals I had the advantage of passing at that place. This sojourn was, I think, an important circumstance in my education. Nothing contributes more to nourish elevation of sentiments in a people, than the large and free character of their habitations. The middle-age architecture, the baronial hall, and the spacious and lofty rooms, of this fine old place, so unlike the mean and cramped externals of English middle class life,[†] gave the sentiment of a larger and freer existence, and were to me a sort of poetic cultivation, aided also by the character of the grounds in which the Abbey stood; which were riant and secluded, umbrageous, and full of the sound of falling waters.

I owed another of the fortunate circumstances in my education, a year's residence in France,[†] to Mr. Bentham's brother, General Sir Samuel Bentham.[†] I had seen Sir Samuel Bentham and his family at their house near Gosport[†] in the course of the tour already mentioned (he being then Superintendant of the Dockyard at Portsmouth), and during a stay of a few days which they made at Ford Abbey shortly after the peace, before going to live on the Continent. In 1820 they invited me for a six months visit to them in the South of France, which their kindness ultimately prolonged to nearly a twelvemonth. Sir Samuel Bentham, though of a character of mind different from that of his illustrious brother, was a man of very considerable attainments and general powers, with a decided genius for mechanical art. His wife, a daughter of the celebrated chemist Dr. Fordyce, was a woman of strong will and decided character, much general knowledge, and great practical good sense of the Edgeworth kind:[†] she was the ruling spirit of the household, as she deserved, and was well qualified, to be. Their family consisted of one son (the eminent botanist) and three daughters, the youngest about two years my senior. I am indebted to them for much and various instruction, and for an almost parental interest in my welfare. When I first joined them, in May 1820, they occupied the Château of Pompignan[†] (still belonging to a descendant of Voltaire's enemy) on the heights overlooking the plain of the Garonne between Montauban and Toulouse. I accompanied them in an excursion to the Pyrenees, including a stay of some duration at Bagnères de Bigorre, a journey to Pau,[†] Bayonne, and Bagnères de

Luchon, and an ascent of the Pic du Midi de Bigorre. This first introduction to the highest order of mountain scenery made the deepest impression on me, and gave a colour to my tastes through life. In October we proceeded by the beautiful mountain route of Castres and St. Pons, from Toulouse to Montpellier, in which last neighbourhood Sir Samuel had just bought the estate of Restinclière, near the foot of the singular mountain of St. Loup. During this residence in France I acquired a familiar knowledge of the French language, and acquaintance with the ordinary French literature; I took lessons in various bodily exercises, in none of which however I made any proficiency; and at Montpellier I attended the excellent winter courses of lectures at the Faculté des Sciences, those of M. Anglada on chemistry, of M. Provençal on zoology, and of a very accomplished representative of the eighteenth century metaphysics, M. Gergonne, on logic, under the name of Philosophy of the Sciences. I also went through a course of the higher mathematics under the private tuition of M. Lenthéric, a professor at the Lycée of Montpellier. But the greatest, perhaps, of the many advantages which I owed to this episode in my education, was that of having breathed for a whole year the free and genial atmosphere of Continental life. This advantage was not the less real though I could not then estimate, nor even consciously feel it. Having so little experience of English life, and the few people I knew being mostly such as had public objects, of a large and personally disinterested kind, at heart, I was ignorant of the low moral tone of what, in England, is called society; the habit of, not indeed professing, but taking for granted in every mode of implication, that conduct is of course always directed towards low and petty objects;† the absence of high feelings which manifests itself by sneering depreciation of all demonstrations of them, and by general abstinence (except among a few of the stricter religionists) from professing any high principles of action at all, except in those preordained cases in which such profession is put on as part of the costume and formalities of the occasion. I could not then know or estimate the difference between this manner of existence, and that of a people like the French, whose faults, if equally real, are at all events different; among whom sentiments, which by comparison at least may be called elevated, are the current coin of human intercourse, both in books and in private life; and though often evaporating in profession, are yet kept alive in the nation at large by constant exercise, and stimulated by sympathy, so as to form a living and active part of the existence of great numbers of persons, and to

31

be recognized and understood by all. Neither could I then appreciate the general culture of the understanding, which results from the habitual exercise of the feelings, and is thus carried down into the most uneducated classes of several countries on the Continent, in a degree not equalled in England among the so called educated, except where an unusual tenderness of conscience leads to a habitual exercise of the intellect on questions of right and wrong. I did not know the way in which, among the ordinary English, the absence of interest in things of an unselfish kind, except occasionally in a special thing here and there, and the habit of not speaking to others, nor much even to themselves, about the things in which they do feel interest, causes both their feelings and their intellectual faculties to remain undeveloped, or to develop themselves only in some single and very limited direction; reducing them, considered as spiritual beings, to a kind of negative existence. All these things I did not perceive till long afterwards; but I even then felt, though without stating it clearly to myself, the contrast between the frank sociability and amiability of French personal intercourse, and the English mode of existence in which everybody acts as if everybody else (with few, or no, exceptions) was either an enemy or a bore. In France, it is true, the bad as well as the good points both of individual and of national character, come more to the surface, and break out more fearlessly in ordinary intercourse, than in England: but the general habit of the people is to shew, as well as to expect, friendly feeling in every one towards every other, wherever there is not some positive cause for the opposite. In England it is only of the best bred people, in the upper or upper middle ranks, that anything like this can be said.

In my way through Paris, both going and returning, I passed some time in the house of M. Say,† the eminent political economist, who was a friend and correspondent of my father, having become acquainted with him on a visit to England a year or two after the peace. He was a man of the later period of the French Revolution, a fine specimen of the best kind of French republican, one of those who had never bent the knee to Bonaparte though courted by him to do so; a truly upright, brave, and enlightened man. He lived a quiet and studious life, made happy by warm affections, public and private. He was acquainted with many of the chiefs of the Liberal party, and I saw various noteworthy persons while staying at his house; among whom I have pleasure in the recollection of having once seen Saint-Simon,† not yet the founder either of a philosophy or a religion, and considered only as a clever *original*. The chief fruit which I carried away from the society I saw, was a strong and permanent interest in Continental Liberalism, of which I ever afterwards kept myself *au courant*, as much as of English politics: a thing not at all usual in those days with Englishmen, and which had a very salutary influence on my development, keeping me free from the error always prevalent in England, and from which even my father with all his superiority to prejudice was not exempt, of judging universal questions by a merely English standard. After passing a few weeks at Caen with an old friend of my father's,[†] I returned to England in July 1821; and my education resumed its ordinary course.

CHAPTER III

Last Stage of Education, and First of Self-Education

❦

For the first year or two after my visit to France, I continued my old studies, with the addition of some new ones. When I returned, my father was just finishing for the press his *Elements of Political Economy*,† and he made me perform an exercise on the manuscript, which Mr. Bentham practised on all his own writings, making what he called 'marginal contents'; a short abstract of every paragraph, to enable the writer more easily to judge of, and improve, the order of the ideas, and the general character of the exposition. Soon after, my father put into my hands Condillac's *Traité des Sensations*, and the logical and meta-physical volumes of his *Cours d'Etudes*;† the first (notwithstanding the superficial resemblance between Condillac's psychological system and my father's) quite as much for a warning as for an example. I am not sure whether it was in this winter or the next that I first read a history of the French Revolution.† I learnt with astonishment, that the princi-ples of democracy, then apparently in so insignificant and hopeless a minority everywhere in Europe, had borne all before them in France thirty years earlier, and had been the creed of the nation. As may be supposed from this, I had previously a very vague idea of that great commotion. I knew only that the French had thrown off the absolute monarchy of Louis XIV. and XV.,† had put the king and queen to death,† guillotined many persons, one of whom was Lavoisier,† and had ultimately fallen under the despotism of Bonaparte.† From this time, as was natural, the subject took an immense hold of my feelings. It allied itself with all my juvenile aspirations to the character of a democratic champion. What had happened so lately, seemed as if it might easily happen again: and the most transcendant glory I was capable of conceiving, was that of figuring, successful or unsuccessful, as a Girondist† in an English Convention.

During the winter of 1821/2, Mr. John Austin,† with whom at the time of my visit to France my father had but lately become acquainted,

kindly allowed me to read Roman law with him. My father, notwithstanding his abhorrence of the chaos of barbarism called English
Law, had turned his thoughts towards the bar as on the whole less
ineligible for me than any other profession: and these readings with
Mr. Austin, who had made Bentham's best ideas his own, and added
much to them from other sources and from his own mind, were not
only a valuable introduction to legal studies, but an important
portion of general education. With Mr. Austin I read Heineccius on
the Institutes, his Roman Antiquities, and part of his exposition of the
Pandects; to which was added a considerable portion of Blackstone.†
It was at the commencement of these studies that my father, as a
needful accompaniment to them, put into my hands Bentham's
principal speculations, as interpreted to the Continent, and indeed
to all the world, by Dumont, in the *Traité de Législation*.† The reading
of this book was an epoch in my life; one of the turning points in my
mental history.

My previous education had been, in a certain sense, already a
course of Benthamism. The Benthamic standard of 'the greatest
happiness' was that which I had always been taught to apply; I was
even familiar with an abstract discussion of it, forming an episode in
an unpublished dialogue on Government, written by my father on
the Platonic model. Yet in the first pages of Bentham it burst upon
me with all the force of novelty. What thus impressed me was the
chapter in which Bentham passed judgment on the common modes
of reasoning in morals and legislation, deduced from phrases like 'law
of nature,' 'right reason,' 'the moral sense,' 'natural rectitude,' and
the like, and characterized them as dogmatism in disguise imposing
its sentiments upon others under cover of sounding expressions
which convey no reason for the sentiment, but set up the sentiment
as its own reason. It had not struck me before, that Bentham's
principle put an end to all this. The feeling rushed upon me, that all
previous moralists were superseded, and that here indeed was the
commencement of a new era in thought. This impression was
strengthened by the manner in which Bentham put into scientific
form the application of the happiness principle to the morality of
actions, by analyzing the various classes and orders of their consequences. But what struck me at that time most of all, was the
Classification of Offences, which is much more clear, compact, and
imposing in Dumont's *rédaction*, than in the original work of
Bentham from which it was taken. Logic, and the dialectics of Plato,
which had formed so large a part of my previous training, had given

me a strong relish for accurate classification. This taste had been strengthened and enlightened by the study of botany, on the principles of what is called the Natural Method, which I had taken up with great zeal, though only as an amusement, during my stay in France; and when I found scientific classification applied to the great and complex subject of Punishable Acts, under the guidance of the ethical principle of Pleasurable and Painful Consequences, followed out in the method of detail introduced into these subjects by Bentham, I felt taken up to an eminence from which I could survey a vast mental domain, and see stretching out into the distance intellectual results beyond all computation. As I proceeded farther, there seemed to be added to this intellectual clearness, the most inspiring prospects of practical improvement in human affairs. To Bentham's general views of the construction of a body of law I was not altogether a stranger, having read with attention that admirable compendium, my father's article 'Jurisprudence': but I had read it with little profit, and scarcely any interest, no doubt from its extremely general and abstract character, and also because it concerned the form more than the substance of the *corpus juris*,† the logic rather than the ethics of law. But Bentham's subject was Legislation, of which Jurisprudence is only the formal part: and at every page he seemed to open a clearer and broader conception of what human opinions and institutions ought to be, how they might be made what they ought to be, and how far removed from it they now are. When I laid down the last volume of the *Traité* I had become a different being. The 'principle of utility,' understood as Bentham understood it, and applied in the manner in which he applied it through these three volumes, fell exactly into its place as the keystone which held together the detached and fragmentary component parts of my knowledge and beliefs. It gave unity to my conceptions of things. I now had opinions; a creed, a doctrine, a philosophy; in one among the best senses of the word, a religion; the inculcation and diffusion of which could be made the principal outward purpose of a life. And I had a grand conception laid before me of changes to be effected in the condition of mankind through that doctrine. The *Traité de Législation* wound up with what was to me a most impressive picture of human life as it would be made by such opinions and such laws as were recommended in the treatise. The anticipations of practicable improvement were studiously moderate, deprecating and discountenancing as reveries of vague enthusiasm many things which will one day seem so natural to human beings, that injustice will probably be done to those who once thought them chimerical. But, in my state of mind, this appearance of superiority to illusion added to the effect which Bentham's doctrines produced on me, by heightening the impression of mental power. And the vista of improvement which he did open was sufficiently large and brilliant to light up my life, as well as to give a definite shape to my aspirations.

After this I read, from time to time, the most important of the other works of Bentham which had then seen the light, either as written by himself or as edited by Dumont. This was my private reading: while, under my father's direction, my studies were carried into the higher branches of analytic psychology. I now read Locke's *Essay*,† and wrote out an account of it, consisting of a complete abstract of every chapter, with such remarks as occurred to me: which was read by, or (I think) to, my father, and discussed throughout. I performed the same process with Helvetius† *De l'Esprit*, which I read of my own choice. This preparation of abstracts, subject to my father's censorship, was of great service to me, by compelling precision in conceiving and expressing psychological doctrines, whether accepted as truths or only regarded as the opinions of others. After Helvetius, my father made me study what he deemed the really master-production in the philosophy of mind, Hartley's *Observations on Man*.† This book, though it did not, like the *Traité de Législation*, give a new colour to my existence, made a very similar impression on me in regard to its immediate subject. Hartley's explanation, incomplete as in many points it is, of the more complex mental phenomena by the law of association, commended itself to me at once as a real analysis, and made me feel by contrast the insufficiency of the merely verbal generalizations of Condillac, and even of the instructive gropings and feelings about for psychological explanations, of Locke. It was at this very time that my father commenced writing his *Analysis of the Mind*,† which carried Hartley's mode of explaining the mental phenomena to so much greater length and depth. He could only command the concentration of thought necessary for this work, during the complete leisure of his holiday of a month or six weeks annually; and he commenced it in the summer of 1822, in the first holiday he passed at Dorking; in which neighbourhood, from that time to the end of his life, with the exception of two years, he lived, as far as his official duties permitted, for six months of every year. He worked at the *Analysis* during several successive vacations, up to the year 1829, when it was published, and allowed me to read the manuscript, portion by portion, as it advanced. The other principal English writers

38

on mental philosophy I read as I felt inclined, particularly Berkeley,[†] Hume's Essays,[†] Reid,[†] Dugald Stewart,[†] and Brown on Cause and Effect.[†] Brown's *Lectures* I did not read until two or three years later, nor at that time had my father himself read them.

Among the works read in the course of this year which contributed materially to my development, I ought to mention a book (written on the foundation of some of Bentham's manuscripts and published under the pseudonyme of Philip Beauchamp) entitled *Analysis of the Influence of Natural Religion on the Temporal Happiness of Mankind.*[†] This was an examination not of the truth, but of the usefulness of religious belief, in the most general sense, apart from the peculiarities of any special Revelation; which, of all the parts of the discussion concerning religion, is the most important in this age, in which real belief in any religious doctrine is feeble and precarious, but the opinion of its necessity for moral and social purposes almost universal;[†] and when those who reject revelation, very generally take refuge in an optimistic Deism,[†] a worship of the order of Nature, and the supposed course of Providence, at least as full of contradictions, and perverting to the moral sentiments, as any of the forms of Christianity, if only it is as completely realized.[‡] Yet, very little, with any claim to a philosophical character, has been written by sceptics against the usefulness of this form of belief. The volume bearing the name of Philip Beauchamp had this for its special object. Having been shown to my father in manuscript, it was put into my hands by him, and I made a marginal analysis of it as I had done of the *Elements of Political Economy.* Next to the *Traité de Législation*, it was one of the books which by the searching character of its analysis produced the greatest effect upon me. On reading it lately after an interval of many years, I find it to have some of the defects as well as the merits of the Benthamic modes of thought, and to contain, as I now think, many weak arguments, but with a great overbalance of sound ones, and much good material for a more completely philosophic and conclusive treatment of the subject.

I have now, I believe, mentioned all the books which had any considerable effect on my early mental developement. From this point I began to carry on my intellectual cultivation by writing still more than by reading. In the summer of 1822 I wrote my first argumentative essay. I remember very little about it, except that it was an attack on what I regarded as the aristocratic prejudice, that the rich were, or were likely to be, superior in moral qualities to the poor. My performance was entirely argumentative, without any of the declamation having half finished what he undertook. From this mental infirmity (of which he is not the sole example among the accomplished and able men whom I have known), combined with liability to frequent attacks of disabling though not dangerous ill health, he accomplished, through life, little in comparison with what he seemed capable of; but what he did produce is held in the very highest estimation by the most competent judges; and, like Coleridge,[†] he might plead as a set-off that he had been to many persons, through his conversation, a source not only of much instruction but of great elevation of character. On me his influence was most salutary. It was moral in the best sense. He took a sincere and kind interest in me, far beyond what could have been expected towards a mere youth from a man of his age, standing, and what seemed austerity of character. There was in his conversation and demeanour a tone of highmindedness which did not shew itself so much, if the quality existed as much, in any of the other persons with whom at that time I associated.[‡] My intercourse with him was the more beneficial, owing to his being of a different mental type from all other intellectual men whom I frequented, and he from the first set himself decidedly against the prejudices and narrownesses which are almost sure to be found in a young man formed by a particular mode of thought or a particular social circle.

His younger brother, Charles Austin,[†] of whom at this time and for the next year or two I saw much,[‡] had also a great effect on me, though of a very different description. He was but a few years older than myself, and had then just left the University, where he had shone with great éclat as a man of intellect and a brilliant orator and converser. The effect he produced on his Cambridge cotemporaries deserves to be accounted an historical event; for to it may in part be traced the tendency towards Liberalism in general, and the Benthamic and politico-economic form of it in particular, which shewed itself in a portion of the more active-minded young men of the higher classes from this time to 1830. The Union Debating Society, at that time at the height of its reputation, was an arena where what were then thought extreme opinions, in politics and philosophy, were weekly asserted, face to face with their opposites, before audiences consisting of the élite of the Cambridge youth: and though many persons afterwards of more or less note (of whom Lord Macaulay[†] is the most celebrated) gained their first oratorical laurels in those debates, the really influential mind among these intellectual gladiators was Charles Austin. He continued, after leaving the University, to be, by his conversation and personal ascendancy, a leader among the same class of young men who had been his associates there; and he attached me among others to his car. Through him I became acquainted with Macaulay, Hyde† and Charles Villiers,† Strutt (now Lord Belper),† Romilly† (now Lord Romilly and Master of the Rolls), and various others who subsequently figured in literature or politics, and among whom I heard discussions on many topics, as yet to a certain degree new to me. The influence of Charles Austin over me differed from that of the persons I have hitherto mentioned, in being not the influence of a man over a boy, but that of an elder cotemporary. It was through him that I first felt myself, not a pupil under teachers, but a man among men. He was the first person of intellect whom I met on a ground of equality, though as yet much his inferior on that common ground. He was a man who never failed to impress greatly those with whom he came in contact, even when their opinions were the very reverse of his. The impression he gave was that of boundless strength, together with talents which, combined with such apparent force of will and character, seemed capable of dominating the world. Those who knew him, whether friendly to him or not, always anticipated that he would play a conspicuous part in public life. It is seldom that men produce so great an immediate effect by speech, unless they, in some degree, lay themselves out for it; and he did this in no ordinary degree. He loved to strike, and even to startle. He knew that decision is the greatest element of effect, and he uttered his opinions with all the decision he could throw into them, never so well pleased as when he astonished any one by their audacity. Very unlike his brother, who made war against the narrower interpretations and applications of the principles they both professed, he on the contrary presented the Benthamic doctrines in the most startling form of which they were susceptible, exaggerating every thing in them which tended to consequences offensive to any one's preconceived feelings. All which, he defended with such verve and vivacity, and carried off by a manner so agreeable as well as forcible, that he always either came off victor, or divided the honours of the field. It is my belief that much of the notion popularly entertained of the tenets and sentiments of what are called Benthamites or Utilitarians had its origin in para-doxes thrown out by Charles Austin. It must be said, however, that his example was followed, *haud passibus æquis*,† by younger proselytes, and that to *outrer* whatever was by anybody considered offensive in the doctrines and maxims of Benthamism, became at one time the badge of a small coterie of youths. All of these who had anything in them, myself among others, quickly outgrew this boyish vanity; and those who had not, became tired of differing from other people, and gave up both the good and the bad part of the heterodox opinions they had for some time professed.

It was in the winter of 1822/23 that I formed the plan of a little society, to be composed of young men agreeing in fundamental principles – acknowledging Utility as their standard in ethics and politics, and a certain number of the principal corollaries drawn from it in the philosophy I had accepted – and meeting once a fortnight to read essays and discuss questions conformably to the premises thus agreed on. The fact would hardly be worth mentioning, but for the circumstance, that the name I gave to the society I had planned was the Utilitarian Society. It was the first time that any one had taken the title of Utilitarian;† and the term made its way into the language from this humble source. I did not invent the word, but found it in one of Galt's novels, the *Annals of the Parish*,† in which the Scotch clergyman, of whom the book is a supposed autobiography, is represented as warning his parishioners not to leave the Gospel and become utilitarians. With a boy's fondness for a name and a banner I seized on the word, and for some years called myself and others by it as a sectarian appellation; and it came to be occasionally used by some others holding the opinions which it was intended to designate. As those opinions attracted more notice, the term was repeated by strangers and opponents, and got into rather common use just about the time when those who had originally assumed it, laid down that along with other sectarian characteristics. The Society so called consisted at first of no more than three members, one of whom, being Mr. Bentham's amanuensis,† obtained for us permission to hold our meetings in his house. The number never, I think, reached ten, and the society was broken up in 1826. It had thus an existence of about three years and a half. The chief effect of it as regards myself, over and above the benefit of practice in oral discussion, was that of bringing me in contact with several young men at that time less advanced than myself, among whom, as they professed the same opinions, I was for some time a sort of leader, and had considerable influence on their mental progress. Any young man of education who fell in my way, and whose opinions were not incompatible with those of the Society, I endeavoured to press into its service; and some others I probably should never have known, had they not joined it. Those of the members who became my intimate companions – no one of whom was in any sense of the word a disciple, but all of them independent thinkers on their own basis – were William Eyton Tooke,† son of the eminent political economist, a young man of singular worth both moral and intellectual, lost to the world by an early death; his friend William Ellis,[†] an original thinker in the field of political economy, now honourably known by his apostolic exertions for the improvement of education; George Graham, afterwards an official assignee of the Bankruptcy Court, a thinker of originality and power on almost all abstract subjects; and (from the time when he came first to England to study for the bar in 1824 or 1825) a man who has made considerably more noise in the world than any of these, John Arthur Roebuck.[†]

In May 1823,[†] my professional occupation and status for the next thirty-five years of my life, were decided by my father's obtaining for me an appointment from the East India Company, in the office of the Examiner of India Correspondence, immediately under himself. I was appointed in the usual manner, at the bottom of the list of clerks, to rise, at least in the first instance, by seniority; but with the understanding, that I should be employed from the beginning in preparing drafts of despatches, and be thus trained up as a successor to those who then filled the higher departments of the office. My drafts of course required, for some time, much revision from my immediate superiors, but I soon became well acquainted with the business, and by my father's instructions and the general growth of my own powers, I was in a few years qualified to be, and practically was, the chief conductor of the correspondence with India in one of the leading departments, that of the Native States. This continued to be my official duty until I was appointed Examiner, only two years before the time when the abolition of the East India Company as a political body determined my retirement. I do not know any one of the occupations by which a subsistence can now be gained, more suitable than such as this to any one who, not being in independent circumstances, desires to devote a part of the twenty-four hours to private intellectual pursuits. Writing for the press, cannot be recommended as a permanent resource to any one qualified to accomplish anything in the higher departments of literature or thought: not only on account of the uncertainty of this means of livelihood, especially if the writer has a conscience, and will not consent to serve any opinions except his own; but also because the writings by which one can live, are not the writings which themselves live, and are never those in which the writer his best. Books destined to form future thinkers take too much time to write, and when written come in general too slowly into notice and repute, to be relied on for subsistence. Those who have to support themselves by their pen must depend on literary

45

drudgery, or at best on writings addressed to the multitude; and can employ in the pursuits of their own choice only such time as they can spare from those of necessity; which is generally less than the leisure allowed by office occupations, while the effect on the mind is far more enervating and fatiguing. For my own part, I have, through life, found office duties an actual rest from the other mental occupations which I have carried on simultaneously with them. They were sufficiently intellectual not to be a distasteful drudgery, without being such as to cause any strain upon the mental powers of a person used to abstract thought, or to the labour of careful literary composition. The drawbacks, for every mode of life has its drawbacks, were not, however, unfelt by me. I cared little for the loss of the chances of riches and honours held out by some of the professions, particularly the bar, which had been, as I have already said, the profession thought of for me. But I was not indifferent to exclusion from Parliament,[†] and public life: and I felt very sensibly the more immediate unpleasantness of confinement to London; the holiday allowed by India-house practice not exceeding a month in the year, while my taste was strong for a country life, and my sojourn in France had left behind it an ardent desire of travelling. But though these tastes could not be freely indulged, they were at no time entirely sacrificed. I passed most Sundays, throughout the year, in the country, taking long rural walks on that day even when residing in London. The month's holiday was, for a few years, passed at my father's house in the country: afterwards a part or the whole was spent in tours, chiefly pedestrian, with some one or more of the young men who were my chosen companions; and at a later period, in longer journeys or excursions, alone or with other friends.[†] France, Belgium, and Rhenish Germany were within easy reach of the annual holiday: and two longer absences, one of three, the other of six months, under medical advice, added Switzerland, the Tyrol, and Italy to my list. Fortunately, also, both these journeys occurred rather early, so as to give the benefit and charm of the remembrance to a large portion of life.

I am disposed to agree with what has been surmised by others, that the opportunity which my official position gave me of learning by personal observation the necessary conditions of the practical conduct of public affairs, has been of considerable value to me as a theoretical reformer of the opinions and institutions of my time. Not, indeed, that public business transacted on paper, to take effect on the other side of the globe, was of itself calculated to give much practical knowledge of life. But the occupation accustomed me to see and hear the difficulties of every course, and the means of obviating them, stated and discussed deliberately, with a view to execution; it gave me opportunities of perceiving when public measures, and other political facts, did not produce the effects which had been expected of them, and from what causes; above all it was valuable to me by making me, in this portion of my activity, merely one wheel in a machine, the whole of which had to work together. As a speculative writer, I should have had no one to consult but myself, and should have encountered in my speculations none of the obstacles which would have started up whenever they came to be applied to practice. But as a Secretary conducting political correspondence, I could not issue an order or express an opinion, without satisfying various persons very unlike myself, that the thing was fit to be done. I was thus in a good position for finding out by practice the mode of putting a thought which gives it easiest admittance into minds not prepared for it by habit; while I became practically conversant with the difficulties of moving bodies of men, the necessities of compromise, the art of sacrificing the non-essential to preserve the essential. I learnt how to obtain the best I could, when I could not obtain everything; instead of being indignant or dispirited because I could not have entirely my own way, to be pleased and encouraged when I could have the smallest part of it; and when even that could not be, to bear with complete equanimity the being overruled altogether. I have found, through life, these acquisitions to be of the greatest possible importance for personal happiness, and they are also a very necessary condition for enabling any one, either as theorist or as practical man, to effect the greatest amount of good compatible with his opportunities.

CHAPTER IV

Youthful Propagandism.
The Westminster Review

❦

The occupation of so much of my time by office work did not relax my attention to my own pursuits, which were never carried on more vigorously. It was about this time that I began to write in newspapers. The first writings of mine which got into print were two letters published towards the end of 1822, in the *Traveller* evening newspaper. The *Traveller* (which afterwards grew into the *Globe and Traveller* by the purchase and incorporation of the *Globe*) was then the property of the well known political economist Colonel Torrens. Under the editorship of an able man, Mr. Walter Coulson† (who after being an amanuensis of Mr. Bentham, became a reporter, then an editor, next a barrister and conveyancer, and died Counsel to the Home Office), it had become one of the most important newspaper organs of liberal politics. Col. Torrens himself wrote much of the political economy of his paper; and had at this time made an attack upon some opinion of Ricardo and my father, to which at my father's instigation I attempted an answer, and Coulson out of consideration for my father and goodwill to me, inserted it. There was a reply by Torrens, to which I again rejoined.† I soon after attempted something considerably more ambitious. The prosecutions of Richard Carlile† and his wife and sister for publications hostile to Christianity, were then exciting much attention, and nowhere more than among the people I frequented. Freedom of discussion even in politics, much more in religion, was at that time far from being, even in theory, the conceded point which it at least seems to be now; and the holders of obnoxious opinions had to be always ready to argue and reargue for the liberty of expressing them. I wrote a series of five letters, under the signature of Wickliffe, going over the whole length and breadth of the question of free publication of all opinions on religion, and offered them to the *Morning Chronicle.*† Three of them were published in January and February 1823; the other two, containing things too outspoken for

49

that journal, never appeared at all. But a paper which I wrote soon after on the same subject, *à propos* of a debate in the House of Commons, was inserted as a leading article;† and during the whole of this year, 1823, a considerable number of my contributions were printed in the *Chronicle* and *Traveller*: sometimes notices of books, but oftener letters, commenting on some nonsense talked in Parliament, or some defect of the law, or misdoings of the magistracy or the courts of justice. In this last department the *Chronicle* was now rendering signal service. After the death of Mr. Perry,† the editorship and management of the paper had devolved on Mr. John Black,† long a reporter on its establishment; a man of most extensive reading and information, great honesty and simplicity of mind; a particular friend of my father, imbued with many of his and Bentham's ideas, which he reproduced in his articles, among other valuable thoughts, with great facility and skill. From this time the *Chronicle* ceased to be the merely Whig organ it was before, and during the next ten years became to a considerable extent a vehicle of the opinions of the Utilitarian radicals. This was mainly by what Black himself wrote, with some assistance from Fonblanque,† who first shewed his eminent qualities as a writer by articles and *jeux d'esprit* in the *Chronicle*. The defects of the law, and of the administration of justice, were the subject on which that paper rendered most service to improvement. Up to that time hardly a word had been said, except by Bentham and my father, against that most peccant part of English institutions and of their administration. It was the almost universal creed of Englishmen, that the law of England, the judicature of England, the unpaid magistracy of England, were models of excellence. I do not go beyond the mark in saying, that after Bentham, who supplied the principal materials, the greatest share of the merit of breaking down this wretched superstition belongs to Black, as editor of the *Morning Chronicle*. He kept up an incessant fire against it, exposing the absurdities and vices of the law and the court of justice, paid and unpaid, until he forced some sense of them into people's minds. On many other questions he became the organ of opinions much in advance of any which had ever before found regular advocacy in the newspaper press. Black was a frequent visitor of my father, and Mr. Grote used to say that he always knew by the Monday morning's article, whether Black had been with my father on the Sunday. Black was one of the most influential of the many channels through which my father's conversation and personal influence made his opinions tell on the world; co-operating with the effect of his writings in making him a power in the

50

country, such as it has rarely been the lot of an individual in a private station to be, through the mere force of intellect and character: and a power which was often acting the most efficiently where it was least seen and suspected. I have already noticed how much of what was done by Ricardo, Hume, and Grote, was the result, in part, of his prompting and persuasion. He was the good genius by the side of Brougham† in most of what he did for the public, either on education, law reform, or any other subject. And his influence flowed in minor streams too numerous to be specified. This influence was now about to receive a great extension, by the foundation of the *Westminster Review*.†

Contrary to what may have been supposed, my father was in no degree a party to setting up the *Westminster Review*. The need of a Radical organ to make head against the *Edinburgh* and *Quarterly*† (then in the period of their greatest reputation and influence) had been a topic of conversation between him and Mr. Bentham many years earlier, and it had been a part of their *château en Espagne* that my father should be the editor, but the idea had never assumed any practical shape. In 1823, however, Mr. Bentham determined to establish the review at his own cost, and offered the editorship to my father, who declined it as incompatible with his India House appointment. It was then entrusted to Mr. (now Sir John) Bowring,† at that time a merchant in the City. Mr. Bowring had been for two or three years previous an assiduous frequenter of Mr. Bentham, to whom he was recommended by many personal good qualities, by an ardent admiration for Bentham, a zealous adoption of many though not all of his opinions, and, not least, by an extensive acquaintanceship and correspondence with Liberals of all countries, which seemed to qualify him for being a powerful agent in spreading Bentham's fame and doctrines through all quarters of the world. My father had seen little of Bowring, but knew enough of him to have formed a strong opinion, that he was a man of an entirely different type from what my father considered suitable for conducting a political and philosophical review: and he augured so ill of the enterprise that he regretted it altogether, feeling persuaded not only that Mr. Bentham would lose his money, but that discredit would probably be brought upon radical principles. He could not however desert Mr. Bentham, and he consented to write an article for the first number.† As it had been a favorite portion of the scheme formerly talked of, that part of the work should be devoted to reviewing the other Reviews, this article of my father's was to be a general criticism of the *Edinburgh Review* from its commencement. Before writing it he made me read through all the volumes of the Review, or as much of each as seemed of any importance (which was not so arduous a task in 1823 as it would be now), and make notes for him of the articles which I thought he would wish to examine, either on account of their good or their bad qualities. This paper of my father's was the chief cause of the sensation which the *Westminster Review* produced at its first appearance, and is, both in conception and in execution, one of the most striking of all his writings. He began by an analysis of the tendencies of periodical literature in general; pointing out, that it cannot, like books, wait for success, but must succeed immediately, or not at all, and is hence almost certain to profess and inculcate the opinions already held by the public to which it addresses itself, instead of attempting to rectify or improve those opinions. He next, to characterize the position of the *Edinburgh Review* as a political organ, entered into a complete analysis, from the Radical point of view, of the British Constitution. He held up to notice its thoroughly aristocratic character: the nomination of a majority of the House of Commons by a few hundred families; the entire identification of the more independent portion, the county members, with the great landholders; the different classes whom this narrow oligarchy was induced, for convenience, to admit to a share of power; and finally, what he called its two props, the Church, and the legal profession. He pointed out the natural tendency of an aristocratic body of this composition, to group itself into two parties, one of them in possession of the executive, the other endeavouring to supplant the former and become the predominant section by the aid of public opinion, without any essential sacrifice of the aristocratical predominance. He described the course likely to be pursued, and the political ground occupied, by an aristocratic party in opposition, coquetting with popular principles for the sake of popular support. He shewed how this idea was realized in the conduct of the Whig party, and of the *Edinburgh Review* as its chief literary organ. He described, as their main characteristic, what he termed 'seesaw'; writing alternately on both sides of every question which touched the power or interest of the governing classes; sometimes in different articles, sometimes in different parts of the same article: and illustrated his position by copious specimens. So formidable an attack on the Whig party and policy had never before been made; nor had so great a blow been ever struck, in this country, for radicalism; nor was there, I believe, any living person capable of writing that article, except my father.[1]

In the meantime the nascent review had formed a junction with another project, of a purely literary periodical, to be edited by Mr. Henry Southern,[†] afterwards a diplomatist, then a literary man by profession. The two editors agreed to unite their corps, and divide the editorship, Bowring taking the political, Southern the literary department. Southern's review was to have been published by Longman, and that firm, though part proprietors of the *Edinburgh*, were willing to be the publishers of the new journal. But when all the arrangements had been made, and the prospectuses sent out, the Longmans saw my father's attack on the *Edinburgh*, and drew back. My father was now appealed to for his interest with his own publisher, Baldwin, which was exerted with a successful result. And so, in April 1824, amidst anything but hope on my father's part, and that of most of those who afterwards aided in carrying on the review, the first number made its appearance.[†]

That number was an agreeable surprise to most of us. The average of the articles was of much better quality than had been expected. The literary and artistic department had rested chiefly on Mr. Bingham,[†] a barrister (subsequently a Police Magistrate) who had been for some years a frequenter of Bentham, was a friend of both the Austins, and had adopted with great ardour Mr. Bentham's philosophical opinions. Partly from accident, there were in the first number as many as five articles by Bingham; and we were extremely pleased with them. I well remember the mixed feeling I myself had about the Review; the joy at finding, what we did not at all expect, that it was sufficiently good to be capable of being made a creditable organ of those who held the opinions it professed; and extreme vexation, since it was so good on the whole, at what we thought the blemishes of it.[‡] When, however, in addition to our generally favourable opinion of it, we learned that it had an extraordinarily large sale for a first number, and found that the appearance of a Radical review, with pretensions equal to those of the established organs of parties, had excited much attention, there could be no room for hesitation, and we all became eager in doing everything we could to strengthen and improve it.[‡]

---

[1] The continuation of this article in the second number of the review was written by me under my father's eye, and (except as practice in composition, in which respect it was, to me, more useful than anything else I ever wrote) was of little or no value.

My father continued to write occasional articles. The *Quarterly Review* received its exposure, as a sequel to that of the *Edinburgh*. Of his other contributions, the most important were an attack on Southey's *Book of the Church*,[†] in the fifth number, and a political article in the twelfth.[†] Mr. Austin only contributed one paper, but one of great merit, an argument against primogeniture, in reply to an article then lately published in the *Edinburgh Review* by McCulloch.[†] Grote also was a contributor only once; all the time he could spare being already taken up with his *History of Greece*.[†] The article he wrote was on his own subject, and was a very complete exposure and castigation of Mitford.[†] Bingham and Charles Austin continued to write for some time; Fonblanque was a frequent contributor from the third number. Of my particular associates, Ellis was a regular writer up to the ninth number; and about the time when he left off, others of the set began; Eyton Tooke, Graham, and Roebuck. I was myself the most frequent writer of all, having contributed, from the second number to the eighteenth, thirteen articles;[‡] reviews of books on history and political economy, or discussions on special political topics, as corn laws, game laws, law of libel.[†] Occasional articles of merit came in from other acquaintances of my father's and, in time, of mine; and some of Mr. Bowring's writers turned out well. On the whole, however, the conduct of the Review was never satisfactory to any of the persons strongly interested in its principles, with whom I came in contact. Hardly ever did a number come out without containing several things extremely offensive to us, either in point of opinion, of taste, or by mere want of ability. The unfavorable judgments passed by my father, Grote, the two Austins, and others, were reechoed with exaggeration by us younger people; and as our youthful zeal rendered us by no means backward in making complaints, we led the two editors a sad life. From my knowledge of what I then was, I have no doubt that we were at least as often wrong as right; and I am very certain that if the Review had been carried on according to our notions (I mean those of the juniors) it would have been no better, perhaps not even so good as it was. But it is worth noting as a fact in the history of Benthamism, that the periodical organ, by which it was best known, was from the first extremely unsatisfactory to those, whose opinions on all subjects it was supposed specially to represent.[†]

Meanwhile, however, the Review made considerable noise in the world, and gave a recognised *status*, in the arena of opinion and discussion, to the Benthamic type of radicalism, out of all proportion to the number of its adherents, and to the personal merits and abilities, at that time, of most of those who could be reckoned among them. It was a time, as is known, of rapidly rising Liberalism. When the fears and animosities accompanying the war with France had been brought to an end, and people had once more a place in their thoughts for home politics, the tide began to set towards reform. The renewed oppression of the Continent by the old reigning families, the countenance apparently given by the English Government to the conspiracy against liberty called the Holy Alliance,[†] and the enormous weight of the national debt and taxation occasioned by so long and costly a war, rendered the government and parliament very unpopular. Radicalism, under the leadership of the Burdetts[†] and Cobbetts,[†] had assumed a character and importance which seriously alarmed the Administration: and their alarm had scarcely been temporarily assuaged by the celebrated Six Acts,[†] when the trial of Queen Caroline[†] roused a still wider and deeper feeling of hatred. Though the outward signs of this hatred passed away with its exciting cause, there arose on all sides a spirit which had never shewn itself before, of opposition to abuses in detail. Mr. Hume's persevering scrutiny of the public expenditure, forcing the House of Commons to a division on every objectionable item in the estimates, had begun to tell with great force on public opinion, and had extorted many minor retrenchments from an unwilling Administration. Political economy had asserted itself with great vigour in public affairs, by the Petition of the Merchants of London for Free Trade, drawn up in 1820 by Mr. Tooke and presented by Mr. Alexander Baring;[†] and by the noble exertions of Ricardo during the few years of his parliamentary life. His writings, following up the impulse given by the Bullion controversy, and followed up in their turn by the expositions and comments of my father and McCulloch (whose writings in the *Edinburgh Review* during those years were most valuable), had drawn general attention to the subject, making at least partial converts in the Cabinet itself; and Huskisson,[†] supported by Canning,[†] had commenced that gradual demolition of the protective system, which one of their colleagues virtually completed in 1846,[†] though the last vestiges were only swept away by Mr. Gladstone in 1860.[†] Mr. Peel,[†] then Home Secretary, was entering cautiously into the untrodden and peculiarly Benthamic path of Law Reform. At this period, when Liberalism seemed to be becoming the tone of the time, when improvement of institutions was preached from the highest places, and a complete change of the constitution of Parliament was loudly demanded in the lowest, it is not strange that attention should have been roused by the regular appearance in controversy of what seemed a new school of writers, claiming to be the legislators and theorists of this new tendency. The air of strong conviction‡ with which they wrote, when scarcely any one else seemed to have an equally strong faith in as definite a creed; the boldness with which they tilted against the very front of both the existing political parties; their uncompromising profession of opposition to many of the generally received opinions, and the suspicion they lay under of holding others still more heterodox than they professed; the talent and verve of at least my father's articles, and the appearance of a corps behind him sufficient to carry on a review; and finally, the fact that the review was bought and read, made the so called Bentham school in philosophy and politics fill a greater place in the public mind than it had held before, or has ever again held since other equally earnest schools of thought have arisen in England. As I was in the head quarters of it, knew of what it was composed, and as one of the most active of its very small number, might say without undue assumption, *quorum pars magna fui*,† it belongs to me more than to most others to give some account of it.

This supposed school, then, had no other existence than what was constituted by the fact, that my father's writings and conversation drew round him a certain number of young men who had already imbibed, or who imbibed from him, a greater or smaller portion of his very decided political and philosophical opinions. The notion that Bentham was surrounded by a band of disciples who received their opinions from his lips, is a fable to which my father did justice in his *Fragment on Mackintosh*,† and which, to all who knew Mr. Bentham's habits of life and manner of conversation,‡ is simply ridiculous. The influence which Bentham exercised was by his writings. Through them he has produced, and is producing, effects on the condition of mankind, wider and deeper, no doubt, than any which can be attributed to my father. He is a much greater name in history. But my father exercised a far greater personal ascendancy. He *was* sought for the vigour and instructiveness of his conversation, and did use it largely as an instrument for the diffusion of his opinions. I have never known any man who could do such ample justice to his best thoughts in colloquial discussion. His perfect command over his great mental resources, the terseness and expressiveness of his language, and the moral earnestness as well as intellectual force of his delivery, made him one of the most striking of all argumentative conversers: and he was full of anecdote, a hearty laugher, and when with people whom he liked, a most lively and amusing companion. It was not solely, or even chiefly, in diffusing his merely intellectual convictions, that his power shewed itself: it was still more through the influence of a quality, of which I have only since learnt to appreciate the extreme rarity:‡ that exalted public spirit and regard above all things to the good of the whole, which warmed into life and activity every germ of similar virtue that existed in the minds he came in contact with: the desire he made them feel for his approbation, the shame at his disapproval; the moral support which his conversation and his very existence gave to those who were aiming at the same objects, and the encouragement he afforded to the faint-hearted or desponding among them, by the firm confidence which (though the reverse of sanguine as to the results to be expected in any one particular case) he always felt in the power of reason, the general progress of improvement, and the good which individuals could do by judicious effort.

It was my father's opinions which gave the distinguishing character to the Benthamic or utilitarian propagandism of that time. They fell singly scattered from him in many directions, but they flowed from him in a continued stream principally in three channels. One was through me, the only mind directly formed by his instructions, and through whom considerable influence was exercised over various young men who became, in their turn, propagandists. A second was through some of the Cambridge cotemporaries of Charles Austin, who, either initiated by him or under the general mental impulse which he gave, had adopted many opinions allied to those of my father, and some of the more considerable of whom afterwards sought my father's acquaintance and frequented his house. Among these may be mentioned Strutt, afterwards Lord Belper, and the present Lord Romilly, with whose eminent father, Sir Samuel,† my father had of old been on terms of friendship. The third channel was that of a younger generation of Cambridge undergraduates, cotemporary not with Austin but with Eyton Tooke, who were drawn to that estimable person by affinity of opinions, and introduced by him to my father: the most notable of these was Charles Buller.† Various other persons individually received and transmitted a considerable amount of my father's influence: for example, Black (as before mentioned) and Fonblanque: most of these however we accounted only partial allies; Fonblanque, for instance, was always divergent from us on many important points. But indeed there was by no means complete unanimity among any portion of us, nor had any of us adopted implicitly all my father's opinions. For example, although his Essay on Government† was regarded probably by all of us as a masterpiece of political wisdom, our adhesion by no means extended to the paragraph of it, in which he maintains that women may consistently with good government, be excluded from the suffrage, because their interest is the same with that of men. From this doctrine, I, and all those who formed my chosen associates, most positively dissented. It is due to my father to say that he denied having intended to affirm that women *should* be excluded, any more than men under the age of forty, concerning whom he maintained, in the very next paragraph, an exactly similar thesis. He was, as he truly said, not discussing whether the suffrage had better be restricted, but only (assuming that it is to be restricted) what is the utmost limit of restriction, which does not necessarily involve a sacrifice of the securities for good government. But I thought then, as I have always thought since, that the opinion which he acknowledged, no less than that which he disclaimed, is as great an error as any of those against which the Essay was directed;† that the interest of women is included in that of men exactly as much and no more, as the interest of subjects is included in that of kings; and that every reason which exists for giving the suffrage to anybody, demands that it should not be withheld from women. This was also the general opinion of the younger proselytes; and it is pleasant to be able to say that Mr. Bentham, on this important point, was wholly on our side.

But though none of us, probably, agreed in every respect with my father, his opinions, as I said before, were the principal element which gave its colour and character to the little group of young men who were the first propagators of what was afterwards called 'philosophic radicalism.' Their mode of thinking was not character-ized by Benthamism in any sense which has relation to Bentham as a chief or guide, but rather by a combination of Bentham's point of view with that of the modern political economy, and with the Hartleian metaphysics.† Malthus's population principle† was quite as much a banner, and point of union among us, as any opinion spe-cially belonging to Bentham. This great doctrine, originally brought forward as an argument against the indefinite improvability of human affairs, we took up with ardent zeal in the contrary sense, as indicating the sole means of realizing that improvability by securing full employment at high wages to the whole labouring population through a voluntary restriction of the increase of their numbers.† The other leading characteristics of the creed, which we held in common with my father, may be stated as follows:

In politics, an almost unbounded confidence‡ in the efficacy of two things: representative government, and complete freedom of discussion. So complete was my father's reliance on the influence of reason over the minds of mankind,[†] whenever it is allowed to reach them, that he felt as if all would be gained if the whole population were taught to read, if all sorts of opinions were allowed to be addressed to them by word and in writing, and if by means of the suffrage they could nominate a legislature to give effect to the opinions they adopted. He thought that when the legislature no longer represented a class interest, it would aim at the general interest, honestly and with adequate wisdom; since the people would be sufficiently under the guidance of educated intelligence, to make in general a good choice of persons to represent them, and having done so, to leave to those whom they had chosen a liberal discretion. Accordingly aristocratic rule, the government of the Few in any of its shapes, being in his eyes the only thing which stood between mankind and an administration of their affairs by the best wisdom to be found among them, was the object of his sternest disapprobation, and a democratic suffrage the principal article of his political creed, not on the ground of liberty, Rights of Man, or any of the phrases, more or less significant, by which, up to that time, democracy had usually been defended, but as the most essential of 'securities for good government.' In this, too, he held fast only to what he deemed essentials; he was comparatively indifferent to monarchical or republican forms – far more so than Bentham, to whom a king, in the character of 'corrupter-general,'[†] appeared necessarily very noxious. Next to aristocracy, an established church, or corporation of priests, as being by position the great depravers of religion, and interested in opposing the progress of the human mind, was the object of his greatest detestation; though he disliked no clergyman personally who did not deserve it, and was on terms of sincere friendship with several.[‡] In ethics, his moral feelings were energetic and rigid on all points which he deemed important to human well being, while he was supremely indifferent in opinion (though his indifference did not shew itself in personal conduct) to all those doctrines of the common morality, which he thought had no foundation but in asceticism and priestcraft. He looked forward, for example, to a considerable increase of freedom in the relations between the sexes, though without pretending to define exactly what would be, or ought to be, the precise conditions of that freedom.[†] This opinion was connected in him with no sensuality either of a theoretical or of a practical kind. He anticipated, on the contrary, as one of the beneficial effects of increased freedom, that the imagination would no longer dwell upon the physical relation and its adjuncts, and swell this into one of the principal objects of life; a perversion of the imagination and feelings, which he regarded as one of the deepest seated and most pervading evils in the human mind.† In psychology, his fundamental doctrine was the formation of all human character by circumstances, through the universal Principle of Association, and the consequent unlimited possibility of improving the moral and intellectual condition of mankind by education. Of all his doctrines none was more important than this, or needs more to be insisted on: unfortunately there is none which is more contradictory to the prevailing tendencies of speculation, both in his time and since.†

These various opinions were seized on with youthful fanaticism by the little knot of young men of whom I was one: and we put into them a sectarian spirit, from which, in intention at least, my father was wholly free. What we (or rather a phantom substituted in the place of us) were sometimes, by a ridiculous exaggeration, called by others, namely a 'school,' some of us for a time really hoped and aspired to be. The French *philosophes* of the eighteenth century were the example we sought to imitate, and we hoped to accomplish no less results. No one of the set went to so great excesses in this boyish ambition as I did; which might be shewn by many particulars, were it not a useless waste of space and time.‡

All this, however, is properly only the outside of our existence; or at least, the intellectual part alone, and no more than one side of that. In attempting to penetrate inward, and give any indication of what we were as human beings, I must be understood as speaking only of myself, of whom alone I can speak from sufficient knowledge; and I do not believe that the picture would suit any of my companions without many and great modifications.

I conceive that the description so often given of a Benthamite, as a mere reasoning machine, though extremely inapplicable to most of those who have been designated by that title, was during two or three years of my life not altogether untrue of me. It was perhaps as applicable to me as it can well be to any one just entering into life, to whom the common objects of desire must in general have at least the attraction of novelty. There is nothing very extraordinary in this fact: no youth of the age I then was, can be expected to be more than one thing, and this was the thing I happened to be. Ambition‡ and desire of distinction, I had in abundance; and zeal for what I thought the good of mankind was my strongest sentiment, mixing with and colouring all others. But my zeal was as yet little else, at that period of my life, than zeal for speculative opinions. It had not its root in genuine benevolence, or sympathy with mankind; though these qualities held their due place in my ethical standard. Nor was it connected with any high enthusiasm for ideal nobleness. Yet of this feeling I was imaginatively very susceptible; but there was at that time an intermission of its natural aliment, poetical culture, while there was a superabundance of the discipline antagonistic to it, that of mere logic and analysis. Add to this that, as already mentioned, my father's teachings tended to the undervaluing of feeling. It was not that he was himself cold-hearted or insensible; I believe it was rather from the contrary quality; he thought that feeling could take care of itself; that there was sure to be enough of it if actions were properly cared about. Offended by the frequency with which, in ethical and philosophical controversy, feeling is made the ultimate reason and justification of conduct, instead of being itself called on for a justification, while, in practice, actions, the effect of which on human happiness is mis-chievous, are defended as being required by feeling, and the character of a person of feeling obtains a credit for desert, which he thought only due to actions, he had a real impatience of attributing praise to feeling, or of any but the most sparing reference to it either in the estimation of persons or in the discussion of things. In addition to the influence which this characteristic in him had on me and others, we found all the opinions to which we attached most importance, constantly attacked on the ground of feeling. Utility was denounced as cold calculation; political economy as hard-hearted; anti-population doctrines as repulsive to the natural feelings of mankind. We retorted by the word 'sentimentality,' which, along with 'declamation' and 'vague generalities,' served us as common terms of opprobrium. Although we were generally in the right, as against those who were opposed to us, the effect was that the cultivation of feeling (except the feelings of public and private duty) was not in much esteem among us, and had very little place in the thoughts of most of us, myself in particular.‡ What we principally thought of, was to alter people's opinions; to make them believe according to evidence, and know what was their real interest, which when they once knew, they would, we thought, by the instrument of opinion, enforce a regard to it upon one another. While fully recognizing the superior excellence of unselfish benevolence and love of justice, we did not expect the regeneration of mankind from any direct action on those sentiments, but from the effect of educated intellect, enlightening the selfish feelings. Although this last is prodigiously important as a means of improvement in the hands of those who are themselves impelled by nobler principles of action, I do not believe that any one of the survivors of the Benthamites or Utilitarians of that day, now relies mainly upon it for the general amendment‡ of human conduct.

From this neglect both in theory and in practice of the cultivation of feeling, naturally resulted among other things an undervaluing of poetry, and of Imagination generally as an element of human nature. It is, or was, part of the popular notion of Benthamites, that they are enemies of poetry: this was partly true of Bentham himself; he used to say that 'all poetry is misrepresentation':† but, in the sense in which he said it, the same might have been said of all impressive speech; of all representation or inculcation more oratorical in its character than a sum in arithmetic. An article of Bingham's in the first number of the *Westminster Review*, in which he offered as an explanation of something which he disliked in Moore, that 'Mr. Moore *is* a poet, and therefore is *not* a reasoner,'† did a good deal to attach the notion of hating poetry to the writers in the Review. But the truth was that many of us were great readers of poetry; Bingham himself had been a writer of it, while as regards me (and the same thing might be said of my father) the correct statement would be not that I disliked poetry, but that I was theoretically indifferent to it. I disliked any sentiments in poetry which I should have disliked in prose; and that included a great deal. And I was wholly blind to its place in human culture, as a means of educating the feelings. But I was always personally very susceptible to some kinds of it. In the most sectarian period of my Benthamism I happened to look into Pope's *Essay on Man*,† and though every opinion in it was contrary to mine, I well remember how powerfully it acted on my imagination. Perhaps at that time poetical composition of any higher type than eloquent discussion in verse, might not have produced a similar effect on me: at all events I seldom gave it an opportunity. This, however, was a mere passing state. Long before I had enlarged in any considerable degree, the basis of my intellectual creed, I had obtained in the natural course of my mental progress, poetic culture of the most valuable kind, by means of reverential admiration for the lives and characters of heroic persons; especially the heroes of philosophy. The same inspiring effect which so many of the benefactors of mankind have left on record that they had experienced from Plutarch's *Lives*, was produced on me by Plato's pictures of Socrates, and by some modern biographies, above all by Condorcet's *Life of Turgot*;† a book well calculated to rouse the best sort of enthusiasm, since it contains one of the wisest and noblest of lives, delineated by one of the wisest and noblest of men. The heroic virtue of these glorious representatives of the opinions with which I sympathized, deeply affected me, and I perpetually recurred to them as others do to a favorite poet, when needing to be carried up into the more elevated regions of feeling and thought. I may observe by the way that this book cured me of my sectarian follies. The two or three pages beginning 'Il regardait toute secte comme nuisible,' and explaining why Turgot always kept himself perfectly distinct from the Encyclopedists, sank deeply into my mind. I left off designating myself and others as Utilitarians, and by the pronoun 'we,' or any other collective designation, I ceased to *afficher* sectarianism. My real inward sectarianism I did not get rid of till later, and much more gradually.

About the end of 1824, or beginning of 1825, Mr. Bentham, having lately got back his papers on Evidence from M. Dumont (whose *Traité des Preuves Judiciaires*, grounded on them, was then first completed and published), resolved to have them printed in the original, and bethought himself of me as capable of preparing them for the press; in the same manner as his *Book of Fallacies* had been recently edited by Bingham.† I gladly undertook this task, and it occupied nearly all my leisure for about a year, exclusive of the time afterwards spent in seeing the five large volumes through the press. Mr. Bentham had begun this treatise three times, at considerable intervals, each time in a different manner, and each time without reference to the preceding: two of the three times he had gone over nearly the whole subject. These three masses of manuscript it was my business to condense into a single treatise; adopting the one last written as the groundwork, and incorporating with it as much of the two others as it had not completely superseded. I had also to unroll such of Bentham's involved and parenthetical sentences, as seemed to overpass by their complexity the measure of what readers were likely to take the pains to understand. It was further Mr. Bentham's particular desire that I should, from myself, endeavour to supply any *lacunæ*† which he had left; and at his instance I read, for this purpose, the most authoritative treatises on the English Law of Evidence, and commented on a few of the objectionable points of the English rules, which had escaped Bentham's notice. I also replied to the objections which had been made to some of his doctrines, by reviewers of Dumont's book, and added a few supplementary remarks on some of the more abstract parts of the subject, such as the theory of improbability and impossibility. The controversial part of these editorial additions was written in a more assuming tone, than became one so young and inexperienced as I was: but indeed I had never contemplated coming forward in my own person; and, as an anonymous editor of Bentham, I fell into the tone of my author, not thinking it unsuitable to him or to the subject, however it might be so to me. My name as editor was put to the book after it was printed, at Mr. Bentham's positive desire, which I in vain attempted to persuade him to forego.†

The time occupied in this editorial work was extremely well employed in respect to my own improvement. The *Rationale of Judicial Evidence* is one of the richest in matter of all Bentham's productions. The theory of evidence being in itself one of the most important of his subjects, and ramifying into most of the others, the book contains, very fully developed, a great proportion of all his best thoughts: while, among more special things, it comprises the most elaborate exposure of the vices and defects of English law, as it then was, which is to be found in his works: not confined to the law of evidence, but including, by way of illustrative episode, the entire procedure or practice of Westminster Hall.† The direct knowledge, therefore, which I obtained from the book, and which was imprinted upon me much more thoroughly than it could have been by mere reading, was itself no small acquisition. But this occupation did for me what might seem less to be expected; it gave a great start to my powers of composition. Everything which I wrote subsequently to this editorial employment, was markedly superior to anything that I had written before it. Bentham's later style, as the world knows, was heavy and cumbersome, from the excess of a good quality, the love of precision, which made him introduce clause within clause into the heart of every sentence, that the reader might receive into his mind all the modifications and qualifications simultaneously with the main proposition: and the habit grew on him until his sentences became, to those not accustomed to them, most laborious reading. But his earlier style, that of the *Fragment on Government, Plan of a Judicial Establishment*,† &c., is a model of liveliness and ease combined with fulness of matter, scarcely ever surpassed: and of this earlier style there were many striking specimens in the manuscripts on Evidence, all of which I endeavoured to preserve. So long a course of this admirable writing had a considerable effect upon my own; and I added to it by the assiduous reading of other writers, both French and English, who combined, in a remarkable degree, ease with force, such as Goldsmith,† Fielding,† Pascal,† Voltaire,† and Courier.†‡ Through these influences my writing lost the jejuneness of my early compositions; the bones and cartilages began to clothe themselves with flesh, and the style became, at times, lively and almost light.

This improvement was first exhibited in a new field. Mr. Marshall, of Leeds, father of the present generation of Marshalls, the same who was brought into Parliament for Yorkshire, when the representation forfeited by Grampound was transferred to it – an earnest parliamentary reformer, and a man of large fortune, of which he made a liberal use, had been much struck with Bentham's *Book of Fallacies*:[†] and the thought had occurred to him that it would be useful to publish annually the Parliamentary Debates, not in the chronological order of *Hansard*,[†] but classified according to subjects, and accompanied by a commentary pointing out the fallacies of the speakers. With this intention, he very naturally addressed himself to the editor of *The Book of Fallacies*; and Bingham, with the assistance of Charles Austin, undertook the editorship. The work was called *Parliamentary History and Review*.[†] Its sale was not sufficient to keep it in existence, and it only lasted three years. It excited, however, some attention among parliamentary and political people. The best strength of the party was put forth in it; and its execution did them much more credit, than that of the *Westminster Review* had ever done. Bingham and Charles Austin wrote much in it;[†] as did Strutt, Romilly, and several other liberal lawyers. My father wrote one article in his best style; the elder Austin another. Coulson wrote one of great merit. It fell to my lot to lead off the first number by an article on the principal topic of the session (that of 1825), the Catholic Association and the Catholic disabilities.[†] In the second number I wrote an elaborate Essay on the commercial crisis of 1825 and the Currency Debates. In the third I had two articles, one on a minor subject, the other on the Reciprocity principle in commerce, *à propos* of a celebrated diplomatic correspondence between Canning and Gallatin. These writings were no longer mere reproductions and applications of the doctrines I had been taught; they were original thinking, as far as that name can be applied to old ideas in new forms and connexions: and I do not exceed the truth in saying that there was a maturity, and a well-digested character about them, which there had not been in any of my previous performances. In execution, therefore, they were not at all juvenile; but their subjects have either gone by, or have been so much better treated since, that they are entirely superseded, and should remain buried in the same oblivion with my contributions to the first dynasty of the *Westminster Review*.

While thus engaged in writing for the public, I did not neglect other modes of self-cultivation. It was at this time that I learnt German;

beginning it in the Hamiltonian method, for which purpose I and several of my companions formed a class. For several years from this period, our social studies assumed a shape which contributed very much to my mental progress. The idea occurred to us of carrying on, by reading and conversation, a joint study of several of the branches of science which we wished to be masters of. We assembled to the number of a dozen or more. Mr. Grote lent a room of his house in Threadneedle Street† for the purpose, and his partner Prescott,† one of the three original members of the Utilitarian Society, made one among us. We met two mornings in every week, from half-past eight till ten, at which hour most of us were called off to our daily occupations. Our first subject was Political Economy. We chose some systematic treatise as our text-book; my father's *Elements* being our first choice. One of us read aloud a chapter, or some smaller portion, of the book. The discussion was then opened, and any one who had an objection or other remark to make, made it. Our rule was to discuss thoroughly every point raised, whether great or small, prolonging the discussion until all who took part were satisfied with the conclusion they had individually arrived at; and to follow up every topic of collateral speculation which the chapter or the conversation suggested, never leaving it until we had untied every knot which we found. We repeatedly kept up the discussion of some one point for several weeks, thinking intently on it during the intervals of our meetings, and contriving solutions of the new difficulties which had risen up in the last morning's discussion. When we had finished in this way my father's *Elements*, we went in the same manner through Ricardo's *Principles of Political Economy,*† and Bailey's *Dissertation on Value.*† These close and vigorous discussions were not only improving in a high degree to those who took part in them, but brought out new views of some topics of abstract Political Economy. The theory of International Values which I afterwards published, emanated from these conversations, as did also the modified form of Ricardo's theory of Profits, laid down in my Essay on Profits and Interest. Those among us with whom new speculations chiefly originated, were Ellis, Graham, and I; though others gave valuable aid to the discussions, especially Prescott and Roebuck, the one by his knowledge, the other by his dialectical acuteness. The theories of International Values and of Profits were excogitated and worked out in about equal proportions by myself and Graham: and if our original project had been executed, my *Essays on Some Unsettled Questions of Political Economy*† would have been brought out along with some papers of his, under our joint names. But when my exposition came to be written, I found that I had so much overestimated my agreement with him, and he dissented so much from the most original of the two Essays, that on International Values, that I was obliged to consider the theory as now exclusively mine, and it came out as such when published many years later. I may mention that among the alterations which my father made in revising his *Elements* for the third edition, several were grounded on criticisms elicited by these Conversations; and in particular, he modified his opinions (though not to the extent of our new speculations) on both the points to which I have adverted.

When we had enough of political economy, we took up the syllogistic logic in the same manner, Grote now joining us. Our first text book was Aldrich,[†] but being disgusted with its superficiality, we reprinted one of the most finished among the many manuals of the school logic, which my father, a great collector of such books, possessed, the *Manuductio ad Logicam* of the Jesuit Du Trieu.[†] After finishing this, we took up Whately's *Logic*,[†] then first republished from the *Encyclopædia Metropolitana*, and finally the 'Computatio sive Logica' of Hobbes.[†] These books, dealt with in our manner, afforded a wide range for original metaphysical speculation: and most of what has been done in the First Book of my *System of Logic*,[†] to rationalize and correct the principles and distinctions of the school logicians, and to improve the theory of the Import of Propositions, had its origin in these discussions; Graham and I originating most of the novelties, while Grote and others furnished an excellent tribunal or test. From this time I formed the project of writing a book on Logic, though on a much humbler scale than the one I ultimately executed.

Having done with Logic, we launched into analytic psychology, and having chosen Hartley for our text book, we raised Priestley's edition[†] to an extravagant price by searching through London to furnish each of us with a copy. When we had finished Hartley, we suspended our meetings; but, my father's *Analysis of the Mind* being published soon after, we reassembled for the purpose of reading it. With this our exercises ended. I have always dated from these conversations my own real inauguration as an original and independent thinker. It was also through them that I acquired, or very much strengthened, a mental habit to which I attribute all that I have ever done, or ever shall do, in speculation; that of never accepting half-solutions of difficulties as complete; never abandoning a puzzle, but again and again returning to it until it was cleared up; never allowing obscure corners of a subject to remain unexplored, because they did not appear important; never thinking that I perfectly understood any part of a subject until I understood the whole.

Our doings from 1825 to 1830 in the way of public speaking filled a considerable place in my life during those years, and as they had important effects on my development, something ought to be said of them.

There was for some time in existence a society of Owenites,† called the Cooperative Society, which met for weekly public discussions in Chancery Lane.† In the early part of 1825, accident brought Roebuck in contact with several of its members, and led to his attending one or two of the meetings and taking part in the debate in opposition to Owenism. Some one of us started the notion of going there in a body and having a general battle: and Charles Austin and some of his friends who did not usually take part in our joint exercises, entered into the project. It was carried out by concert with the principal members of the Society, themselves nothing loth, as they naturally preferred a controversy with opponents to a tame discussion among their own body. The question of population was proposed as the subject of debate: Charles Austin led the case on our side with a brilliant speech, and the fight was kept up by adjournment through five or six weekly meetings before crowded auditories, including along with the members of the Society and their friends, many hearers and some speakers from the Inns of Court.† When this debate was ended, another was commenced on the general merits of Owen's system: and the contest altogether lasted about three months. It was a *lutte corps-à-corps* between Owenites and political economists, whom the Owenites regarded as their most inveterate opponents: but it was a perfectly friendly dispute. We who represented political economy, had the same objects in view as they had, and took pains to shew it; and the principal champion on their side was a very estimable man, with whom I was well acquainted, Mr. William Thompson,† of Cork, author of a book on the Distribution of Wealth, and of an 'Appeal' in behalf of women against the passage relating to them in my father's Essay on Government. Ellis, Roebuck, and I, took an active part in the debate, and among those from the Inns of Court who joined in it I remember Charles Villiers. The other side obtained also, on the population question, very efficient support from without. The well-known Gale Jones, then an elderly man, made one of his florid speeches; but the speaker with whom I was most struck, though I dissented from nearly every word he said, was Thirlwall,† the historian, since Bishop of St. David's, then a Chancery barrister, unknown except by a high reputation for eloquence acquired at the Cambridge Union before the era of Austin and Macaulay. His speech was in answer to one of mine. Before he had uttered ten sentences, I set him down as the best speaker I had ever heard, and I have never since heard any one whom I placed above him.‡

The great interest of these debates predisposed some of those who took part in them, to catch at a suggestion thrown out by McCulloch, the political economist, that a society was wanted in London similar to the Speculative Society at Edinburgh, in which Brougham, Horner† and others first cultivated public speaking. Our experience at the Cooperative Society seemed to give cause for being sanguine as to the sort of men who might be brought together in London for such a purpose. McCulloch mentioned the matter to several young men of influence to whom he was then giving private lessons in political economy. Some of these entered warmly into the project, particularly George Villiers, afterwards Earl of Clarendon. He and his brothers Hyde and Charles, Romilly, Charles Austin, and I, with some others, met and agreed on a plan. We determined to meet once a fortnight, from November to June, at the Freemason's Tavern,† and we had soon a splendid list of members, containing, along with several members of parliament, nearly all the most noted speakers of the Cambridge Union and of the Oxford United Debating Society. It is curiously illustrative of the tendencies of the time that our principal difficulty in recruiting for the Society was to find a sufficient number of Tory speakers. Almost all whom we could press into the service were Liberals, of different orders and degrees. Besides those already named, we had Macaulay, Thirlwall, Praed,† Lord Howick,† Samuel Wilberforce† (afterwards Bishop of Oxford), Charles Poulett Thomson† (afterwards Lord Sydenham), Edward and Henry Lytton Bulwer,† Fonblanque, and many others whom I cannot now recollect, but who made themselves afterwards more or less conspicuous in public or literary life. Nothing could seem more promising. But when the time for action drew near, and it was necessary to fix on a President, and find somebody to open the first debate, none of our celebrities would consent to perform either office. Of the many who were pressed on the subject, the only one who could be prevailed on was a man of whom I knew very little, but who had taken high honours at Oxford and was said to have acquired a great oratorical reputation there; who some time afterwards became a Tory member of parliament.† He accordingly was fixed on, both for filling the President's chair and for making the first speech. The important day arrived; the benches were crowded; all our great speakers were present, to judge of, but not to help our efforts. The Oxford orator's speech was a complete failure. This threw a damp on the whole concern: the speakers who followed were few, and none of them did their best: the affair was a complete *fiasco*; and the oratorical celebrities we had counted on went away never to return, giving to me at least a lesson in knowledge of the world. This unexpected breakdown altered my whole relation to the project. I had not anticipated taking a prominent part, or speaking much or often, particularly at first; but I now saw that the success of the scheme depended on the new men, and I put my shoulder to the wheel. I opened the second question, and from that time spoke in nearly every debate.[†] It was very uphill work for some time. The three Villiers and Romilly stuck to us for some time longer,[‡] but the patience of all the founders of the Society was at last exhausted, except me and Roebuck. In the season following, 1826/27, things began to mend. We had acquired two excellent Tory speakers, Hayward, and Shee[†] (afterwards Sergeant Shee): the radical side was reinforced by Charles Buller, Cockburn,[†] and others of the second generation of Cambridge Benthamites; and with their and other occasional aid, and the two Tories as well as Roebuck and me for regular speakers, almost every debate was a *bataille rangée* between the 'philosophic radicals' and the Tory lawyers; until our conflicts were talked about, and several persons of note and consideration came to hear us. This happened still more in the subsequent seasons, 1828 and 1829, when the Coleridgians, in the persons of Maurice[†] and Sterling,[†] made their appearance in the Society as a second Liberal and even Radical party, on totally different grounds from Benthamism and vehemently opposed to it; bringing into these discussions the general doctrines and modes of thought of the European reaction against the philosophy of the eighteenth century; and adding a third and very important belligerent party to our contests, which were now no bad exponents of the movement of opinion among the most cultivated part of the new generation.[†] Our debates were very different from those of common debating societies, for they habitually consisted of the strongest arguments and most philosophic principles which either side was able to produce, thrown often into close and *serré* confutations of one another. The practice was necessarily very useful to us, and eminently so to me. I never, indeed, acquired real fluency, and had always a bad and ungraceful delivery; but I could make myself listened to:[‡] and as I always wrote my speeches when, from the feelings involved or the

70

nature of the ideas to be developed, expression seemed important, I greatly increased my power of effective writing; acquiring not only an ear for smoothness and rhythm, but a practical sense for *telling* sentences, and an immediate criterion of their telling property, by their effect on a mixed audience.

The Society, and the preparation for it, together with the preparation for the morning conversations which were going on simultaneously, occupied the greater part of my leisure; and made me feel it a relief when, in the spring of 1828, I ceased to write for the *Westminster*. The Review had fallen into difficulties. Though the sale of the first number had been very encouraging, the permanent sale had never, I believe, been sufficient to pay the expenses, on the scale on which the review was carried on. Those expenses had been considerably, but not sufficiently, reduced. One of the editors, Southern, had resigned; and several of the writers, including my father and me, who had been paid like other contributors for our earlier articles, had latterly written without payment. Nevertheless, the original funds‡ were nearly or quite exhausted, and if the Review was to be continued some new arrangement of its affairs had become indispensable. My father and I had several conferences with Bowring on the subject. We were willing to do our utmost for maintaining the Review as an organ of our opinions, but not under Bowring's editorship: while the impossibility of its any longer supporting a paid editor, afforded a ground on which, without affront to him, we could propose to dispense with his services. We, and some of our friends, were prepared to carry on the Review as unpaid writers, either finding among ourselves an unpaid editor, or sharing the editorship among us. But while this negociation was proceeding, with Bowring's apparent acquiescence, he was carrying on another in a different quarter (with Colonel Perronet Thompson), of which we received the first intimation in a letter from Bowring as editor, informing us merely that an arrangement had been made, and proposing to us to write for the next number, with promise of payment. We did not dispute Bowring's right to bring about, if he could, an arrangement more favorable to himself than the one we had proposed; but we thought the concealment which he had practised towards us, while seemingly entering into our own project, an affront: and even had we not thought so, we were indisposed to expend any more of our time and trouble in attempting to write up the Review under his management. Accordingly my father excused himself from writing; though two or three years later, on great pressure, he did write one more political article.[†] As for me, I positively refused. And thus ended my connexion with the original *Westminster*. The last article which I wrote in it had cost me more labour than any previous; but it was a labour of love, being a defence of the early French Revolutionists against the Tory misrepresentations of Sir Walter Scott,[†] in the introduction to his *Life of Napoleon*. The number of books which I read for this purpose, making notes and extracts – even the number I had to buy (for in those days there was no public or subscription library from which books of reference could be taken home), far exceeded the worth of the immediate object; but I had at that time a half formed intention of writing a History of the French Revolution; and though I never executed it, my collections afterwards were very useful to Carlyle [†] for a similar purpose.

CHAPTER V

A Crisis in My Mental History.
One Stage Onward

❦

For some years after this time I wrote very little, and nothing regularly, for publication: and great were the advantages which I derived from the intermission. It was of no common importance to me, at this period, to be able to digest and mature my thoughts for my own mind only, without any immediate call for giving them out in print. Had I gone on writing, it would have much disturbed the important transformation in my opinions and character, which took place during those years. The origin of this transformation, or at least the process by which I was prepared for it, can only be explained by turning some distance back.

From the winter of 1821, when I first read Bentham, and especially from the commencement of the *Westminster Review*, I had what might truly be called an object in life; to be a reformer of the world. My conception of my own happiness was entirely identified with this object. The personal sympathies I wished for were those of fellow labourers in this enterprise. I endeavoured to pick up as many flowers as I could by the way; but as a serious and permanent personal satisfaction to rest upon, my whole reliance was placed on this: and I was accustomed to felicitate myself on the certainty of a happy life which I enjoyed, through placing my happiness in something durable and distant, in which some progress might be always making, while it could never be exhausted by complete attainment. This did very well for several years, during which the general improvement going on in the world and the idea of myself as engaged with others in struggling to promote it, seemed enough to fill up an interesting and animated existence. But the time came when I awakened from this as from a dream. It was in the autumn of 1826. I was in a dull state of nerves, such as everybody is occasionally liable to; unsusceptible to enjoyment or pleasurable excitement; one of those moods when what is pleasure at other times, becomes insipid or indifferent; the state,

I should think, in which converts to Methodism usually are, when smitten by their first 'conviction of sin.' In this frame of mind it occurred to me to put the question directly to myself, 'Suppose that all your objects in life were realized; that all the changes in institutions and opinions which you are looking forward to, could be completely effected at this very instant: would this be a great joy and happiness to you?' And an irrepressible self-consciousness distinctly answered, 'No!' At this my heart sank within me: the whole foundation on which my life was constructed fell down. All my happiness was to have been found in the continual pursuit of this end. The end had ceased to charm, and how could there ever again be any interest in the means? I seemed to have nothing left to live for.

At first I hoped that the cloud would pass away of itself; but it did not. A night's sleep, the sovereign remedy for the smaller vexations of life, had no effect on it. I awoke to a renewed consciousness of the woful fact. I carried it with me into all companies, into all occupations. Hardly anything had power to cause me even a few minutes oblivion of it. For some months the cloud seemed to grow thicker and thicker. The lines in Coleridge's 'Dejection'† – I was not then acquainted with them – exactly describe my case:

> A grief without a pang, void, dark and drear,
> A drowsy, stifled, unimpassioned grief,
> Which finds no natural outlet or relief
> In word, or sigh, or tear.

In vain I sought relief from my favourite books; those memorials of past nobleness and greatness, from which I had always hitherto drawn strength and animation. I read them now without feeling, or with the accustomed feeling *minus* all its charm; and I became persuaded, that my love of mankind, and of excellence for its own sake, had worn itself out. I sought no comfort by speaking to others of what I felt. If I had loved any one sufficiently to make confiding my griefs a necessity, I should not have been in the condition I was. I felt, too, that mine was not an interesting, or in any way respectable distress. There was nothing in it to attract sympathy. Advice, if I had known where to seek it, would have been most precious. The words of Macbeth to the physician often occurred to my thoughts.† But there was no one on whom I could build the faintest hope of such assistance. My father, to whom it would have been natural to me to have recourse in any practical difficulties, was the last person to whom, in such a case as this, I looked for help. Everything convinced me that he had no knowledge of any such mental state as I was suffering from, and that even if he could be made to understand it, he was not the physician who could heal it. My education, which was wholly his work, had been conducted without any regard to the possibility of its ending in this result; and I saw no use in giving him the pain of thinking that his plans had failed, when the failure was probably irremediable, and at all events, beyond the power of *his* remedies. Of other friends, I had at that time none to whom I had any hope of making my condition intelligible. It was however abundantly intelligible to myself; and the more I dwelt upon it, the more hopeless it appeared.

My course of study had led me to believe, that all mental and moral feelings and qualities, whether of a good or of a bad kind, were the results of association; that we love one thing and hate another, take pleasure in one sort of action or contemplation, and pain in another sort, through the clinging of pleasurable or painful ideas to those things, from the effect of education or of experience. As a corollary from this, I had always heard it maintained by my father, and was myself convinced, that the object of education should be to form the strongest possible associations of the salutary class; associations of pleasure with all things beneficial to the great whole, and of pain with all things hurtful to it. This doctrine appeared inexpugnable; but it now seemed to me on retrospect, that my teachers had occupied themselves but superficially with the means of forming and keeping up these salutary associations. They seemed to have trusted altogether to the old familiar instruments, praise and blame, reward and punishment. Now I did not doubt that by these means, begun early and applied unremittingly, intense associations of pain and pleasure, especially of pain, might be created, and might produce desires and aversions capable of lasting undiminished to the end of life. But there must always be something artificial and casual in associations thus produced. The pains and pleasure thus forcibly associated with things, are not connected with them by any natural tie; and it is therefore, I thought, essential to the durability of these associations, that they should have become so intense and inveterate as to be practically indissoluble, before the habitual exercise of the power of analysis had commenced. For I now saw, or thought I saw, what I had always before received with incredulity – that the habit of analysis has a tendency to wear away the feelings: as indeed it has when no other mental habit is cultivated, and the analysing spirit remains without its natural complements and correctives. The very excellence of analysis

75

(I argued) is that it tends to weaken and undermine whatever is the result of prejudice; that it enables us mentally to separate ideas which have only casually clung together: and no associations whatever could ultimately resist this dissolving force, were it not that we owe to analysis our clearest knowledge of the permanent sequences in nature; the real connexions between Things, not dependent on our will and feelings; natural laws, by virtue of which, in many cases, one thing is inseparable from another in fact; which laws, in proportion as they are clearly perceived and imaginatively realized, cause our ideas of things which are always joined together in Nature, to cohere more and more closely in our thoughts. Analytic habits may thus even strengthen the associations between causes and effects, means and ends, but tend altogether to weaken those which are, to speak familiarly, a *mere* matter of feeling. They are therefore (I thought) favourable to prudence and clearsightedness, but a perpetual worm at the root both of the passions and of the virtues; and above all, fearfully undermine all desires, and all pleasures, which are the effects of association, that is, according to the theory I held, all except the purely physical and organic; of the entire insufficiency of which to make life desirable, no one had a stronger conviction than I had. These were the laws of human nature by which, as it seemed to me, I had been brought to my present state. All those to whom I looked up, were of opinion that the pleasure of sympathy with human beings, and the feelings which made the good of others, and especially of mankind on a large scale, the object of existence, were the greatest and surest sources of happiness. Of the truth of this I was convinced, but to know that a feeling would make me happy if I had it, did not give me the feeling. My education, I thought, had failed to create these feelings in sufficient strength to resist the dissolving influence of analysis, while the whole course of my intellectual cultivation had made precocious and premature analysis the inveterate habit of my mind. I was thus, as I said to myself, left stranded at the commence-ment of my voyage, with a well equipped ship and a rudder, but no sail; without any real desire for the ends which I had been so carefully fitted out to work for: no delight in virtue or the general good, but also just as little in anything else. The fountains of vanity and ambition seemed to have dried up within me, as completely as those of benevo-lence. I had had (as I reflected) some gratification of vanity at too early an age: I had obtained some distinction, and felt myself of some importance, before the desire of distinction and of importance had grown into a passion: and little as it was which I had attained, yet having been attained too early, like all pleasures enjoyed too soon, it had made me *blasé* and indifferent to the pursuit. Thus neither selfish nor unselfish pleasures were pleasures to me. And there seemed no power in nature sufficient to begin the formation of my character anew, and create in a mind now irretrievably analytic, fresh associations of pleasure with any of the objects of human desire.

These were the thoughts which mingled with the dry heavy dejection of the melancholy winter of 1826–7. During this time I was not incapable of my usual occupations. I went on with them mechanically, by the mere force of habit. I had been so drilled in a certain sort of mental exercise, that I could still carry it on when all the spirit had gone out of it. I even composed and spoke several speeches at the debating society, how, or with what degree of success I know not. Of four years continual speaking at that society, this is the only year of which I remember next to nothing. Two lines of Coleridge, in whom alone of all writers I have found a true description of what I felt, were often in my thoughts, not at this time (for I had never read them), but in a later period of the same mental malady:

> Work without hope draws nectar in a sieve,
> And hope without an object cannot live.†

In all probability my case was by no means so peculiar as I fancied it, and I doubt not that many others have passed through a similar state; but the idiosyncrasies of my education had given to the general phenomenon a special character, which made it seem the natural effect of causes that it was hardly possible for time to remove. I frequently asked myself, if I could, or if I was bound to go on living, when life must be passed in this manner. I generally answered to myself, that I did not think I could possibly bear it beyond a year. When, however, not more than half that duration of time had elapsed, a small ray of light broke in upon my gloom. I was reading, accidentally, Marmontel's *Memoirs*,† and came to the passage which relates his father's death, the distressed position of the family, and the sudden inspiration by which he, then a mere boy, felt and made them feel that he would be everything to them – would supply the place of all that they had lost. A vivid conception of the scene and its feelings came over me, and I was moved to tears. From this moment my burthen grew lighter. The oppression of the thought that all feeling was dead within me, was gone. I was no longer hopeless: I was not a stock or a stone. I had still, it seemed, some of the material out of which all worth of character, and all capacity for happiness, are made. Relieved from my ever present sense of irremediable wretchedness, I gradually found that the ordinary incidents of life could again give me some pleasure; that I could again find enjoyment, not intense, but sufficient for cheerfulness, in sunshine and sky, in books, in conversation, in public affairs; and that there was, once more, excitement, though of a moderate kind, in exerting myself for my opinions, and for the public good. Thus the cloud gradually drew off, and I again enjoyed life: and though I had several relapses, some of which lasted many months, I never again was as miserable as I had been.

The experiences of this period had two very marked effects on my opinions and character. In the first place, they led me to adopt a theory of life, very unlike that on which I had before acted, and having much in common with what at that time I certainly had never heard of, the anti-self-consciousness theory of Carlyle.[†] I never, indeed, wavered in the conviction that happiness is the test of all rules of conduct, and the end of life. But I now thought that this end was only to be attained by not making it the direct end. Those only are happy (I thought) who have their minds fixed on some object other than their own happiness; on the happiness of others, on the improvement of mankind, even on some art or pursuit, followed not as a means, but as itself an ideal end. Aiming thus at something else, they find happiness by the way. The enjoyments of life (such was now my theory) are sufficient to make it a pleasant thing, when they are taken *en passant*, without being made a principal object. Once make them so, and they are immediately felt to be insufficient. They will not bear a scrutinizing examination. Ask yourself whether you are happy, and you cease to be so. The only chance is to treat, not happiness, but some end external to it, as the purpose of life. Let your self-consciousness, your scrutiny, your self-interrogation, exhaust themselves on that; and if otherwise fortunately circumstanced you will inhale happiness with the air you breathe, without dwelling on it or thinking about it, without either forestalling it in imagination, or putting it to flight by fatal questioning. This theory now became the basis of my philosophy of life. And I still hold to it as the best theory for all those who have but a moderate degree of sensibility and of capacity for enjoyment, that is, for the great majority of mankind.

The other important change which my opinions at this time underwent, was that I, for the first time, gave its proper place, among the prime necessities of human well-being, to the internal culture of the individual. I ceased to attach almost exclusive importance to the ordering of outward circumstances, and the training of the human being for speculation and for action. I had now learnt by experience that the passive susceptibilities needed to be cultivated as well as the active capacities, and required to be nourished and enriched as well as guided. I did not, for an instant, lose sight of, or undervalue, that part of the truth which I had seen before; I never turned recreant to intellectual culture, or ceased to consider the power and practice of analysis as an essential condition both of individual and of social improvement. But I thought that it had consequences which required to be corrected, by joining other kinds of cultivation with it. The maintenance of a due balance among the faculties, now seemed to me of primary importance. The cultivation of the feelings became one of the cardinal points in my ethical and philosophical creed. And my thoughts and inclinations turned in an increasing degree towards whatever seemed capable of being instrumental to that object.

I now began to find meaning in the things which I had read or heard about the importance of poetry and art as instruments of human culture. But it was some time longer before I began to know this by personal experience. The only one of the imaginative arts in which I had from childhood taken great pleasure, was music; the best effect of which (and in this it surpasses perhaps every other art) consists in exciting enthusiasm; in winding up to a high pitch those feelings of an elevated kind which are already in the character, but to which this excitement gives a glow and a fervour, which though transitory at its utmost height, is precious for sustaining them at other times. This effect of music I had often experienced; but like all my pleasurable susceptibilities, it was suspended during the gloomy period. I had sought relief again and again from this quarter, but found none. After the tide had turned, and I was in process of recovery, I had been helped forward by music, but in a much less elevated manner. I at this time first became acquainted with Weber's *Oberon*,† and the extreme pleasure which I drew from its delicious melodies did me good, by shewing me a source of pleasure to which I was as susceptible as ever. The good however was much impaired by the thought, that the pleasure of music (as is quite true of such pleasure as this was, that of mere tune) fades with familiarity, and requires either to be revived by intermittence, or fed by continual novelty. And it is very characteristic both of my then state, and of the general tone of my mind at this period of my life, that I was seriously tormented by the thought of the exhaustibility of musical combinations. The octave consists only of five tones and two semi-tones, which can be put together in only a limited number of ways, of which but a small proportion are beautiful: most of these, it seemed to me, must have been already discovered, and there could not be room for a long succession of Mozarts† and Webers, to strike out as these had done, entirely new and surpassingly rich veins of musical beauty. This source of anxiety may perhaps be thought to resemble that of the philosophers of Laputa,† who feared lest the sun should be burnt out. It was, however, connected with the best feature in my character, and the only good point to be found in my very unromantic and in no way honorable distress. For though my dejection, honestly looked at, could not be called other than egotistical, produced by the ruin, as I thought, of my fabric of happiness, yet the destiny of mankind in general was ever in my thoughts, and could not be separated from my own. I felt that the flaw in my life, must be a flaw in life itself; that the question was, whether, if the reformers of society and government could succeed in their objects, and every person in the community were free and in a state of physical comfort, the pleasures of life, being no longer kept up by struggle and privation, would cease to be pleasures. And I felt that unless I could see my way to some better hope than this for human happiness in general, my dejection must continue; but that if I could see such an outlet, I should then look on the world with pleasure; content as far as I was myself concerned, with any fair share of the general lot.

This state of my thoughts and feelings made the fact of my reading Wordsworth for the first time (in the autumn of 1828)† an important event in my life. I took up the collection of his poems from curiosity, with no expectation of mental relief from it, though I had before resorted to poetry with that hope. In the worst period of my depression I had read through the whole of Byron† (then new to me) to try whether a poet, whose peculiar department was supposed to be that of the intenser feelings, could rouse any feeling in me. As might be expected, I got no good from this reading, but the reverse. The poet's state of mind was too like my own. His was the lament of a man who had worn out all pleasures, and who seemed to think that life, to all who possess the good things of it, must necessarily be the vapid uninteresting thing which I found it. His Harold† and Manfred† had the same burthen on them which I had; and I was not in a frame of mind to derive any comfort from the vehement sensual passion of his Giaours,† or the sullenness of his Laras.† But while Byron was exactly what did not suit my condition, Wordsworth was exactly what did.

I had looked into *The Excursion*[†] two or three years before, and found little in it; and I should probably have found as little, had I read it at this time. But the miscellaneous poems, in the two-volume edition of 1815 (to which little of value was added in the latter part of the author's life), proved to be the precise thing for my mental wants at that particular juncture.

In the first place, these poems addressed themselves powerfully to one of the strongest of my pleasurable susceptibilities, the love of rural objects and natural scenery; to which I had been indebted not only for much of the pleasure of my life, but quite recently for relief from one of my longest relapses into depression.[‡] In this power of rural beauty over me, there was a foundation laid for taking pleasure in Wordsworth's poetry; the more so, as his scenery lies mostly among mountains, which, owing to my early Pyrenean excursion, were my ideal of natural beauty. But Wordsworth would never have had any great effect on me, if he had merely placed before me beautiful pictures of natural scenery. Scott does this still better than Wordsworth, and a very second-rate landscape does it more effectually than any poet. What made Wordsworth's poems a medicine for my state of mind, was that they expressed, not mere outward beauty, but states of feeling, and of thought coloured by feeling, under the excitement of beauty. They seemed to be the very culture of the feelings, which I was in quest of. In them I seemed to draw from a source of inward joy, of sympathetic and imaginative pleasure, which could be shared in by all human beings; which had no connexion with struggle or imperfection, but would be made richer by every improvement in the physical or social condition of mankind. From them I seemed to learn what would be the perennial sources of happiness, when all the greater evils of life shall have been removed. And I felt myself at once better and happier as I came under their influence.[‡] There have certainly been, even in our own age, greater poets than Wordsworth; but poetry of deeper and loftier feeling could not have done for me at that time what his did. I needed to be made to feel that there was real, permanent happiness in tranquil contemplation. Wordsworth taught me this, not only without turning away from, but with a greatly increased interest in, the common feelings and common destiny of human beings. And the delight which these poems gave me, proved that with culture of this sort, there was nothing to dread from the most confirmed habit of analysis. At the conclusion of the Poems came the famous 'Ode,' falsely called Platonic, 'Intimations of Immortality':[†] in which, along with more

81

than his usual sweetness of melody and rhythm, and along with the two passages of grand imagery but bad philosophy so often quoted, I found that he too had had similar experience to mine; that he also had felt that the first freshness of youthful enjoyment of life was not lasting; but that he had sought for compensation, and found it, in the way in which he was now teaching me to find it. The result was that I gradually, but completely, emerged from my habitual depression, and was never again subject to it. I long continued to value Wordsworth less according to his intrinsic merits, than by the measure of what he had done for me. Compared with the greatest poets, he may be said to be the poet of unpoetical natures,† possessed of quiet and contemplative tastes. But unpoetical natures are precisely those which require poetic cultivation. This cultivation Wordsworth is much more fitted to give, than poets who are intrinsically far more poets than he.

It so fell out that the merits of Wordsworth were the occasion of my first public declaration of my new way of thinking, and separation from those of my habitual companions who had not undergone a similar change. The person with whom at that time I was most in the habit of comparing notes on such subjects was Roebuck, and I induced him to read Wordsworth, in whom he also at first seemed to find much to admire: but I, like most Wordsworthians, threw myself into strong antagonism to Byron, both as a poet and as to his influence on the character. Roebuck, all whose instincts were those of action and struggle, had, on the contrary, a strong relish and great admiration of Byron, whose writings he regarded as the poetry of human life, while Wordsworth's, according to him, was that of flowers and butterflies. We agreed to have the fight out at our Debating Society, where we accordingly discussed for two evenings the comparative merits of Byron and Wordsworth, propounding and illustrating by long recitations our respective theories of poetry: Sterling also, in a brilliant speech, putting forward his particular theory.† This was the first debate on any weighty subject in which Roebuck and I had been on opposite sides. The schism between us widened from this time more and more, though we continued for some years longer to be companions. In the beginning, our chief divergence related to the cultivation of the feelings. Roebuck was in many respects very different from the vulgar notion of a Benthamite or Utilitarian. He was a lover of poetry and of most of the fine arts. He took great pleasure in music, in dramatic performances, especially in painting, and himself drew and designed landscapes with great facility and beauty. But he never could be made to see that these things have any value as aids in the formation of character. Personally, instead of being, as Benthamites are supposed to be, void of feeling, he had very quick and strong sensibilities. But, like most Englishmen who have feelings, he found his feelings stand very much in his way. He was much more susceptible to the painful sympathies than to the pleasurable, and looking for his happiness elsewhere, he wished that his feelings should be deadened rather than quickened. And in truth the English character, and English social circumstances, make it so seldom possible to derive happiness from the exercise of the sympathies, that it is not wonderful if they count for little in an Englishman's scheme of life. In most other countries the paramount importance of the sympathies as a constituent of individual happiness is an axiom, taken for granted rather than needing any formal statement; but most English thinkers almost seem to regard them as necessary evils,† required for keeping men's actions benevolent and compassionate. Roebuck was, or appeared to be, this kind of Englishman. He saw little good in any cultivation of the feelings, and none at all in cultivating them through the imagination, which he thought was only cultivating illusions. It was in vain I urged on him that the imaginative emotion which an idea when vividly conceived excites in us, is not an illusion but a fact, as real as any of the other qualities of objects; and far from implying anything erroneous and delusive in our mental apprehension of the object, is quite consistent with the most accurate knowledge and most perfect practical recognition of all its physical and intellectual laws and relations.† The intensest feeling of the beauty of a cloud lighted by the setting sun, is no hindrance to my knowing that the cloud is vapour of water, subject to all the laws of vapours in a state of suspension; and I am just as likely to allow for, and act on, these physical laws whenever there is occasion to do so, as if I had been incapable of perceiving any distinction between beauty and ugliness.‡

While my intimacy with Roebuck diminished, I fell more and more into friendly intercourse with our Coleridgian adversaries in the Society, Frederick Maurice and John Sterling, both subsequently so well known, the former by his writings, the latter through the biographies by Hare and Carlyle.† Of these two friends, Maurice was the thinker, Sterling the orator, and impassioned expositor of thoughts which, at this period, were almost entirely formed for him by Maurice. With Maurice I had for some time been acquainted through Eyton Tooke, who had known him at Cambridge, and though my discussions with him were almost always disputes, I had carried away from them much that helped to build up my new fabric of thought, in the same way as I was deriving much from Coleridge, and from the writings of Goethe† and other German authors which I read during those years. I have so deep a respect for Maurice's character and purposes, as well as for his great mental gifts, that it is with some unwillingness I say anything which may seem to place him on a less high eminence than I would gladly be able to accord to him. But I have always thought that there was more intellectual power wasted in Maurice than in any other of my cotemporaries. Few of them certainly have had so much to waste. Great powers of generalization, rare ingenuity and subtlety, and a wide perception of important and unobvious truths, served him not for putting something better into the place of the worthless heap of received opinions on the great subjects of thought, but for proving to his own mind that the Church of England had known everything from the first, and that all the truths on the ground of which the Church and orthodoxy have been attacked (many of which he saw as clearly as any one) are not only consistent with the Thirty-nine articles,† but are better understood and expressed in those articles than by any one who rejects them. I have never been able to find any other explanation of this, than by attributing it to that timidity of conscience, combined with original sensitiveness of temperament, which has so often driven highly gifted men into Romanism from the need of a firmer support than they can find in the independent conclusions of their own judgment. Any more vulgar kind of timidity no one who knew Maurice would ever think of imputing to him, even if he had not given public proof of his freedom from it, by his ultimate collision with some of the opinions commonly regarded as orthodox, and by his noble origination of the Christian Socialist movement. The nearest parallel to him, in a moral point of view, is Coleridge, to whom, in merely intellectual power, apart from poetical genius, I think him decidedly superior. At this time, however, he might be described as a disciple of Coleridge, and Sterling as a disciple of Coleridge and of him. The modifications which were taking place in my old opinions gave me some points of contact with them; and both Maurice and Sterling were of considerable use to my development. With Sterling I soon became very intimate, and was more attached to him than I have ever been to any other man. He was indeed one of the most loveable of men. His frank, cordial, affection-ate and expansive character; a love of truth alike conspicuous in the highest things and the humblest; a generous and ardent nature which threw itself with impetuosity into the opinions it adopted, but was as eager to do justice to the doctrines and the men it was opposed to, as to make war on what it thought their errors; and an equal devotion to the two cardinal points of Liberty and Duty, formed a combination of qualities as attractive to me, as to all others who knew him as well as I did. With his open mind and heart, he found no difficulty in joining hands with me across the gulf which as yet divided our opinions. He told me how he and others had looked upon me (from hearsay information) as a 'made' or manufactured man, having had a certain impress of opinion stamped on me which I could only reproduce; and what a change took place in his feelings when he found, in the discussion on Wordsworth and Byron, that Wordsworth, and all which that name implies, 'belonged' to me as much as to him and his friends. The failure of his health soon scattered all his plans of life, and compelled him to live at a distance from London, so that after the first year or two of our acquaintance, we only saw each other at distant intervals. But (as he said himself in one of his letters to Carlyle) when we did meet it was like brothers. Though he was never, in the full sense of the word, a profound thinker, his openness of mind, and the moral courage in which he greatly surpassed Maurice, made him outgrow the dominion which Maurice and Coleridge had once exercised over his intellect; though he retained to the last a great but discriminating admiration of both, and towards Maurice a warm affection. Except in that short and transitory phasis of his life, during which he made the mistake of becoming a clergyman, his mind was ever progressive; and the advance he always seemed to have made when I saw him after an interval, made me apply to him what Goethe said of Schiller, 'Er hatte eine fürchtliche Fortschreitung.'† He and I started from intellectual points almost as wide apart as the poles, but the distance between us was always diminishing: if I made steps towards some of his opinions, he, during his short life, was constantly approximating more and more to several of mine: and if he had lived, and had health and vigour to prosecute his ever assiduous self-culture, there is no knowing how much further this spontaneous assimilation might have proceeded.‡

After 1829 I withdrew from attendance on the Debating Society. I had had enough of speech-making, and was glad to carry on my private studies and meditations without any immediate call for outward assertion of their results. I found the fabric of my old and taught opinions giving way in many fresh places, and I never allowed it to fall to pieces, but was incessantly occupied in weaving it anew. I never, in the course of my transition, was content to remain, for ever so short a time, confused and unsettled. When I had taken in any new idea, I could not rest till I had adjusted its relation to my old opinions, and ascertained exactly how far its effect ought to extend in modifying or superseding them.

The conflicts which I had so often had to sustain in defending the theory of government laid down in Bentham's and my father's writings, and the acquaintance I had obtained with other schools of political thinking, made me aware of many things which that doctrine, professing to be a theory of government in general, ought to have made room for, and did not. But these things, as yet, remained with me rather as corrections to be made in applying the theory to practice, than as defects in the theory. I felt that politics could not be a science of specific experience; and that the accusations against the Benthamic theory of *being* a theory, of proceeding *à priori*, by way of general reasoning, instead of Baconian experiment, shewed complete ignorance of Bacon's principles,[†] and of the necessary conditions of experimental investigation. At this juncture appeared, in the *Edinburgh Review*, Macaulay's famous attack on my father's Essay on Government.[†] This gave me much to think about. I saw that Macaulay's conception of the logic of politics was erroneous; that he stood up for the empirical mode of treating political phenomena, against the philosophical; that even in physical science, his notion of philosophizing might have recognised Kepler, but would have excluded Newton and Laplace. But I could not help feeling, that though the tone was unbecoming (an error for which the writer, at a later period, made the most ample and honorable amends), there was truth in several of his strictures on my father's treatment of the subject; that my father's premises were really too narrow, and included but a small number of the general truths, on which, in politics, the important consequences depend. Identity of interest between the governing body and the community at large, is not, in any practical sense which can be attached to it, the only thing on which good government depends; neither can this identity of interest be secured by the mere conditions of election. I was not at all satisfied with the mode in which my father met the criticisms of Macaulay. He did not, as I thought he ought to have done, justify himself by saying, 'I was not writing a scientific treatise on politics. I was writing an argument for parliamentary reform.' He treated Macaulay's argument as simply irrational; an attack upon the reasoning faculty; an example of the saying of Hobbes, that when reason is against a man, a man will be against reason.[†] This made me think that there was really something more fundamentally erroneous in my father's conception of philosophical Method, as applicable to politics, than I had hitherto supposed there was. But I did not at first see clearly what the error might be. At last it flashed upon me all at once in the course of other studies. In the early part of 1830 I had begun to put on paper the ideas on Logic (chiefly on the distinctions among Terms, and the import of Propositions) which had been suggested and in part worked out in the morning conversations already spoken of. Having secured these thoughts from being lost, I pushed on into the other parts of the subject, to try whether I could do anything further towards clearing up the theory of Logic generally. I grappled at once with the problem of Induction, postponing that of Reasoning, on the ground that it is necessary to obtain premises before we can reason from them. Now, Induction is mainly a process for finding the causes of effects: and in attempting to fathom the mode of tracing causes and effects in physical science, I soon saw that in the more perfect of the sciences, we ascend, by generalization from particulars, to the tendencies of causes considered singly, and then reason downward from those separate tendencies, to the effect of the same causes when combined. I then asked myself, what is the ultimate analysis of this deductive process; the common theory of the syllogism evidently throwing no light upon it. My practice (learnt from Hobbes and my father) being to study abstract principles by means of the best concrete instances I could find, the Composition of Forces, in dynamics, occurred to me as the most complete example of the logical process I was investigating. On examining, accordingly, what the mind does when it applies the principle of the Composition of Forces, I found that it performs a simple act of addition. It adds the separate effect of the one force to the separate effect of the other, and puts down the sum of these separate effects as the joint effect. But is this a legitimate process? In dynamics, and in all the mathematical branches of physics, it is; but in some other cases, as in chemistry, it is not; and I then recollected that something not unlike this was pointed out as one of the distinctions between chemical and mechanical phenomena, in the introduction to that favorite of my boyhood, Thomson's *System of Chemistry*. This distinction at once made my mind clear as to what was perplexing me in respect to the philosophy of politics. I now saw, that a science is either deductive or experimental, according as, in the province it deals with, the effects of causes when conjoined, are or are not the sums of the effects which the same causes produce when separate. It followed that politics must be a deductive science. It thus appeared, that both Macaulay and my father were wrong; the one in assimilating the method of philosophizing in politics to the purely experimental method of chemistry; while the other, though right in adopting a deductive method, had made a wrong selection of one, having taken as the type of deduction, not the appropriate process, that of the deductive branches of natural philosophy, but the inappropriate one of pure geometry, which not being a science of causation at all, does not require or admit of any summing-up of effects. A foundation was thus laid in my thoughts for the principal chapters of what I afterwards published on the Logic of the Moral Sciences;† and my new position in respect to my old political creed now became perfectly definite.‡

If I am asked what system of political philosophy I substituted for that which, as a philosophy, I had abandoned, I answer, no system: only a conviction, that the true system was something much more complex and many sided than I had previously had any idea of, and that its office was to supply, not a set of model institutions, but principles from which the institutions suitable to any given circumstances might be deduced. The influences of European, that is to say, Continental, thought, and especially those of the reaction of the nineteenth century against the eighteenth, were now streaming in upon me. They came from various quarters: from the writings of Coleridge, which I had begun to read with interest even before the change in my opinions; from the Coleridgians with whom I was in personal intercourse; from what I had read of Goethe; from Carlyle's early articles in the *Edinburgh* and *Foreign* Reviews,† though for a long time I saw nothing in these (as my father saw nothing in them to the last) but insane rhapsody. From these sources, and from the acquaintance I kept up with the French literature of the time, I derived, among other ideas which the general turning upside down of the opinions of European thinkers had brought uppermost, these in particular: That the human mind has a certain order of possible progress, in which some things must precede others, an order which governments and public instructors can modify to some, but not to an unlimited extent: That all questions of political institutions are relative, not absolute, and that different stages of human progress not only *will* have, but *ought* to have, different institutions: That government is always either in the hands, or passing into the hands, of whatever is the strongest power in society, and that what this power is, does not depend on institutions, but institutions on it: That any general theory or philosophy of politics supposes a previous theory of human progress, and that this is the same thing with a philosophy of history. These opinions, true in the main, were held in an exaggerated and violent manner by the thinkers with whom I was now most accustomed to compare notes, and who, as usual with a reaction, ignored that half of the truth which the thinkers of the eighteenth century saw. But though, at one period of my progress, I for some time undervalued that great century, I never joined in the reaction against it, but kept as firm hold of one side of the truth as I took of the other. The fight between the nineteenth century and the eighteenth always reminded me of the battle about the shield, one side of which was white and the other black. I marvelled at the blind rage with which the combatants rushed against one another. I applied to them, and to Coleridge himself, many of Coleridge's sayings about half truths; and Goethe's device, 'many-sidedness,'† was one which I would most willingly, at this period, have taken for mine.

The writers by whom, more than by any others, a new mode of political thinking was brought home to me, were those of the St. Simonian school in France. In 1829 and 1830 I became acquainted with some of their writings. They were then only in the earlier stages of their speculations. They had not yet dressed out their philosophy as a religion, nor had they organized their scheme of Socialism. They were just beginning to question the principle of hereditary property. I was by no means prepared to go with them even this length; but I was greatly struck with the connected view which they for the first time presented to me, of the natural order of human progress; and especially with their division of all history into organic periods and critical periods. During the organic periods (they said) mankind accept with firm conviction some positive creed, claiming jurisdiction over all their actions, and containing more or less of truth and adaptation to the needs of humanity. Under its influence they make all the progress compatible with the creed, and finally outgrow it; when a period follows of criticism and negation, in which mankind lose their old convictions without acquiring any new ones, of a general or authoritative character, except the conviction that the old are false. The period of Greek and Roman polytheism, so long as really believed in by instructed Greeks and Romans, was an organic period, succeeded by the critical or sceptical period of the Greek philosophers. Another organic period came in with Christianity. The corresponding critical period began with the Reformation, has lasted ever since, still lasts, and cannot altogether cease until a new organic period has been inaugurated by the triumph of a yet more advanced creed. These ideas, I knew, were not peculiar to the St. Simonians; on the contrary, they were the general property of Europe, or at least of

Germany and France, but they had never, to my knowledge, been so completely systematized as by these writers, nor the distinguishing characteristics of a critical period so powerfully set forth; for I was not then acquainted with Fichte's Lectures on *The Characteristics of the Present Age.*† In Carlyle, indeed, I found bitter denunciations of an 'age of unbelief,' and of the present age as such, which I, like most people at that time, supposed to be passionate protests in favour of the old modes of belief. But all that was true in these denunciations I thought that I found more calmly and philosophically stated by the St. Simonians. Among their publications, too, there was one which seemed to me far superior to the rest; in which the general idea was matured into something much more definite and instructive. This was an early work of Auguste Comte,† who then called himself, and even announced himself in the title page as, a pupil of Saint-Simon. In this tract M. Comte first put forth the doctrine which he afterwards so copiously illustrated, of the natural succession of three stages in every department of human knowledge – first the theological, next the metaphysical, and lastly, the positive stage; and contended, that social science must be subject to the same law; that the feudal and Catholic system was the concluding phasis of the theological state of the social science, Protestantism the commencement and the doctrines of the French Revolution the consummation of the metaphysical, and that its positive state was yet to come. This doctrine harmonized well with my existing notions, to which it seemed to give a scientific shape. I already regarded the methods of physical science as the proper models for political. But the chief benefit which I derived at this time from the trains of thought suggested by the St. Simonians and by Comte, was, that I obtained a clearer conception than ever before of the peculiarities of an era of transition in opinion, and ceased to mistake the moral and intellectual characteristics of such an era, for the normal attributes of humanity. I looked forward, through the present age of loud disputes but generally weak convictions, to a future which shall unite the best qualities of the critical with the best qualities of the organic periods; unchecked liberty of thought, unbounded freedom of individual action in all modes not hurtful to others; but also, convictions as to what is right and wrong, useful and pernicious, deeply engraven on the feelings by early education and general unanimity of sentiment, and so firmly grounded in reason and in the true exigencies of life, that they shall not, like all former and present creeds, religious, ethical, and political, require to be periodically thrown off and replaced by others.

90

M. Comte soon left the St. Simonians, and I lost sight of him and his writings for a number of years. But the St. Simonians I continued to cultivate. I was kept *au courant* of their progress by one of their most enthusiastic disciples, M. Gustave d'Eichthal, who about that time passed a considerable interval in England. I was introduced to their chiefs, Bazard and Enfantin,† in 1830; and as long as their public teachings and proselytism continued, I read nearly everything they wrote. Their criticisms on the common doctrines of Liberalism seemed to me full of important truth; and it was partly by their writings that my eyes were opened to the very limited and temporary value of the old political economy, which assumes private property and inheritance as indefeasible facts, and freedom of production and exchange as the *dernier mot* of social improvement. The scheme gradually unfolded by the St. Simonians, under which the labour and capital of society would be managed for the general account of the community, every individual being required to take a share of labour, either as thinker, teacher, artist, or producer, all being classed according to their capacity, and remunerated according to their works, appeared to me a far superior description of Socialism to Owen's. Their aim seemed to me desirable and rational, however their means might be inefficacious; and though I neither believed in the practicability, nor in the beneficial operation of their social machinery, I felt that the proclamation of such an ideal of human society could not but tend to give a beneficial direction to the efforts of others to bring society, as at present constituted, nearer to some ideal standard. I honoured them most of all for what they have been most cried down for – the boldness and freedom from prejudice with which they treated the subject of family, the most important of any, and needing more fundamental alterations than remain to be made in any other great social institution, but on which scarcely any reformer has the courage to touch. In proclaiming the perfect equality of men and women, and an entirely new order of things in regard to their relations with one another, the St. Simonians in common with Owen and Fourier† have entitled themselves to the grateful remembrance of future generations.

In giving an account of this period of my life, I have only specified such of my new impressions as appeared to me, both at the time and since, to be a kind of turning points, marking a definite progress in my mode of thought. But these few selected points give a very insufficient idea of the quantity of thinking which I carried on respecting a host of subjects during these years of transition. Much of this, it is true, consisted in rediscovering things known to all the world, which I had previously disbelieved, or disregarded. But the rediscovery was to me a discovery, giving me plenary possession of the truths not as traditional platitudes but fresh from their source: and it seldom failed to place them in some new light, by which they were reconciled with, and seemed to confirm while they modified, the truths less generally known which lay in my early opinions, and in no essential part of which I at any time wavered. All my new thinking only laid the foundation of these more deeply and strongly, while it often removed misapprehension and confusion of ideas which had perverted their effect. For example, during the later returns of my dejection, the doctrine of what is called Philosophical Necessity weighed on my existence like an incubus. I felt as if I was scientifically proved to be the helpless slave of antecedent circumstances; as if my character and that of all others had been formed for us by agencies beyond our control, and was wholly out of our own power. I often said to myself, what a relief it would be if I could disbelieve the doctrine of the formation of character by circumstances; and remembering the wish of Fox† respecting the doctrine of resistance to governments, that it might never be forgotten by kings, nor remembered by subjects, I said that it would be a blessing if the doctrine of necessity could be believed by all *quoad*† the characters of others, and disbelieved in regard to their own. I pondered painfully on the subject, till gradually I saw light through it. I perceived, that the word Necessity, as a name for the doctrine of Cause and Effect applied to human action, carried with it a misleading association; and that this association was the operative force in the depressing and paralysing influence which I had experienced. I saw that though our character is formed by circumstances, our own desires can do much to shape those circumstances; and that what is really inspiriting and ennobling in the doctrine of freewill, is the conviction that we have real power over the formation of our own character; that our will, by influencing some of our circumstances, can modify our future habits or capabilities of willing. All this was entirely consistent with the doctrine of circumstances, or rather, was that doctrine itself, properly understood. From that time I drew, in my own mind, a clear distinction between the doctrine of circumstances, and Fatalism; discarding altogether the misleading word Necessity. The theory, which I now for the first time rightly apprehended, ceased altogether to be discouraging, and besides the relief to my spirits, I no longer suffered under the burthen, so heavy to one who aims at being a reformer in opinions, of thinking one doctrine true, and the contrary doctrine morally beneficial. The train of thought which had extricated me from this dilemma, seemed to me, in after years, fitted to render a similar service to others; and it now forms the chapter on Liberty and Necessity in the concluding Book of my *System of Logic*.[†]

Again, in politics, though I no longer accepted the doctrine of the Essay on Government as a scientific theory; though I ceased to consider representative democracy as an absolute principle, and regarded it as a question of time, place, and circumstance; though I now looked upon the choice of political institutions as a moral and educational question more than one of material interests, thinking that it ought to be decided mainly by the consideration, what great improvement in life and culture stands next in order for the people concerned, as the condition of their further progress, and what institutions are most likely to promote that; nevertheless this change in the premises of my political philosophy did not alter my practical political creed as to the requirements of my own time and country. I was as much as ever a radical and democrat, for Europe, and especially for England. I thought the predominance of the aristocratic classes, the noble and the rich, in the English Constitution, an evil worth any struggle to get rid of; not on account of taxes, or any such comparatively small inconvenience, but as the great demoralizing agency in the country. Demoralizing, first, because it made the conduct of the government an example of gross public immorality, through the predominance of private over public interests in the State,[†] and the abuse of the powers of legislation for the advantage of classes. Secondly, and in a still greater degree, because the respect of the multitude always attaching itself principally to that which, in the existing state of society, is the chief passport to power; and under English institutions, riches, hereditary or acquired, being the almost exclusive source of political importance; riches, and the signs of riches, were almost the only things really respected, and the life of the people was mainly devoted to the pursuit of them. I thought, that while the higher and richer classes held the power of government, the instruction and improvement of the mass of the people were contrary to the self interest of those classes, because tending to render the people more powerful for throwing off the yoke: but if the democracy obtained a large, and perhaps the principal, share in the governing power, it would become the interest of the opulent classes to promote their education, in order to ward off really mischievous errors, and especially those which would lead to unjust violations of property. On these grounds

I was not only as ardent as ever for democratic institutions, but earnestly hoped that Owenite, St. Simonian, and all other anti-property doctrines might spread widely among the poorer classes; not that I thought those doctrines true, or desired that they should be acted on, but in order that the higher classes might be made to see that they had more to fear from the poor when uneducated, than when educated.

In this frame of mind the French Revolution of July† found me. It roused my utmost enthusiasm, and gave me, as it were, a new existence. I went at once to Paris, was introduced to Lafayette,† and laid the groundwork of the intercourse I afterwards kept up with several of the active chiefs of the extreme popular party. After my return I entered warmly, as a writer, into the political discussions of the time; which soon became still more exciting, by the coming in of Lord Grey's† ministry, and the proposing of the Reform Bill.† For the next few years I wrote copiously in newspapers. It was about this time that Fonblanque, who had for some time written the political articles in the *Examiner*, became the proprietor and editor of the paper. It is not forgotten with what verve and talent, as well as fine wit, he carried it on, during the whole period of Lord Grey's ministry, and what importance it assumed as the principal representative, in the newspaper press, of radical opinions. The distinguishing character of the paper was given to it entirely by his own articles, which formed at least three fourths of all the original writing contained in it: but of the remaining fourth I contributed during those years a much larger share than any one else. I wrote nearly all the articles on French subjects, including a weekly summary of French politics, often extending to considerable length; together with many leading articles on general politics, commercial and financial legislation, and any miscellaneous subjects in which I felt interested, and which were suitable to the paper, including occasional reviews of books. Mere newspaper articles on the occurrences or questions of the moment gave no opportunity for the development of any general mode of thought; but I attempted, in the beginning of 1831, to embody in a series of articles, headed 'The Spirit of the Age,'† some of my new opinions, and especially to point out in the character of the present age, the anomalies and evils characteristic of the transition from a system of opinions which had worn out, to another only in process of being formed. These articles were, I fancy, lumbering in style, and not lively or striking enough to be at any time acceptable to newspaper readers; but had they been far more attractive, still, at that particular moment, when great political changes were impending, and engrossing all minds, these discussions were ill timed, and missed fire altogether.⁺ The only effect which I know to have been produced by them, was that Carlyle, then living in a secluded part of Scotland, read them in his solitude, and saying to himself (as he afterwards told me) 'here is a new Mystic,' enquired on coming to London that autumn respecting their authorship; an enquiry which was the immediate cause of our becoming personally acquainted.

I have already mentioned Carlyle's earlier writings as one of the channels through which I received the influences which enlarged my early narrow creed; but I do not think that those writings, by themselves, would ever have had any effect on my opinions. What truths they contained, though of the very kind which I was already receiving from other quarters, were presented in a form and vesture less suited than any other to give them access to a mind trained as mine had been. They seemed a haze of poetry and German metaphysics, in which almost the only clear thing was a strong animosity to most of the opinions which were the basis of my mode of thought; religious scepticism, utilitarianism, the doctrine of circumstances, and the attaching any importance to democracy, logic, or political economy. Instead of my having been taught anything, in the first instance, by Carlyle, it was only in proportion as I came to see the same truths, through media more suited to my mental constitution, that I recognized them in his writings. Then, indeed, the wonderful power with which he put them forth made a deep impression upon me, and I was during a long period one of his most fervent admirers; but the good his writings did me, was not as philosophy to instruct, but as poetry to animate. Even at the time when our acquaintance commenced, I was not sufficiently advanced in my new modes of thought, to appreciate him fully; a proof of which is, that on his shewing me the manuscript of *Sartor Resartus*,† his best and greatest work, which he had just then finished, I made little of it; though when it came out about two years afterwards in *Fraser's Magazine*, I read it with enthusiastic admiration and the keenest delight. I did not seek and cultivate Carlyle less on account of the fundamental differences in our philosophy. He soon found out that I was not 'another mystic,' and when for the sake of my own integrity I wrote to him a distinct profession of all those of my opinions which I knew he most disliked, he replied that the chief difference between us was that I 'was as yet consciously nothing of a mystic.'† I do not know at what period he gave up the expectation that I was destined to become one; but though both his and my opinions underwent in subsequent years considerable changes, we never approached much nearer to each other's modes of thought than we were in the first years of our acquaintance. I did not, however, deem myself a competent judge of Carlyle. I felt that he was a poet,† and that I was not; that he was a man of intuition, which I was not; and that as such, he not only saw many things long before me, which I could only, when they were pointed out to me, hobble after and prove, but that it was highly probable he could see many things which were not visible to me even after they were pointed out. I knew that I could not see round him, and could never be certain that I saw over him; and I never presumed to judge him with any definiteness, until he was interpreted to me by one greatly the superior of us both – who was more a poet than he, and more a thinker than I† – whose own mind and nature included his, and infinitely more.

Among the persons of intellect whom I had known of old, the one with whom I had now most points of agreement was the elder Austin. I have mentioned that he always set himself in opposition to our early sectarianism; and latterly he had, like myself, come under new influences. Having been appointed Professor of Jurisprudence in the London University (now University College), he had lived for some time at Bonn to study for his Lectures;† and the influences of German literature and of the German character and state of society had made a very perceptible change in his views of life. His personal disposition was much softened; he was less militant and polemic; his tastes had begun to turn themselves towards the poetic and contemplative. He attached much less importance than formerly to outward changes, unless accompanied by a better cultivation of the inward nature. He had a strong distaste for the general meanness of English life, the absence of enlarged thoughts and unselfish desires, the low objects on which the faculties of all classes of the English are intent. Even the kind of public interests which Englishmen care for, he held in very little esteem. He thought that there was more practical good government, and (which is true enough) infinitely more care for the education and mental improvement of all ranks of the people, under the Prussian monarchy, than under the English representative government: and he held, with the French Economistes, that the real security for good government is 'un peuple éclairé,' which is not always the fruit of popular institutions, and which if it could be had without them, would do their work better than they. Though he approved of the Reform Bill, he predicted, what in fact occurred, that it would not produce the great immediate improvements in government, which many expected from it. The men, he said, who could do these great things, did not exist in the country. There were many points of sympathy between him and me, both in the new opinions he had adopted and in the old ones which he retained. Like me, he never ceased to be an utilitarian, and with all his love of the Germans, and enjoyment of their literature, never became in the smallest degree reconciled to the innate-principle metaphysics. He cultivated more and more a kind of German religion, a religion of poetry and feeling with little if anything of positive dogma; while, in politics (and here it was that I most differed with him) he acquired an indifference, bordering on contempt, for the progress of popular institutions: though he rejoiced in that of Socialism, as the most effectual means of compelling the powerful classes to educate the people, and to impress on them the only real means of permanently improving their material condition, a limitation of their numbers. Neither was he, at this time, fundamentally opposed to Socialism in itself, as an ultimate result of improvement. He professed great disrespect for what he called 'the universal principles of human nature of the political economists,' and insisted on the evidence which history and daily experience afford of the 'extraordinary pliability of human nature'[†] (a phrase which I have somewhere borrowed from him); nor did he think it possible to set any positive bounds to the moral capabilities which might unfold themselves in mankind, under an enlightened direction of social and educational influences. Whether he retained all these opinions to the end of life I know not. Certainly the modes of thinking of his later years and especially of his last publication were much more Tory in their general character, than those which he held at this time.[‡]

My father's tone of thought and feeling, I now felt myself at a great distance from: greater, indeed, than a full and calm explanation and reconsideration on both sides, might have shewn to exist in reality. But my father was not one with whom calm and full explanations on fundamental points of doctrine could be expected, at least with one whom he might consider as, in some sort, a deserter from his standard. Fortunately we were almost always in strong agreement on the political questions of the day, which engrossed a large part of his interest and of his conversation. On those matters of opinion on which we differed, we talked little. He knew that the habit of thinking for myself, which his mode of education had fostered, sometimes led me to opinions different from his, and he perceived from time to time that I did not always tell him how different. I expected no good, but only pain to both of us, from discussing our differences: and I never expressed them but when he gave utterance to some opinion or feeling repugnant to mine, in a manner which would have made it disingenuousness on my part to remain silent.

It remains to speak of what I wrote during these years, which, independently of my contributions to newspapers, was considerable. In 1830 and 1831 I wrote the five Essays since published under the title of *Essays on Some Unsettled Questions of Political Economy*, almost as they now stand, except that in 1833 I partially rewrote the fifth Essay.[†] They were written with no immediate purpose of publication; and when, some years later, I offered them to a publisher, he declined them. They were only printed in 1844, after the success of the *System of Logic*. I also resumed my speculations on this last subject, and puzzled myself, like others before me, with the great paradox of the discovery of new truths by general reasoning. As to the fact, there could be no doubt. As little could it be doubted, that all reasoning is resolvable into syllogisms, and that in every syllogism the conclusion is actually contained and implied in the premises. How, being so contained and implied, it could be new truth, and how the theorems of geometry, so different, in appearance, from the definitions and axioms, could be all contained in these, was a difficulty which no one, I thought, had sufficiently felt, and which at all events no one had succeeded in clearing up. The explanations offered by Whately and others, though they might give a temporary satisfaction, always, in my mind, left a mist still hanging over the subject. At last, when reading a second or third time the chapters on Reasoning in the second volume of Dugald Stewart,[†] interrogating myself on every point, and following out as far as I knew how, every topic of thought which the book suggested, I came upon an idea of his respecting the use of axioms in ratiocination, which I did not remember to have before noticed, but which now, in meditating on it, seemed to me not only true of axioms, but of all general propositions whatever, and to be the key of the whole perplexity. From this germ grew the theory of the Syllogism propounded in the second Book of the *Logic*; which I immediately fixed by writing it out. And now, with greatly increased hope of being able to produce a work on Logic, of some originality and value, I proceeded to write the First Book, from the rough and imperfect draft I had already made. What I now wrote became the basis of that part of the subsequent Treatise; except that it did not contain the Theory of Kinds, which was a later addition, suggested by otherwise inextricable difficulties which met me in my first attempt to work out the subject of some of the concluding chapters of the Third Book. At the point which I have now reached 1 made a halt, which lasted five years. I had come to the end of my tether; I could make nothing satisfactory of Induction, at this time. I continued to read any book which seemed to promise light on the subject, and appropriated, as well as I could, the results; but for a long time I found nothing which seemed to open to me any very important vein of meditation.

In 1832 I wrote several papers for the first series of *Tait's Magazine*,† and one for a quarterly periodical called the *Jurist*,† which had been founded and for a short time carried on by a set of friends, all lawyers and law reformers, with several of whom I was acquainted. The paper in question is the one on the rights and duties of the State respecting Corporation and Church Property, now standing first among the collected *Dissertations and Discussions*;† where one of my articles in *Tait*, 'The Currency Juggle,' also appears. In the whole mass of what I wrote previous to these, there is nothing of sufficient permanent value to justify reprinting. The paper in the *Jurist*, which I still think a very complete discussion of the rights of the State over Foundations, shewed both sides of my opinions, asserting as firmly as I should have done at any time, the doctrine that all endowments are national property, which the government may and ought to control; but not, as I should once have done, condemning endowments in themselves, and proposing that they should be taken to pay off the national debt. On the contrary, I urged strenuously the importance of having a provision for education, not dependent on the mere demand of the market, that is, on the knowledge and discernment of average parents, but calculated to establish and keep up a higher standard of instruction than is likely to be spontaneously demanded by the buyers of the article. All these opinions have been confirmed and strengthened by the whole course of my subsequent reflections.

CHAPTER VI

Commencement of the Most Valuable Friendship of My Life. My Father's Death. Writings and Other Proceedings up to 1840

It was at the period of my mental progress which I have now reached that I formed the friendship which has been the honour and chief blessing of my existence, as well as the source of a great part of all that I have attempted to do, or hope to effect hereafter, for human improvement. My first introduction to the lady who, after a friendship of twenty years, consented to become my wife,[†] was in 1830, when I was in my twenty-fifth and she in her twenty-third year. With her husband's family it was the renewal of an old acquaintanceship. His grandfather lived in the next house to my father's in Newington Green, and I had sometimes when a boy been invited to play in the old gentleman's garden. He was a fine specimen of the old Scotch puritan; stern, severe, and powerful, but very kind to children, on whom such men make a lasting impression. Although it was years after my introduction to Mrs. Taylor before my acquaintance with her became at all intimate or confidential, I very soon felt her to be the most admirable person I had ever known. It is not to be supposed that she was, or that any one, at the age at which I first saw her, could be, all that she afterwards became. Least of all could this be true of her, with whom self-improvement, progress in the highest and in all senses, was a law of her nature; a necessity equally from the ardour with which she sought it, and from the spontaneous tendency of faculties which could not receive an impression or an experience without making it the source or the occasion of an accession of wisdom. Up to the time when I first saw her, her rich and powerful nature had chiefly unfolded itself according to the received type of feminine genius. To her outer circle she was a beauty and a wit, with an air of natural distinction, felt by all who approached her: to the inner, a woman of deep and strong feeling, of penetrating and intuitive intelligence, and of an eminently meditative and poetic

101

nature. Married at a very early age, to a most upright, brave, and honourable man, of liberal opinions and good education, but without the intellectual or artistic tastes which would have made him a companion for her – though a steady and affectionate friend, for whom she had true esteem and the strongest affection through life, and whom she most deeply lamented when dead; shut out by the social disabilities of women from any adequate exercise of her highest faculties in action on the world without; her life was one of inward meditation, varied by familiar intercourse with a small circle of friends, of whom one only (long since deceased)[†] was a person of genius, or of capacities of feeling or intellect kindred with her own, but all had more or less of alliance with her in sentiments and opinions. Into this circle I had the good fortune to be admitted, and I soon perceived that she possessed in combination, the qualities which in all other persons whom I had known I had been only too happy to find singly. In her, complete emancipation from every kind of superstition (including that which attributes a pretended perfection to the order of nature and the universe), and an earnest protest against many things which are still part of the established constitution of society, resulted not from the hard intellect but from strength of noble and elevated feeling, and coexisted with a highly reverential nature. In general spiritual characteristics, as well as in temperament and organisation, I have often compared her, as she was at this time, to Shelley:[†] but in thought and intellect, Shelley, so far as his powers were developed in his short life, was but a child compared with what she ultimately became. Alike in the highest regions of speculation and in the smallest practical concerns of daily life, her mind was the same perfect instrument, piercing to the very heart and marrow of the matter; always seizing the essential idea or principle. The same exactness and rapidity of operation, pervading as it did her sensitive as well as her mental faculties, would with her gifts of feeling and imagination have fitted her to be a consummate artist, as her fiery and tender soul and her vigorous eloquence would certainly have made her a great orator, and her profound knowledge of human nature and discernment and sagacity in practical life, would in the times when such a *carrière* was open to women, have made her eminent among the rulers of mankind. Her intellectual gifts did but minister to a moral character at once the noblest and the best balanced which I have ever met with in life. Her unselfishness was not that of a taught system of duties, but of a heart which thoroughly identified itself with the feelings of others, and often went to excess in consideration for them, by imaginatively investing their feelings with the intensity of its own. The passion of justice might have been thought to be her strongest feeling, but for her boundless generosity, and a lovingness ever ready to pour itself forth upon any or all human beings who were capable of giving the smallest feeling in return. The rest of her moral characteristics were such as naturally accompany these qualities of mind and heart: the most genuine modesty combined with the loftiest pride; a simplicity and sincerity which were absolute, towards all who were fit to receive them; the utmost scorn of whatever was mean and cowardly, and a burning indignation at everything brutal or tyrannical, faithless or dishonorable in conduct and character; while making the broadest distinction between *mala in se*† and mere *mala prohibita*† – between acts giving evidence of intrinsic badness in feeling and character, and those which are only violations of conventions either good or bad, violations which whether in themselves right or wrong, are capable of being committed by persons in every other respect loveable or admirable.

To be admitted into any degree of mental intercourse with a being of these qualities, could not but have a most beneficial influence on my development; though the effect was only gradual, and many years elapsed before her mental progress and mine went forward in the complete companionship they at last attained. The benefit I received was far greater than any which I could hope to give; though to her, who had at first reached her opinions by the moral intuition of a character of strong feeling, there was doubtless help as well as encouragement to be derived from one who had arrived at many of the same results by study and reasoning: and in the rapidity of her intellectual growth, her mental activity, which converted everything into knowledge, doubtless drew from me, as it did from other sources, many of its materials. What I owe, even intellectually, to her, is in its detail, almost infinite; of its general character, a few words will give some, though a very imperfect, idea. With those who, like all the best and wisest of mankind, are dissatisfied with human life as it is, and whose feelings are wholly identified with its radical amendment, there are two main regions of thought. One is the region of ultimate aims; the constituent elements of the highest realizable ideal of human life. The other is that of the immediately useful and practically attainable. In both these departments I have acquired more from her teaching, than from all other sources taken together. And, to say truth, it is in these two extremes principally, that real certainty lies. My own strength lay wholly in the uncertain and slippery intermediate region, that of theory, or moral and political science: respecting the conclusions of which, in any of the forms in which I have received or originated them, whether as political economy, analytic psychology, logic, philosophy of history, or anything else, it is not the least of my intellectual obligations to her that I have derived from her a wise scepticism, which, while it has not hindered me from following out the honest exercise of my thinking faculties to whatever conclusions might result from it, has put me on my guard against holding or announcing those conclusions with a degree of confidence which the nature of such speculations does not warrant, and has kept my mind not only open to admit, but prompt to welcome and eager to seek, even on the questions on which I have most meditated, any prospect of clearer perceptions and better evidence. I have often received praise, which in my own right I only partially deserve, for the greater practicality which is supposed to be found in my writings, compared with those of most thinkers who have been equally addicted to large generalizations. The writings in which this quality has been observed, were not the work of one mind, but of the fusion of two, one of them as preeminently practical in its judgments and perceptions of things present, as it was high and bold in its anticipations for a remote futurity.‡

At the present period, however, this influence was only one among many which were helping to shape the character of my future development: and even after it became, I may truly say, the presiding principle of my mental progress, it did not alter the path, but only made me move forward more boldly and at the same time more cautiously in the same course. The only actual revolution which has ever taken place in my modes of thinking, was already complete. My new tendencies had to be confirmed in some respects, moderated in others: but the only substantial changes of opinion that were yet to come, related to politics, and consisted, on one hand, in a greater approximation, so far as regards the ultimate prospects of humanity, to a qualified Socialism, and on the other, a shifting of my political ideal from pure democracy, as commonly understood by its partisans, to the modified form of it, which is set forth in my *Considerations on Representative Government*.†

The last change, which took place very gradually, dates its commencement from my reading, or rather study, of M. de Tocqueville's *Democracy in America*,† which fell into my hands immediately after its first appearance. In that remarkable work, the excellencies of Democracy were pointed out in a more conclusive, because a more specific manner than I had ever known them to be even by the most enthusiastic democrats; while the specific dangers which beset Democracy, considered as the government of the numerical majority, were brought into equally strong light, and subjected to a masterly analysis, not as reasons for resisting what the author considered as an inevitable result of human progress, but as indications of the weak points of popular government, the defences by which it needs to be guarded, and the correctives which must be added to it in order that while full play is given to its beneficial tendencies, those which are of a different nature may be neutralized or mitigated. I was now well prepared for speculations of this character, and from this time onward my own thoughts moved more and more in the same channel, though the consequent modifications in my practical political creed were spread over many years, as would be shewn by comparing my first review of *Democracy in America*, written and published in 1835,[†] with the one in 1840 (reprinted in the *Dissertations*), and this last, with the *Considerations on Representative Government*.

A collateral subject on which also I derived great benefit from the study of Tocqueville, was the fundamental question of Centralization. The powerful philosophic analysis which he applied to American and to French experience, led him to attach the utmost importance to the performance of as much of the collective business of society, as can safely be so performed, by the people themselves, without any intervention of the executive government, either to supersede their agency, or to dictate the manner of its exercise. He viewed this practical political activity of the individual citizen, not only as one of the most effectual means of training the social feelings and practical intelligence of the people, so important in themselves and so indispensable to good government, but also as the specific counteractive to some of the characteristic infirmities of Democracy, and a necessary protection against its degenerating into the only despotism of which in the modern world there is real danger – the absolute rule of the head of the executive over a congregation of isolated individuals, all equals but all slaves. There was, indeed, no immediate peril from this source on the British side of the channel, where nine tenths of the internal business which elsewhere devolves on the government, was transacted by agencies independent of it; where Centralization was, and is, the subject not only of rational disapprobation, but of unreasoning prejudice; where jealousy of Government interference was a blind feeling preventing or resisting even the most beneficial exertion of legislative authority to correct the abuses of what pretends to be local self-government, but is, too often, selfish mismanagement of local interests, by a jobbing and *borné* local oligarchy. But the more certain the public were to go wrong on the side opposed to Centralization, the greater danger was there lest philosophic reformers should fall into the contrary error, and overlook the mischiefs of which they had been spared the painful experience. I was myself, at this very time, actively engaged in defending important measures, such as the great Poor Law Reform of 1834,[†] against an irrational clamour grounded on the Anti-Centralization prejudice: and had it not been for the lessons of Tocqueville, I do not know that I might not, like many reformers before me, have been hurried into the excess opposite to that which, being the one prevalent in my own country, it was generally my business to combat. As it is, I have steered carefully between the two errors, and whether I have or have not drawn the line between them exactly in the right place, I have at least insisted with equal emphasis upon the evils on both sides, and have made the means of reconciling the advantages of both, a subject of serious study.

In the meanwhile had taken place the election of the first Reformed Parliament, which included several of the most notable of my Radical friends and acquaintances; Grote, Roebuck, Buller, Sir William Molesworth, John and Edward Romilly, and several more; besides Warburton, Strutt, and others, who were in parliament already. These who thought themselves, and were called by their friends, the philosophic radicals, had now, it seemed, a fair opportunity, in a more advantageous position than they had ever before occupied, for shewing what was in them; and I, as well as my father, founded great hopes on them. These hopes were destined to be disappointed. The men were honest, and faithful to their opinions, as far as votes were concerned; often in spite of much discouragement. When measures were proposed, flagrantly at variance with their principles, such as the Irish Coercion Bill,[†] or the Canada coercion in 1837,[†] they came forward manfully, and braved any amount of hostility and prejudice rather than desert the right. But on the whole they did very little to promote any opinions; they had little enterprise, little activity: they left the lead of the radical portion of the House to the old hands, to Hume and O'Connell.[†‡] A partial exception must be made in favour of one or two of the younger men; and in the case of Roebuck, it is his title to permanent remembrance, that in the very first year during which he sat in Parliament he originated (or reoriginated after the unsuccessful attempt of Mr. Brougham) the parliamentary movement for National Education; and that he was the first to commence, and for years carried on almost alone, the contest for the self-government of

106

the Colonies. Nothing, on the whole equal to these two things, was done by any other individual, even of those from whom most was expected. And now, on a calm retrospect, I can perceive that the men were less in fault than we supposed, and that we had expected too much from them. They were in unfavourable circumstances. Their lot was cast in the ten years of inevitable reaction, when, the Reform excitement being over, and the few legislative improvements which the public really called for having been rapidly effected, power gravitated back in its natural direction, to those who were for keeping things as they were; when the public mind desired rest, and was less disposed than at any other period since the peace, to let itself be moved by attempts to work up the reform feeling into fresh activity in favour of new things. It would have required a great political leader, which no one is to be blamed for not being, to have effected really great things by parliamentary discussion when the nation was in this mood. My father and I had hoped that some competent leader might arise; some man of philosophic attainments and popular talents, who could have put heart into the many younger or less distinguished men that would have been ready to join him – could have made them available, to the extent of their talents, in bringing advanced ideas before the public – could have used the House of Commons as a rostra or a teacher's chair for instructing and impelling the public mind; and would either have forced the Whigs to receive their measures from him, or have taken the lead of the Reform party out of their hands. Such a leader there would have been, if my father had been in Parliament.[†] For want of such a man, the instructed Radicals sank into a mere *côté gauche* of the Whig party. With a keen, and as I now think, an exaggerated sense of the possibilities which were open to the Radicals if they made even ordinary exertion for their opinions, I laboured from this time till 1839, both by personal influence with some of them, and by writings, to put ideas into their heads and purpose into their hearts. I did some good with Charles Buller, and some with Sir William Molesworth;[†] both of whom did valuable service, but were unhappily cut off almost in the beginning of their usefulness. On the whole, however, my attempt was vain. To have had a chance of succeeding in it, required a different position from mine. It was a task only for one who, being himself in Parliament, could have mixed with the radical members in daily consultation, could himself have taken the initiative, and instead of urging others to lead, could have summoned them to follow.

What I could do by writing, I did. During the year 1833 I continued working in the *Examiner* with Fonblanque, who at that time was zealous in keeping up the fight for radicalism against the Whig ministry. During the session of 1834 I wrote comments on passing events, of the nature of newspaper articles (under the title 'Notes on the Newspapers'), in the *Monthly Repository*,[†] a magazine conducted by Mr. Fox,[†] well known as a preacher and political orator, and subsequently as member of parliament for Oldham; with whom I had lately become acquainted, and for whose sake chiefly I wrote in his Magazine. I contributed several other articles to this periodical, the most considerable of which (on the theory of poetry), is reprinted in the *Dissertations*.[†] Altogether, the writings (independently of those in newspapers) which I published from 1832 to 1834, amount to a large volume. This, however, includes abstracts of several of Plato's Dialogues, with introductory remarks, which, though not published until 1834,[†] had been written several years earlier; and which I afterwards, on various occasions, found to have been read, and their authorship known, by more people than were aware of anything else which I had written, up to that time. To complete the tale of my writings at this period, I may add that in 1833, at the request of Bulwer, who was just then completing his *England and the English*[†] (a work, at that time, greatly in advance of the public mind), I wrote for him a critical account of Bentham's philosophy, a small part of which he incorporated in his text, and printed the rest (with an honorable acknowledgment), as an Appendix. In this, along with the favorable, a part also of the unfavourable side of my estimation of Bentham's doctrines, considered as a complete philosophy, was for the first time put into print.

But an opportunity soon offered by which, as it seemed, I might have it in my power to give more effectual aid, and at the same time, stimulus, to the 'philosophic radical' party, than I had done hitherto. One of the projects occasionally talked of between my father and me, and some of the parliamentary and other Radicals who frequented his house, was the foundation of a periodical organ of philosophic radicalism, to take the place which the *Westminster Review* had been intended to fill: and the scheme had gone so far as to bring under discussion the pecuniary contributions which could be looked for, and the choice of an editor. Nothing however came of it for some time: but in the summer of 1834 Sir William Molesworth, himself a laborious student, and a precise and metaphysical thinker capable of aiding the cause by his pen as well as by his purse, spontaneously proposed to establish a Review, provided I would consent to be the real, if I could not be the ostensible, editor. Such a proposal was not to be refused; and the review was founded, at first under the title of the *London Review*, and afterwards under that of the *London and Westminster*, Molesworth having bought the *Westminster* from its proprietor General Thompson, and merged the two into one. In the years between 1834 and 1840 the conduct of this review occupied the greater part of my spare time. In the beginning, it did not, as a whole, by any means represent my opinions. I was under the necessity of conceding much to my inevitable associates. The Review was established to be the representative of the 'philosophic radicals,' with most of whom I was now at issue on many essential points, and among whom I could not even claim to be the most important individual. My father's cooperation as a writer we all deemed indispensable, and he wrote largely in it until prevented by his last illness. The subjects of his articles, and the strength and decision with which his opinions were expressed in them, made the Review at first derive its tone and colouring from him much more than from any of the other writers.[†] I could not exercise editorial control over his articles, and I was sometimes obliged to sacrifice to him portions of my own. The old *Westminster Review* doctrines, but little modified, thus formed the staple of the review; but I hoped, by the side of these, to introduce other ideas and another tone, and to obtain for my own shade of opinion a fair representation, along with those of other members of the party. With this end chiefly in view, I made it one of the peculiarities of the work that every article should bear an initial, or some other signature, and be held to express the opinions solely of the individual writer; the editor being only responsible for its being worth publishing, and not in conflict with the objects for which the Review was set on foot. I had an opportunity of putting in practice my scheme of conciliation between the old and the new 'philosophic radicalism' by the choice of a subject for my own first contribution. Professor Sedgwick,[†] a man of eminence in a particular walk of natural science, but who should not have trespassed into philosophy, had lately published his *Discourse on the Studies of Cambridge*,[†] which had as its most prominent feature an intemperate assault on analytic psychology and utilitarian ethics, in the form of an attack on Locke and Paley.[†] This had excited great indignation in my father and others, which I thought it fully deserved. And here, I imagined, was an opportunity of at the same time repelling an unjust attack, and inserting into my defence of Hartleianism and Utilitarianism a number of the opinions which constituted my view of those subjects, as distinguished from that of my old associates. In this I partially succeeded, though my relation to my father would have made it painful to me in any case, and impossible in a review for which he wrote, to speak out my whole mind on the subject at this time.

I am, however, inclined to think that my father was not so much opposed as he seemed, to the modes of thought in which I believed myself to differ from him; that he did injustice to his own opinions by the unconscious exaggerations of an intellect emphatically polemical; and that when thinking without an adversary in view, he was willing to make room for a great portion of the truths he seemed to deny. I have frequently observed that he made large allowance in practice for considerations which seemed to have no place in his theory. His *Fragment on Mackintosh*, which he wrote and published about this time, although I greatly admired some parts of it, I read as a whole with more pain than pleasure; yet on reading it again, long after, I found little in the opinions it contains, but what I think in the main just; and I can even sympathize in his disgust at the *verbiage* of Mackintosh, though his asperity towards it went not only beyond what was judicious, but beyond what was even fair. One thing which I thought, at the time, of good augury, was the very favourable reception he gave to Tocqueville's *Democracy in America*. It is true, he said and thought much more about what Tocqueville said in favour of Democracy, than about what he said of its disadvantages. Still, his high appreciation of a book which was at any rate an example of a mode of treating the question of government almost the reverse of his – wholly inductive and analytical, instead of purely ratiocinative – gave me great encouragement. He also approved of an article which I published in the first number following the junction of the two reviews, the Essay reprinted in the *Dissertations* under the title 'Civilization';[†] into which I threw many of my new opinions, and criticized rather emphatically the mental and moral tendencies of the time, on grounds and in a manner which I certainly had not learnt from him.

All speculation, however, on the possible future developments of my father's opinions, and on the probabilities of permanent co-operation between him and me in the promulgation of our thoughts, was doomed to be cut short. During the whole of 1835 his health had been declining: his symptoms became unequivocally those of pulmonary consumption, and after lingering to the last stage of debility, he died on the 23rd of June 1836. Until the last few days of his life there was no apparent abatement of intellectual vigour; his interest in all things and persons that had interested him through life was undiminished, nor did the approach of death cause the smallest wavering (as in so strong and firm a mind it was impossible that it should) in his convictions on the subject of religion. His principal satisfaction, after he knew that his end was near, seemed to be the thought of what he had done to make the world better than he found it; and his chief regret in not living longer, that he had not had time to do more.

His place is an eminent one in the literary, and even in the political history of his country; and it is far from honourable to the generation which has benefitted by his worth, that he is so seldom mentioned, and, compared with men far his inferiors, so little remembered. This is probably to be ascribed mainly to two causes. In the first place, the thought of him merges too much in the deservedly superior fame of Bentham. Yet he was anything but Bentham's mere follower or disciple. Precisely because he was himself one of the most original thinkers of his time, he was one of the earliest to appreciate and adopt the most important mass of original thought which had been produced by the generation preceding him. His mind and Bentham's were essentially of different construction. He had not all Bentham's high qualities, but neither had Bentham all his. It would, indeed, be ridiculous to claim for him the praise of having accomplished for mankind such splendid services as Bentham's. He did not revolutionize – or rather create – one of the great departments of human thought. But, leaving out of the reckoning all that portion of his labours in which he benefitted by what Bentham had done, and counting only what he achieved in a province in which Bentham had done nothing, that of analytic psychology, he will be known to posterity as one of the greatest names in that most important branch of speculation, on which all the moral and political sciences ultimately rest, and will mark one of the essential stages in its progress.† The other reason, which has made his fame less than he deserved, is that notwithstanding the great number of his opinions which, partly through his own efforts, have now been generally adopted, there was on the whole a marked opposition between his spirit and that of the present time. As Brutus was called the last of the Romans,† so was he the last of the eighteenth century: he continued its tone of thought and sentiment into the nineteenth (though not unmodified nor unimproved), partaking neither in the good nor in the bad influences of the reaction against the eighteenth century, which was the great characteristic of the first half of the nineteenth.† The eighteenth century was a great age, an age of strong and brave men, and he was a fit companion for its strongest and bravest. By his writings and his personal influence he was a great centre of light to his generation. During his later years he was quite as much the head and leader of the intellectual radicals in England, as Voltaire was of the *philosophes* of France. It is only one of his minor merits, that he was the originator of all sound statesmanship in regard to the subject of his largest work, India.[†] He wrote on no subject which he did not enrich with valuable thought, and excepting the *Elements of Political Economy*, a very useful book when first written, but which has now for some time finished its work, it will be long before any of his books will be wholly superseded, or will cease to be instructive reading to students of their subjects. In the power of influencing by mere force of mind and character, the convictions and purposes of others, and in the strenuous exertion of that power to promote freedom and progress, he left, as far as my knowledge extends, no equal among men, and but one among women.[†]

Though acutely sensible of my own inferiority in the qualities by which he acquired his personal ascendancy, I had now to try what it might be possible for me to accomplish without him; and the Review was the instrument on which I built my chief hopes of establishing a useful influence over the liberal and democratic section of the public mind. Deprived of my father's aid, I was also exempted from the restraints and retinences[‡] by which that aid had been purchased. I did not feel that there was any other radical writer or politician to whom I was bound to defer, further than consisted with my own opinions: and having the complete confidence of Molesworth, I resolved henceforth to give full scope to my own opinions and modes of thought, and to open the Review widely to all writers who were in sympathy with Progress as I understood it, even though I should lose by it the support of my former associates. Carlyle, consequently, became from this time a frequent writer in the Review; Sterling, soon after, an occasional one; and though each individual article continued to be the expression of the private sentiments of its writer, the general tone conformed in some tolerable degree to my opinions. For the conduct of the Review, under and in conjunction with me, I associated with myself a young Scotchman of the name of Robertson,[†] who had some ability and information, much industry, and an active scheming head, full of devices for making the Review more saleable, and on whose capacities in that direction I founded a good deal of hope: insomuch that when Molesworth, in the beginning of 1837, became tired of carrying on the Review at a loss, and desirous of getting rid of it (he had done *his* part honourably, and at no small pecuniary cost), I, very imprudently for my own pecuniary interest, and very much from reliance on Robertson's devices, determined to continue it at my own risk, until his plans should have had a fair trial. The devices were good, and I never had any reason to change my opinion of them. But I do not believe that any devices would have made a radical and democratic review defray its expenses, including a paid editor or sub editor, and a liberal payment to writers. I myself and several frequent contributors gave our labour gratuitously, as we had done for Molesworth; but the paid contributors continued to be remunerated on the usual scale of the *Edinburgh* and *Quarterly* Reviews; and this could not be done from the proceeds of the sale.

In the same year, 1837, and in the midst of these occupations, I resumed the *Logic*. I had not touched my pen on the subject for five years, having been stopped and brought to a halt on the threshold of Induction. I had gradually discovered that what was mainly wanting, to overcome the difficulties of that branch of the subject, was a comprehensive and at the same time accurate view of the whole circle of physical science, which I feared it would take me a long course of study to acquire; since I knew not of any book, or other guide, that would spread out before me the generalities and processes of the sciences, and I apprehended that I should have no choice but to extract them for myself, as I best could, from the details. Happily for me, Dr. Whewell,[†] early in this year, published his *History of the Inductive Sciences*. I read it with eagerness, and found in it a considerable approximation to what I wanted. Much, if not most, of the philosophy of the work appeared open to objection; but the materials were there, for my own thoughts to work upon: and the author had given to those materials that first degree of elaboration, which so greatly facilitates and abridges the subsequent labour. I had now obtained what I had been waiting for. Under the impulse given me by the thoughts excited by Dr. Whewell, I read again Sir J. Herschel's *Discourse on the Study of Natural Philosophy*;[†] and I was able to measure the progress my mind had made, by the great help I now found in this work, though I had read and even reviewed it several years before with little profit. I now set myself vigorously to work out the subject in thought and in writing. The time I bestowed on this had to be stolen from occupations more urgent. I had just two months to spare, at this period, in the intervals of writing for the Review. In these two months I completed the first draft of about a third, the most difficult third, of the book. What I had before written I estimate at another third, so that only one third remained. What I wrote at this time consisted of the remainder of the doctrine of Reasoning (the theory of Trains of Reasoning, and Demonstrative Science) and the greater part of the Book on Induction. When this was done, I had, as it seemed to me, untied all the really hard knots, and the completion of the book had become only a question of time. Having got thus far, I had to leave off in order to write two articles for the next number of the Review.† When these were written, I returned to the subject, and now for the first time fell in with Comte's *Cours de Philosophie Positive*,† or rather with the two volumes of it which were all that had at that time been published.

My theory of Induction was substantially completed before I knew of Comte's book; and it is perhaps well that I came to it by a different road from his, since the consequence has been that my treatise contains, what his certainly does not, a reduction of the inductive process to strict rules and to a scientific test, such as the Syllogism is for ratiocination. Comte is always precise and profound on the method of investigation, but he does not even attempt any exact definition of the conditions of proof: and his writings shew that he never attained a just conception of them. This, however, was specifically the problem which, in treating of Induction, I had proposed to myself. Nevertheless, I gained much from Comte, with which to enrich my chapters in the subsequent rewriting: and his book was of essential service to me in some of the parts which still remained to be thought out. As his subsequent volumes successively made their appearance, I read them with avidity, but, when he reached the subject of Social Science, with varying feelings. The fourth volume disappointed me: it contained those of his opinions on social subjects with which I most disagree. But the fifth, containing the connected view of history, rekindled all my enthusiasm; which the sixth (or concluding) volume did not materially abate. In a merely logical point of view, the only leading conception for which I am indebted to him is that of the Inverse Deductive Method, as the one chiefly applicable to the complicated subjects of History and Statistics: a process differing from the more common form of the Deductive Method in this, that instead of arriving at its conclusions by general reasoning and verifying them by specific experience (as is the natural order in the deductive branches of physical science), it obtains its generalizations by a collation of specific experience, and verifies them by ascertaining whether they are such as would follow from known general principles. This was an idea entirely new to me when I found it in Comte: and but for him I might not soon (if ever) have arrived at it.

I had been long an ardent admirer of Comte's writings before I had any communication with himself; nor did I ever, to the last, see him in the body. But for some years we were frequent correspondents, until our correspondence became controversial, and our zeal cooled. I was the first to slacken correspondence; he was the first to drop it. I found, and he probably found likewise, that I could do no good to his mind, and that all the good he could do to mine, he did by his books. This would never have led to discontinuance of intercourse, if the differences between us had been on matters of simple doctrine. But they were chiefly on those points of opinion which blended in both of us with our strongest feelings, and determined the entire direction of our aspirations. I had fully agreed with him when he maintained that the mass of mankind, including even their rulers in all the practical departments of life, must, from the necessity of the case, accept most of their opinions on political and social matters, as they do on physical, from the authority of those who have bestowed more study on those subjects than they generally have it in their power to do. This lesson had been strongly impressed on me by the early work of Comte, to which I have adverted.[†] And there was nothing in his great Treatise which I admired more than his remarkable exposition of the benefits which the nations of modern Europe have historically derived from the separation, during the middle ages, of temporal and spiritual power, and the distinct organization of the latter.[†] I agreed with him that the moral and intellectual ascendancy, once exercised by priests, must in time pass into the hands of philosophers, and will naturally do so when they become sufficiently unanimous, and in other respects worthy to possess it. But when he exaggerated this line of thought into a practical system, in which philosophers were to be organized into a kind of corporate hierarchy, invested with almost the same spiritual supremacy (though without any secular power) once possessed by the Catholic Church; when I found him relying on this spiritual authority as the only security for good government, the sole bulwark against practical oppression, and expecting that by it a system of despotism in the state and despotism in the family would be rendered innocuous and beneficial; it is not surprising, that while as logicians we were nearly at one, as sociologists we could travel together no further. M. Comte lived to carry out these doctrines to their extremest consequences, by planning, in his last work, the *Système de Politique Positive*,[†] the completest system of spiritual and temporal despotism which ever yet emanated from a human brain, unless possibly that of Ignatius Loyola:[†] a system by

115

which the yoke of general opinion, wielded by an organized body of spiritual teachers and rulers, would be made supreme over every action, and as far as is in human possibility, every thought, of every member of the community, as well in the things which regard only himself, as in those which concern the interests of others. It is but just to say that this work is a considerable improvement, in many points of feeling, over Comte's previous writings on the same subjects: but as an accession to social philosophy, the only value it seems to me to possess consists in putting an end to the notion that no effectual moral authority can be maintained over society without the aid of religious belief; for Comte's work recognizes no religion except that of Humanity, yet it leaves an irresistible conviction that any moral beliefs, concurred in by the community generally, may be brought to bear upon the whole conduct and lives of its individual members with an energy and potency truly alarming to think of. The book stands a monumental warning to thinkers on society and politics, of what happens when once men lose sight, in their speculations, of the value of Liberty and of Individuality.

To return to myself: the Review engrossed, for some time longer, nearly all the time I could devote to authorship, or to thinking with authorship in view. The articles from the *London and Westminster Review* which are reprinted in the *Dissertations* are scarcely a fourth part of those I wrote. In the conduct of the Review I had two principal objects. One was to free philosophic radicalism from the reproach of sectarian Benthamism. I desired, while retaining the precision of expression, the definiteness of meaning, the contempt of declamatory phrases and vague generalities, which were so honorably characteristic both of Bentham and of my father, to give a wider basis and a more free and genial character to Radical speculations; to shew that there was a Radical philosophy, better and more complete than Bentham's, while recognizing and incorporating all of Bentham's which is permanently valuable. In this first object I, to a certain extent, succeeded. The other thing I attempted, was to stir up the educated Radicals, in and out of Parliament, to exertion, and induce them to make themselves, what I thought by using the proper means, they might become – a powerful party capable of taking the government of the country, or at least of dictating the terms on which they should share it with the Whigs. This attempt was from the first chimerical: partly because the time was unpropitious, the Reform fervour being in its period of ebb, and the Tory influences powerfully rallying; but, still more, because, as Austin so truly said, 'the country did not contain the men.' Among the Radicals in Parliament there were several qualified to be useful members of an enlightened Radical party, but none capable of forming and leading such a party. The exhortations I addressed to them found no response. One occasion did present itself when there seemed to be room for a bold and successful stroke for Radicalism. Lord Durham[†] had left the ministry, by reason, as was thought, of their not being sufficiently liberal; he afterwards accepted from them the task of ascertaining and removing the causes of the Canadian rebellion: he had shewn a disposition to surround himself at the outset with Radical advisers; one of his earliest measures, a good measure both in intention and in effect, having been disapproved and reversed by the Government at home, he had resigned his post, and placed himself openly in a position of quarrel with the ministers. Here was a possible chief for a Radical party in the person of a man of importance, who was hated by the Tories, and had just been injured by the Whigs. Any one who had the most elementary notions of party tactics, must have attempted to make something of such an opportunity. Lord Durham was bitterly attacked from all sides, inveighed against by enemies, given up by timid friends; while those who would willingly have defended him did not know what to say. He appeared to be returning a defeated and discredited man. I had followed the Canadian events from the beginning; I had been one of the prompters of his prompters; his policy was almost exactly what mine would have been, and I was in a position to defend it. I wrote and published a manifesto in the Review, in which I took the very highest ground in his behalf, claiming for him not mere acquittal, but praise and honour.[†] Instantly a number of other writers took up the tone. I believe there was a portion of truth in what Lord Durham, soon after, with polite exaggeration, said to me – that to this article might be ascribed the almost triumphal reception which he met with on his arrival in England. I believe it to have been the word in season, which, at a critical moment, does much to decide the result; the touch which determines whether a stone, set in motion at the top of an eminence, shall roll down on one side or on the other. All hopes connected with Lord Durham as a politician soon vanished; but with regard to Canadian, and generally to colonial policy, the cause was gained: Lord Durham's report, written by Charles Buller, partly under the inspiration of Wakefield, began a new era; its recommendations, extending to complete internal self-government, were in full operation in Canada within two or three years, and have been since extended to nearly all the other colonies, of European race,

117

which have any claim to the character of important communities. And I may say that in successfully upholding the reputation of Lord Durham and his advisers at the most important moment, I contributed materially to this result.

One other case occurred during my conduct of the Review, which similarly illustrated the effect of taking a prompt initiative. I believe that the early success and reputation of Carlyle's *French Revolution*, were considerably accelerated by what I wrote about it in the Review. Immediately on its publication, and before the commonplace critics, all whose rules and modes of judgment it set at defiance, had time to preoccupy the public with their disapproval of it, I wrote and published a review of the book, hailing it as one of those productions of genius which are above all rules, and are a law to themselves. Neither in this case nor in that of Lord Durham do I ascribe the impression, which I think was produced by what I wrote, to any particular merit of execution: indeed, in at least one of the cases (the article on Carlyle) I do not think the execution was good. And in both instances, I am persuaded that anybody, in a position to be read, who had expressed the same opinion at the same precise time, and had made any tolerable statement of the just grounds for it, would have produced the same effect. But, after the complete failure of my hopes of putting a new life into radical politics by means of the Review, I am glad to look back on these two instances of success in an honest attempt to do immediate service to things and persons that deserved it.

After the last hope of the formation of a Radical party had disappeared, it was time for me to stop the heavy expenditure of time and money which the Review cost me. It had to some extent answered my personal purpose, as a vehicle for my opinions. It had enabled me to express in print much of my altered mode of thought, and to separate myself in a marked manner from the narrower Benthamism of my early writings. This was done by the general tone of all I wrote, including various purely literary articles, but especially by the two papers (reprinted in the *Dissertations*) which attempted a philosophical estimate of Bentham and of Coleridge.† In the first of these, while doing full justice to the merits of Bentham, I pointed out what I thought the errors and deficiencies of his philosophy. The substance of this criticism I still think perfectly just; but I have sometimes doubted whether it was right to publish it at that time. I have often felt that Bentham's philosophy, as an instrument of progress, has been to some extent discredited before it had done its work, and that to lend a hand towards lowering its reputation was doing more harm than service to improvement. Now however when a counter-reaction appears to be setting in towards what is good in Benthamism, I can look with more satisfaction on this criticism of its defects, especially as I have myself balanced it by vindications of the fundamental principles of Bentham's philosophy, which are reprinted along with it in the same collection. In the essay on Coleridge I attempted to characterize the European reaction against the negative philosophy of the eighteenth century: and here, if the effect only of this one paper were to be considered, I might be thought to have erred by giving undue prominence to the favourable side, as I had done in the case of Bentham to the unfavourable. In both cases, the impetus with which I had detached myself from what was untenable in the doctrines of Bentham and of the eighteenth century, may have carried me, though in appearance rather than in reality, too far on the contrary side. But as far as relates to the article on Coleridge, my defence is, that I was writing for Radicals and Liberals, and it was my business to dwell most on that in writers of a different school, from the knowledge of which they might derive most improvement.

The number of the Review which contained the paper on Coleridge, was the last which was published during my proprietorship. In the spring of 1840 I made over the Review to Mr. Hickson,† who had been a frequent and very useful unpaid contributor under my management; only stipulating that the change should be marked by a resumption of the old name, that of *Westminster Review*. Under that name Mr. Hickson conducted it for ten years, on the plan of dividing among contributors only the net proceeds of the Review, giving his own labour as writer and editor gratuitously. Under the difficulty in obtaining writers, which arose from this low scale of payment, it is highly creditable to him that he was able to maintain, in some tolerable degree, the character of the Review as an organ of radicalism and progress. I did not cease altogether to write for the Review, but continued to send it occasional contributions, not, however, exclusively; for the greater circulation of the *Edinburgh Review* induced me from this time to offer articles to it also when I had anything to say for which it appeared to be a suitable vehicle. And the concluding volumes of *Democracy in America* having just then come out, I inaugurated myself as a contributor to the *Edinburgh* by the article on that work, which heads the second volume of the *Dissertations*.

CHAPTER VII

General View of the Remainder of My Life

❦

From this time, what is worth relating of my life will come into a very small compass; for I have no further mental changes to tell of, but only, as I hope, a continued mental progress; which does not admit of a consecutive history, and the results of which, if real, will be best found in my writings. I shall therefore greatly abridge the chronicle of my subsequent years.

The first use I made of the leisure which I gained by disconnecting myself from the Review, was to finish the *Logic*. In July and August 1838 I had found an interval in which to execute what was still undone of the original draft of the Third Book. In working out the logical theory of those laws of nature which are not laws of Causation, nor corollaries from such laws, I was led to recognize Kinds as realities in nature, and not mere distinctions for convenience; a light which I had not obtained when the First Book was written, and which made it necessary for me to modify and enlarge several chapters of that Book. The Book on Language and Classification, and the chapter on the Classification of Fallacies, were drafted in the autumn of the same year; the remainder of the work in the summer and autumn of 1840. From April following to the end of 1841, my spare time was devoted to a complete rewriting of the book from its commencement. It is in this way that all my books have been composed. They were always written at least twice over; a first draft of the entire work was completed to the very end of the subject, then the whole begun again *de novo*;[†] but incorporating, in the second writing, all sentences and parts of sentences of the old draft, which appeared as suitable to my purpose as anything which I could write in lieu of them. I have found great advantages in this system of double redaction. It combines, better than any other mode of composition, the freshness and vigour of the first conception, with the superior precision and completeness resulting from prolonged thought. In my own case, moreover, I have found that the patience necessary for a careful elaboration of the details of composition and expression, costs much less effort after the entire subject has been once gone through, and the substance of all that I find to say has in some manner, however imperfect, been got upon paper. The only thing which I am careful, in the first draft, to make as perfect as I am able, is the arrangement. If that is bad, the whole thread on which the ideas string themselves becomes twisted; thoughts placed in a wrong connexion are not expounded in a manner that suits the right, and a first draft with this original vice is next to useless as a foundation for the final treatment.

During the rewriting of the *Logic*, Dr. Whewell's *Philosophy of the Inductive Sciences*† made its appearance; a circumstance fortunate for me, as it gave me what I greatly desired, a full treatment of the subject by an antagonist, and enabled me to present my ideas with greater clearness and emphasis as well as fuller and more varied development, in defending them against definite objections, and confronting them distinctly with an opposite theory. The controversies with Dr. Whewell, as well as much matter derived from Comte, were first introduced into the book in the course of the rewriting.

At the end of 1841, the book being ready for press, I offered it to Murray, who kept it until too late for publication that season, and then refused it, for reasons which could just as well have been given at first. But I have had no cause to regret a rejection which led to my offering it to Mr. Parker, by whom it was published in the spring of 1843. My original expectations of success were extremely limited. Archbishop Whately had, indeed, rehabilitated the name of Logic, and the study of the forms, rules, and fallacies of Ratiocination; and Dr. Whewell's writings had begun to excite an interest in the other part of my subject, the theory of Induction. A treatise, however, on a matter so abstract, could not be expected to be popular; it could only be a book for students, and students on such subjects were not only (at least in England) few, but addicted chiefly to the opposite school of metaphysics, the ontological and 'innate principles' school. I therefore did not expect that the book would have many readers, or approvers; and looked for little practical effect from it, save that of keeping the tradition unbroken of what I thought a better philosophy. What hopes I had of exciting any immediate attention, were mainly grounded on the polemical propensities of Dr. Whewell; who, I thought, from observation of his conduct in other cases, would probably do something to bring the book into notice, by replying, and that promptly, to the attack on his opinions. He did reply, but not till

1850,† just in time for me to answer him in the third edition.† How the book came to have, for a work of the kind, so much success, and what sort of persons compose the bulk of those who have bought, I will not venture to say read, it, I have never thoroughly understood. But taken in conjunction with the many proofs which have since been given of a revival of speculation, speculation too of a free kind, in many quarters, and above all (where at one time I should have least expected it) in the Universities, the fact becomes partially intelligible. I have never indulged the illusion that the book had made any considerable impression on philosophical opinion. The German, or *à priori* view of human knowledge, and of the knowing faculties, is likely for some time longer (though it may be hoped in a diminishing degree) to predominate among those who occupy themselves with such enquiries, both here and on the Continent. But the *System of Logic* supplies what was much wanted, a text-book of the opposite doctrine – that which derives all knowledge from experience, and all moral and intellectual qualities principally from the direction given to the associations. I make as humble an estimate as anybody of what either an analysis of logical processes, or any possible canons of evidence, can do by themselves, towards guiding or rectifying the operations of the understanding. Combined with other requisites, I certainly do think them of great use; but whatever may be the practical value of a true philosophy of these matters, it is hardly possible to exaggerate the mischiefs of a false one. The notion that truths external to the mind may be known by intuition or consciousness, independently of observation and experience, is, I am persuaded, in these times, the great intellectual support of false doctrines and bad institutions. By the aid of this theory, every inveterate belief and every intense feeling, of which the origin is not remembered, is enabled to dispense with the obligation of justifying itself by reason, and is erected into its own all-sufficient voucher and justification. There never was such an instrument devised for consecrating all deep seated prejudices. And the chief strength of this false philosophy in morals, politics, and religion, lies in the appeal which it is accustomed to make to the evidence of mathematics and of the cognate branches of physical science. To expel it from these, is to drive it from its stronghold: and because this had never been effectually done, the intuitive school, even after what my father had written in his *Analysis of the Mind*, had in appearance, and as far as published writings were concerned, on the whole the best of the argument. In attempting to clear up the real nature of the evidence of mathematical and physical truths, the *System of Logic* met the intuition philosophers on ground on which they had previously been deemed unassailable; and gave its own explanation, from experience and association, of that peculiar character of what are called necessary truths, which is adduced as proof that their evidence must come from a deeper source than experience. Whether this has been done effectually, is still *sub judice*; and even then, to deprive a mode of thought so strongly rooted in human prejudices and partialities, of its mere speculative support, goes but a very little way towards overcoming it; but though only a step, it is a quite indispensable one; for since, after all, prejudice can only be successfully combated by philosophy, no way can really be made against it permanently until it has been shewn not to have philosophy on its side.‡

Being now released from any active concern in temporary politics, and from any literary occupation involving personal communication with contributors and others, I was enabled to indulge the inclination, natural to thinking persons when the age of boyish vanity is once past, for limiting my own society to a very few persons. General society, as now carried on in England, is so insipid an affair, even to the persons who make it what it is, that it is kept up for any reason rather than the pleasure it affords. All serious discussion on matters on which opinions differ, being considered ill bred, and the national deficiency in liveliness and sociability having prevented the cultivation of the art of talking agreeably on trifles, in which the French of the last century so much excelled, the sole attraction of what is called society to those who are not at the top of the tree, is the hope of being aided to climb a little higher in it; while to those who are already at the top, it is chiefly a compliance with custom, and with the supposed requirements of their station. To a person of any but a very common order in thought or feeling, such society, unless he has personal objects to serve by it, must be supremely unattractive: and most people, in the present day, of any really high class of intellect, make their contact with it so slight, and at such long intervals, as to be almost considered as retiring from it altogether. Those persons of any mental superiority who do otherwise, are, almost without exception, greatly deteriorated by it. Not to mention loss of time, the tone of their feelings is lowered: they become less in earnest about those of their opinions respecting which they must remain silent in the society they frequent: they come to look upon their most elevated objects as unpractical, or, at least, too remote from realization to be more than a vision, or a theory; and if, more fortunate than most, they retain their higher principles unimpaired, yet with respect to the persons and affairs of their own day they insensibly adopt the modes of feeling and judgment in which they can hope for sympathy from the company they keep. A person of high intellect should never go into unintellectual society unless he can enter it as an apostle; yet he is the only person with high objects, who can safely enter it at all. Persons even of intellectual aspirations had much better, if they can, make their habitual associates of at least their equals, and, as far as possible, their superiors, in knowledge, intellect, and elevation of sentiment. Moreover, if the character is formed, and the mind made up, on the few cardinal points of human opinion, agreement of conviction and feeling on these, has been felt in all times to be an essential requisite of anything worthy the name of friendship, in a really earnest mind. All these circumstances united, made the number very small of those whose society, and still more whose intimacy, I now voluntarily sought.

Among these, by far the principal was the incomparable friend of whom I have already spoken. At this period she lived mostly, with one young daughter, in a quiet part of the country, and only occasionally in town, with her first husband, Mr. Taylor.[†] I visited her equally in both places; and was greatly indebted to the strength of character which enabled her to disregard the false interpretations liable to be put on the frequency of my visits to her while living generally apart from Mr. Taylor, and on our occasionally travelling together, though in all other respects our conduct during those years gave not the slightest ground for any other supposition than the true one,[†] that our relation to each other at that time was one of strong affection and confidential intimacy only. For though we did not consider the ordinances of society binding on a subject so entirely personal, we did feel bound that our conduct should be such as in no degree to bring discredit on her husband, nor therefore on herself.[‡]

In this third period (as it may be termed) of my mental progress, which now went hand in hand with hers, my opinions gained equally in breadth and depth. I understood more things, and those which I had understood before, I now understood more thoroughly. I had now completely turned back from what there had been of excess in my reaction against Benthamism. I had, at the height of that reaction, certainly become much more indulgent to the common opinions of society and the world, and more willing to be content with seconding the superficial improvement which had begun to take place in those common opinions, than became one whose convictions, on so many points, differed fundamentally from them. I was much more inclined,

125

than I can now approve, to put in abeyance the more decidedly heretical part of my opinions, which I now look upon as almost the only ones, the assertion of which tends in any way to regenerate society. But in addition to this, our opinions were far *more* heretical than mine had been in the days of my most extreme Benthamism. In those days I had seen little further than the old school of political economists into the possibilities of fundamental improvement in social arrangements. Private property as now understood, and inheritance, appeared to me as to them, the *dernier mot* of legislation: and I looked no further than to mitigating the inequalities consequent on these institutions, by getting rid of primogeniture and entails. The notion that it was possible to go further than this in removing the injustice – for injustice it is whether admitting of a complete remedy or not – involved in the fact that some are born to riches and the vast majority to poverty, I then reckoned chimerical; and only hoped that by universal education, leading to voluntary restraint on population, the portion of the poor might be made more tolerable. In short, I was a democrat, but not the least of a Socialist. We were now much less democrats than I had been, because so long as education continues to be so wretchedly imperfect, we dreaded the ignorance and especially the selfishness and brutality of the mass: but our ideal of ultimate improvement went far beyond Democracy, and would class us decidedly under the general designation of Socialists. While we repudiated with the greatest energy that tyranny of society over the individual which most Socialistic systems are supposed to involve, we yet looked forward to a time when society will no longer be divided into the idle and the industrious;‡ when the rule that they who do not work shall not eat,† will be applied not to paupers only, but impartially to all; when the division of the produce of labour, instead of depending, as in so great a degree it now does, on the accident of birth, will be made by concert, on an acknowledged principle of justice; and when it will no longer either be, or be thought to be, impossible for human beings to exert themselves strenuously in procuring benefits which are not to be exclusively their own, but to be shared with the society they belong to. The social problem of the future we considered to be, how to unite the greatest individual liberty of action, with a common ownership in the raw material of the globe, and an equal participation of all in the benefits of combined labour. We had not the presumption to suppose that we could already foresee, by what precise form of institutions these objects could most effectually be attained, or at how near or how distant a period they would become practicable. We saw clearly that to render any such social transformation either possible or desirable, an equivalent change of character must take place both in the uncultivated herd who now compose the labouring masses, and in the immense majority of their employers. Both these classes must learn by practice to labour and combine for generous, or at all events for public and social purposes, and not, as hitherto, solely for narrowly interested ones. But the capacity to do this has always existed in mankind, and is not, nor is ever likely to be, extinct. Education, habit, and the cultivation of the sentiments will make a common man dig or weave for his country, as readily as fight for his country. True enough, it is only by slow degrees, and a system of culture prolonged through successive generations, that men in general can be brought up to this point. But the hindrance is not in the essential constitution of human nature. Interest in the common good is at present so weak a motive in the generality, not because it can never be otherwise, but because the mind is not accustomed to dwell on it as it dwells from morning till night on things which tend only to personal advantage. When called into activity as only self interest now is, by the daily course of life, and spurred from behind by the love of distinction and the fear of shame, it is capable of producing, even in common men, the most strenuous exertions as well as the most heroic sacrifices. The deep rooted selfishness which forms the general character of the existing state of society, is *so* deeply rooted, only because the whole course of existing institutions tends to foster it;[†] modern institutions in some respects more than ancient, since the occasions on which the individual is called on to do anything for the public without receiving its pay, are far less frequent in modern life, than in the smaller commonwealths of antiquity. These considerations did not make us overlook the folly of premature attempts to dispense with the inducements of private interest in social affairs, while no substitute for them has been or can be provided: but we regarded all existing institutions and social arrangements as being (in a phrase I once heard from Austin) 'merely provisional,' and we welcomed with the greatest pleasure and interest all socialistic experiments by select individuals (such as the Cooperative Societies), which, whether they succeeded or failed, could not but operate as a most useful education of those who took part in them, by cultivating their capacity of acting upon motives pointing directly to the general good, or making them aware of the defects which render them and others incapable of doing so.

In the *Principles of Political Economy*, these opinions were promulgated, less clearly and fully in the first edition, rather more so in the second, and quite unequivocally in the third.[†] The difference arose partly from the change of times, the first edition having been written and sent to press before the French Revolution of 1848, after which the public mind became more open to the reception of novelties in opinion, and doctrines appeared moderate which would have been thought very startling a short time before. In the first edition the difficulties of Socialism were stated so strongly, that the tone was on the whole that of opposition to it. In the year or two which followed, much time was given to the study of the best Socialistic writers on the Continent, and to meditation and discussion on the whole range of topics involved in the controversy: and the result was that most of what had been written on the subject in the first edition was cancelled, and replaced by arguments and reflections which represent a more advanced opinion.

The *Political Economy* was far more rapidly executed than the *Logic*, or indeed than anything of importance which I had previously written. It was commenced in the autumn of 1845, and was ready for the press before the end of 1847. In this period of little more than two years there was an interval of six months during which the work was laid aside, while I was writing articles in the *Morning Chronicle* (which unexpectedly entered warmly into my purpose) urging the formation of peasant properties on the waste lands of Ireland.[†] This was during the period of the famine, the winter of 1846/47, when the stern necessities of the time seemed to afford a chance of gaining attention for what appeared to me the only mode of combining relief to immediate destitution with permanent improvement of the social and economical condition of the Irish people. But the idea was new and strange; there was no English precedent for such a proceeding: and the profound ignorance of English politicians and the English public concerning all social phenomena not generally met with in England (however common elsewhere) made my endeavours an entire failure. Instead of a great operation on the waste lands, and the conversion of cottiers into proprietors, Parliament passed a Poor Law[†] for maintaining them as paupers: and if the nation has not since found itself in inextricable difficulties from the joint operation of the old evils and the quack remedy, it is indebted for its deliverance to that most unexpected and surprising fact, the depopulation of Ireland, commenced by famine, and continued by emigration.

The rapid success of the *Political Economy* shewed that the public wanted, and were prepared for such a book. Published early in 1848, an edition of a thousand copies was sold in less than a year. Another similar edition was published in the spring of 1849; and a third, of 1250 copies, early in 1852. It was, from the first, continually cited and referred to as an authority, because it was not a book merely of abstract science, but also of application, and treated Political Economy not as a thing by itself, but as a fragment of a greater whole; a branch of Social Philosophy, so interlinked with all the other branches, that its conclusions, even in its own peculiar province, are only true conditionally, subject to interference and counteraction from causes not directly within its scope: while to the character of a practical guide it has no pretension, apart from other classes of considerations. Political Economy, in truth, has never pretended to give advice to mankind with no lights but its own; though people who knew nothing *but* political economy (and therefore knew that ill) have taken upon themselves to advise, and could only do so by such lights as they had. But the numerous sentimental enemies of political economy, and its still more numerous interested enemies in sentimental guise, have been very successful in gaining belief for this among other unmerited imputations against it. And the *Principles* having, in spite of the freedom of many of its opinions, become for the present the most popular treatise on the subject, has helped to disarm the enemies of so important a study. The amount of its worth as an exposition of the science, and the value of the different applications which it suggests, others of course must judge.

For a considerable time after this, I published no work of magnitude; though I still occasionally wrote in periodicals, and my correspondence (much of it with persons quite unknown to me) on subjects of public interest, swelled to a considerable bulk. During these years I wrote or commenced various Essays, for eventual publication, on some of the fundamental questions of human and social life, with regard to several of which I have already much exceeded the severity of the Horatian precept.† I continued to watch with keen interest the progress of public events. But it was not, on the whole, very encouraging to me. The European reaction after 1848, and the success of an unprincipled usurper in December 1851,† put an end, as it seemed, to all present hope of freedom or social improvement in France and the Continent. In England, I had seen and continued to see many of the opinions of my youth obtain general recognition, and many of the reforms in institutions, for which I had through life contended, either effected or in course of being so. But these changes had been attended with much less benefit to human well being than I should formerly have anticipated, because they had produced very little improvement in that which all real amelioration in the lot of mankind depends on, their intellectual and moral state: and it might even be questioned if the various causes of deterioration which had been at work in the meanwhile, had not more than counterbalanced the tendencies to improvement. I had learnt from experience that many false opinions may be exchanged for true ones, without in the least altering the habits of mind of which false opinions are the result. The English public, for example, are quite as raw and undiscerning on subjects of political economy since the nation has been converted to free trade, as they were before; and are still further from having acquired better habits of thought and feeling, or being in any way better fortified against error, on subjects of a more elevated character. For, though they have thrown off certain errors, the general discipline of their minds, intellectually and morally, is not altered. I am now convinced, that no great improvements in the lot of mankind are possible, until a great change takes place in the fundamental constitution of their modes of thought. The old opinions in religion, morals, and politics, are so much discredited in the more intellectual minds as to have lost the greater part of their efficacy for good, while they have still life enough in them to be a powerful obstacle to the growing up of any better opinions on those subjects. When the philosophic minds of the world can no longer believe its religion, or can only believe it with modifications amounting to an essential change of its character, a transitional period commences, of weak convictions, paralysed intellects, and growing laxity of principle, which cannot terminate until a renovation has been effected in the basis of their belief, leading to the evolution of some faith, whether religious or merely human, which they can really believe: and when things are in this state, all thinking or writing which does not tend to promote such a renovation, is of very little value beyond the moment. Since there was little in the apparent condition of the public mind, indicative of any tendency in this direction, my view of the immediate prospects of human improvement was not sanguine. More recently a spirit of free speculation has sprung up, giving a more encouraging prospect of the gradual mental emancipation of England; and, concurring with the renewal, under better auspices, of the movement for political freedom in the rest of Europe, has given to the present condition of human affairs a more hopeful aspect.

Between the time of which I have now spoken, and the present, took place the most important events of my private life. The first of these was my marriage, in April 1851, to the lady whose incomparable worth had made her friendship the greatest source to me both of happiness and of improvement, during many years in which we never expected to be in any closer relation to one another. Ardently as I should have aspired to this complete union of our lives at any time in the course of my existence at which it had been practicable, I, as much as my wife, would far rather have foregone that privilege for ever, than have owed it to the premature death of one for whom I had the sincerest respect, and she the strongest affection. That event however having taken place in July 1849, it was granted to me to derive from that evil my own greatest good, by adding to the partnership of thought, feeling, and writing‡ which had long existed, a partnership of our entire existence. For seven and a half years that blessing was mine; for seven and a half only! I can say nothing which could describe, even in the faintest manner, what that loss was and is. But because I know that she would have wished it, I endeavour to make the best of what life I have left, and to work on for her purposes with such diminished strength as can be derived from thoughts of her, and communion with her memory.‡

During the years which intervened between the commencement of my married life and the catastrophe which closed it, the principal occurrences of my outward existence (unless I count as such a first attack of the family disease, and a consequent journey of more than six months for the recovery of health, in Italy, Sicily, and Greece) had reference to my position in the India House. In 1856 I was promoted to the rank of chief of the office in which I had served for upwards of thirty-three years. The appointment, that of Examiner of India Correspondence, was the highest, next to that of Secretary, in the East India Company's home service, involving the general superintendance of all the correspondence with the Indian Governments, except the military, naval, and financial. I held this office as long as it continued to exist, being a little more than two years; after which it pleased Parliament, in other words Lord Palmerston, to put an end to the East India Company as a branch of the government of India under the Crown, and convert the administration of that country into a thing to be scrambled for by the second and third class of English parliamentary politicians.† I was the chief manager of the resistance which the Company made to their own political extinction. To the letters and petitions I wrote for them, and the concluding chapter of my treatise on *Representative Government*,† I must refer for my opinions on the folly and mischief of this ill-considered change. Personally I considered myself a gainer by it, as I had given enough of my life to

India, and was not unwilling to retire on the liberal compensation granted. After the change was consummated, Lord Stanley,† the first Secretary of State for India, made me the honorable offer of a seat in the Council, and the proposal was subsequently renewed by the Council itself, on the first occasion of its having to supply a vacancy in its own body. But the conditions of Indian government under the new system made me anticipate nothing but useless vexation and waste of effort from any participation in it: and nothing that has since happened has had any tendency to make me regret my refusal.

During the two years which immediately preceded the cessation of my official life, my wife and I were working together at the *Liberty*. I had first planned and written it as a short essay, in 1854. It was in mounting the steps of the Capitol,† in January 1855, that the thought first arose of converting it into a volume. None of my writings have been either so carefully composed, or so sedulously corrected as this. After it had been written as usual twice over, we kept it by us, bringing it out from time to time and going through it *de novo*, reading, weighing and criticizing every sentence. Its final revision was to have been a work of the winter of 1858/59, the first after my retirement, which we had arranged to pass in the South of Europe. That hope and every other were frustrated by the most unexpected and bitter calamity of her death – at Avignon, on our way to Montpellier, from a sudden attack of pulmonary congestion.

Since then, I have sought for such alleviation as my state admitted of, by the mode of life which most enabled me to feel her still near me. I bought a cottage as close as possible to the place where she is buried, and there her daughter (my fellow-sufferer and now my chief comfort)† and I, live constantly during a great portion of the year. My objects in life are solely those which were hers; my pursuits and occupations those in which she shared, or sympathized, and which are indissolubly associated with her. Her memory is to me a religion, and her approbation the standard by which, summing up as it does all worthiness, I endeavour to regulate my life.‡

In resuming my pen some years after closing the preceding narrative, I am influenced by a desire not to leave incomplete the record, for the sake of which chiefly this biographical sketch was undertaken, of the obligations I owe to those who have either contributed essentially to my own mental developement or had a direct share in my writings and in whatever else of a public nature I have done. In the preceding pages, this record, so far as it relates to my wife, is not so detailed and precise as it ought to be; and since I lost her, I have had other help, not less deserving and requiring acknowledgment.

When two persons have their thoughts and speculations completely in common;‡ when all subjects of intellectual or moral interest are discussed between them in daily life, and probed to much greater depths than are usually or conveniently sounded in writings intended for general readers; when they set out from the same principles and arrive at their conclusions by processes pursued jointly, it is of little consequence in respect to the question of originality which of them holds the pen; the one who contributes least to the composition may contribute most to the thought; the writings which result are the joint product of both, and it must often be impossible to disentangle their respective parts and affirm that this belongs to one and that to the other. In this wide sense, not only during the years of our married life, but during many of the years of confidential friendship which preceded, all my published writings were as much her work as mine; her share in them constantly increasing as years advanced. But in certain cases, what belongs to her can be distinguished, and specially identified. Over and above the general influence which her mind had over mine, the most valuable ideas and features in these joint productions – those which have been most fruitful of important results, and have contributed most to the success and reputation of the works themselves – originated with her; were emanations from her mind, my part in them being no greater than in any of the thoughts which I found in previous writers, and made my own only by incorporating them with my own system of thought. During the greater part of my literary life I have performed the office in relation to her, which from a rather early period I had considered as the most useful part that I was qualified to take in the domain of thought, that of an interpreter of original thinkers, and mediator between them and the public; for I had always a humble opinion of my own powers as an original thinker, except in abstract science (logic, metaphysics, and the theoretic principles of political economy and politics), but thought myself much superior to most of my contemporaries in willingness and ability to learn from everybody; as I found hardly any one who made such a point of examining what was said in defence of all opinions, however new or however old, in the conviction that even if they were errors there might be a substratum of truth underneath them, and that in any case the discovery of what it was that made them plausible, would be a benefit to truth. I had, in consequence, marked out this as a sphere of usefulness in which I was under a special obligation to make myself active: the more so, as the acquaintance

I had formed with the ideas of the Coleridgians, of the German thinkers, and of Carlyle, all of them fiercely opposed to the mode of thought in which I had been brought up, has convinced me that along with much error they possessed much truth, which was veiled from minds otherwise capable of receiving it by the transcendental and mystical phraseology in which they were accustomed to shut it up and from which they neither cared, nor knew how, to disengage it; and I did not despair of separating the truth from the error and expressing it in terms which would be intelligible and not repulsive to those on my own side in philosophy. Thus prepared, it will easily be believed that when I came into close intellectual communion with a person of the most eminent faculties, whose genius, as it grew and unfolded itself in thought, continually struck out truths far in advance of me, but in which I could not, as I had done in those others, detect any mixture of error, the greatest part of my mental growth consisted in the assimilation of those truths, and the most valuable part of my intellectual work was in building the bridges and clearing the paths which connected them with my general system of thought.[1]

---

[1] The steps in my mental growth for which I was indebted to her were far from being those which a person wholly uninformed on the subject would probably suspect. It might be supposed, for instance, that my strong convictions on the complete equality in all legal, political, social and domestic relations, which ought to exist between men and women, may have been adopted or learnt from her. This was so far from being the fact, that those convictions were among the earliest results of the application of my mind to political subjects, and the strength with which I held them was, as I believe, more than anything else, the originating cause of the interest she felt in me. What is true is, that until I knew her, the opinion was, in my mind, little more than an abstract principle. I saw no more reason why women should be held in legal subjection to other people, than why men should. I was certain that their interests required fully as much protection as those of men, and were quite as little likely to obtain it without an equal voice in making the laws by which they are to be bound. But that perception of the vast practical bearings of women's disabilities which found expression in the book on *The Subjection of Women*, was acquired mainly through her teaching. But for her rare knowledge of human nature and comprehension of moral and social influences, though I should doubtless have held my present opinions I should have had a very insufficient perception of the mode in which the consequences of the inferior position of women intertwine themselves with all the evils of existing society and with all the difficulties of human improvement. I am indeed painfully conscious how much of her best thoughts on the subject I have failed to reproduce, and how greatly that little treatise falls short of what would have been given to the world if she had put on paper her entire mind on this question, or had lived to revise and improve, as she certainly would have done, my imperfect statement of the case.

The first of my books in which her share was conspicuous was the *Principles of Political Economy*. The *System of Logic* owed little to her except in the minuter matters of composition, in which respect my writings, both great and small, have largely benefitted by her accurate and clear-sighted criticism.[2] The chapter of the *Political Economy* which has had a greater influence on opinion than all the rest, that on 'the Probable Future of the Labouring Classes,'† is entirely due to her: in the first draft of the book, that chapter did not exist. She pointed out the need of such a chapter, and the extreme imperfection of the book without it: she was the cause of my writing it; and the more general part of the chapter, the statement and discussion of the two opposite theories respecting the proper condition of the labouring classes, was wholly an exposition of her thoughts, often in words taken from her own lips. The purely scientific part of the *Political Economy* I did not learn from her; but it was chiefly her influence that gave to the book that general tone by which it is distinguished from all previous expositions of Political Economy that had any pretension to being scientific, and which has made it so useful in conciliating minds which those previous expositions had repelled. This tone consisted chiefly in making the proper distinction between the laws of the Production of Wealth, which are real laws of nature, dependent on the properties of objects, and the modes of its Distribution, which, subject to certain conditions, depend on human will. The common run of political economists confuse these together, under the designation of economic laws, which they deem incapable of being defeated

---

[2] The only person from whom I received any direct assistance in the preparation of the *System of Logic* was Mr. Bain, since so justly celebrated for his philosophical writings. He went carefully through the manuscript before it was sent to press, and enriched it with a great number of additional examples and illustrations from science; many of which, as well as some detached remarks of his own in confirmation of my logical views, I inserted nearly in his own words.

My obligations to Comte were only to his writings – to the part which had then been published of his *Cours‡ de Philosophie Positive*: and, as has been seen from what I have said in this Narrative, the amount of these obligations is far less than has sometimes been asserted. The first volume, which contains all the fundamental doctrines of the book, was substantially complete before I had seen Comte's treatise. I derived from him many valuable thoughts, conspicuously in the chapter on Hypotheses and in the view taken of the logic of algebra: but it is only in the concluding Book, on the Logic of the Moral Sciences, that I owe to him any radical improvement in my conception of the application of logical methods. This improvement I have stated and characterized in a former part of the present Memoir.

or modified by human effort; ascribing the same necessity to things dependent on the unchangeable conditions of our earthly existence, and to those which, being but the necessary consequences of particular social arrangements, are merely coextensive with these. Given certain institutions and customs, wages, profits, and rent will be determined by certain causes; but this class of political economists drop the indispensable presupposition, and argue that these causes must by an inherent necessity, against which no human means can avail, determine the shares which fall, in the division of the produce, to labourers, capitalists, and landlords. The *Principles of Political Economy* yielded to none of its predecessors in aiming at the scientific appreciation of the action of these causes, under the conditions which they presuppose; but it set the example of not treating those conditions as final. The economic generalisations which depend, not on necessities of nature but on those combined with the existing arrangements of society, it deals with only as provisional, and as liable to be much altered by the progress of social improvement. I had indeed partially learnt this view of things from the thoughts awakened in me by the speculations of the Saint-Simonians; but it was made a living principle pervading and animating the book by my wife's promptings. This example illustrates well the general character of what she contributed to my writings. What was abstract and purely scientific was generally mine; the properly human element came from her: in all that concerned the application of philosophy to the exigencies of human society and progress, I was her pupil, alike in boldness of speculation and cautiousness of practical judgment. For, on the one hand, she was much more courageous and farsighted than without her I should have been, in anticipations of an order of things to come, in which many of the limited generalizations now so often confounded with universal principles will cease to be applicable. Those parts of my writings and especially of the *Political Economy* which contemplate possibilities in the future such as, when affirmed by Socialists, have in general been fiercely denied by political economists, would, but for her, either have been absent, or the suggestions would have been made much more timidly and in a more qualified form. But while she thus rendered me bolder in speculation on human affairs, her practical turn of mind, and her almost unerring estimate of practical obstacles, repressed in me all tendencies that were really visionary. Her mind invested all ideas in a concrete shape, and formed to itself a conception of how they would actually work: and her knowledge of the existing feelings and conduct of mankind was so

136

seldom at fault, that the weak point in any unworkable suggestion seldom escaped her.[3]

The *Liberty* was more directly and literally our joint production than anything else which bears my name, for there was not a sentence of it that was not several times gone through by us together, turned over in many ways, and carefully weeded of any faults, either in thought or expression, that we detected in it. It is in consequence of this that, although it never underwent her final revision, it far surpasses, as a mere specimen of composition, anything which has proceeded from me either before or since. With regard to the thoughts, it is difficult to identify any particular part or element as being more hers than all the rest. The whole mode of thinking of which the book was the expression, was emphatically hers. But I also was so thoroughly imbued with it that the same thoughts naturally occurred to us both. That I was thus penetrated with it, however, I owe in a great degree to her. There was a moment in my mental progress when I might easily have fallen into a tendency towards over-government, both social and political; as there was also a moment when, by reaction from a contrary excess, I might have become a less thorough radical and democrat than I am. In both these points as in many others, she benefitted me as much by keeping me right where I was right, as by leading me to new truths and ridding me of errors. My great readiness and eagerness to learn from everybody, and to make room in my opinions for every new acquisition by adjusting the old and the new to one another, might, but for her steadying influence, have seduced me into modifying my early opinions too much. She was in nothing more valuable to my mental development than by her just measure of the relative importance of different considerations, which often protected me from allowing to truths I had only recently learnt to see, a more important place in my thoughts than was properly their due.‡

The *Liberty* is likely to survive longer than anything else that I have written (with the possible exception of the *Logic*), because the conjunction of her mind with mine has rendered it a kind of philosophic text-book of a single truth, which the changes progressively taking place in modern society tend to bring out into ever stronger relief: the

---

[3] A few dedicatory lines, acknowledging what the book owed to her, were prefixed to some of the presentation copies of the *Political Economy* on its first publication. Her dislike of publicity alone prevented their insertion in the other copies of the work.

the Ballot† (a change of opinion in both of us, in which she rather preceded me) and a claim of representation for minorities; not however at that time going beyond the cumulative vote proposed by Mr. Garth Marshall.† In finishing the pamphlet for publication with a view to the discussions on the Reform Bill of Lord Derby's and Mr. Disraeli's Government in 1859,† I added a third feature, a plurality of votes, to be given, not to property, but to proved superiority of education. This recommended itself to me, as a means of reconciling the irresistible claim of every man or woman to be consulted, and to be allowed a voice, in the regulation of affairs which vitally concern them, with the superiority of weight justly due to opinion grounded on superiority of knowledge. The suggestion however was one which I had never discussed with my almost infallible counsellor, and I have no evidence that she would have concurred in it. As far as I have been able to observe, it has found favour with nobody; all who desire any sort of inequality in the electoral vote, desiring it in favour of property and not of intelligence or knowledge. If it ever overcomes the strong feeling which exists against it, this will only be after the establishment of a systematic National Education by which the various grades of politically valuable acquirement may be accurately defined and authenticated. Without this it will always remain liable to strong, possibly conclusive, objections; and with this, it would perhaps not be needed.

It was soon after the publication of *Thoughts on Parliamentary Reform* that I became acquainted with Mr. Hare's admirable system of Personal Representation,† which, in its present shape, was then for the first time published. I saw in this great practical and philosophical idea, the greatest improvement of which the system of representative government is susceptible; an improvement which, in the most felicitous manner, exactly meets and cures the grand, and what before seemed the inherent, defect of the representative system; that of giving to a numerical majority all power, instead of only a power proportional to its numbers, and enabling the strongest party to exclude all weaker parties from making their opinions heard in the assembly of the nation, except through such opportunity as may be given to them by the accidentally unequal distribution of opinions in different localities. To these great evils nothing more than very imperfect palliations had seemed possible; but Mr. Hare's system affords a radical cure. This great discovery, for it is no less, in the political art, inspired me, as I believe it has inspired all thoughtful persons who have adopted it, with new and more sanguine hopes

140

respecting the prospects of human society; by freeing the form of political institutions towards which the whole civilised world is manifestly and irresistibly tending, from the chief part of what seemed to qualify or render doubtful its ultimate benefits. Minorities, so long as they remain minorities, are, and ought to be, outvoted; but under arrangements which enable any assemblage of voters, amounting to a certain number, to place in the legislature a representative of its own choice, minorities cannot be suppressed. Independent opinions will force their way into the council of the nation and make themselves heard there, a thing which often cannot happen in the existing forms of representative democracy; and the legislature instead of being weeded of individual peculiarities and entirely made up of men who simply represent the creed of great political or religious parties, will comprise a large proportion of the most eminent individual minds in the country placed there without reference to party by voters who appreciate their individual eminence. I can understand that persons, otherwise intelligent, should, for want of sufficient examination, be repelled from Mr. Hare's plan by what they think the complex nature of its machinery. But any one who does not feel the want which the scheme is intended to supply; any one who throws it over as a mere theoretical subtlety or crotchet, tending to no valuable purpose, and unworthy of the attention of practical men, may be pronounced an incompetent statesman, unequal to the politics of the future. I mean, unless he is a minister, or aspires to become one: for we are quite accustomed to a minister continuing to profess unqualified hostility to an improvement almost to the very day when his conscience or his interest induces him to take it up as a public measure and carry it.

Had I met with Mr. Hare's system before the publication of my pamphlet, I should have given an account of it there. Not having done so, I wrote an article in *Fraser's Magazine* (reprinted in my miscellaneous writings)[†] principally for that purpose, though I included in it, along with Mr. Hare's book, a review of two other productions on the question of the day; one of them a pamphlet by my early friend Mr. John Austin,[†] who had in his old age become an enemy to all further parliamentary reform; the other an able and ingenious though partially erroneous work by Mr. Lorimer.[†]

In the course of the same summer I fulfilled a duty particularly incumbent upon me, that of helping (by an article in the *Edinburgh Review*) to make known Mr. Bain's profound treatise on the Mind,[†] just then completed by the publication of its second volume. And I carried through the press a selection of my minor writings, forming the first two volumes of *Dissertations and Discussions*. The selection had been made during my wife's lifetime, but the revision, in concert with her, with a view to republication, had been barely commenced; and when I had no longer the guidance of her judgment I despaired of pursuing it further, and republished the papers as they were, with the exception of striking out such passages as were no longer in accordance with my opinions. My literary work of the year terminated with an essay in *Fraser's Magazine* (afterwards republished in the third volume of *Dissertations and Discussions*,) entitled 'A Few Words on Non-Intervention.' I was prompted to write this paper by a desire, while vindicating England from the imputations commonly brought against her on the Continent, of a peculiar selfishness in matters of foreign policy, to warn Englishmen of the colour given to this imputation by the low tone in which English statesmen are accustomed to speak of English policy as concerned only with English interests, and by the conduct of Lord Palmerston at that particular time in opposing the Suez Canal.† And I took the opportunity of expressing ideas which had long been in my mind (some of them generated by my Indian experience and others by the international questions which then greatly occupied the European public) respecting the true principles of international morality, and the legitimate modifications made in it by difference of times and circumstances; a subject I had already to some extent discussed in the vindication of the French Provisional Government of 1848 against the attacks of Lord Brougham and others which I published at the time in the *Westminster Review* and which I reprinted in the *Dissertations*.†

I had now settled, as I believed for the remainder of my existence, into a purely literary life; if that can be called literary which continued to be occupied in a preeminent degree with politics, and not merely with theoretical, but practical politics, although a great part of the year was spent at a distance of many hundred miles from the chief seat of the politics of my own country, to which, and primarily for which, I wrote. But in truth, the modern facilities of communication have not only removed all the disadvantages, to a political writer in tolerably easy circumstances, of distance from the scene of political action, but have converted them into advantages. The immediate and regular receipt of newspapers and periodicals keeps him *au courant* of even the most temporary politics, and gives him a much more correct view of the state and progress of opinion than he could acquire by personal contact with individuals: for every one's social intercourse is more or less limited to particular sets or classes, whose impressions and no others reach him through that channel; and experience has taught me that those who give their time to the absorbing claims of what is called society, not having leisure to keep up a large acquaintance with the organs of opinion, remain much more ignorant of the general state either of the public mind, or of the active and instructed part of it, than a recluse who reads the newspapers need be. There are, no doubt, disadvantages in too long a separation from one's country – in not occasionally renewing one's impressions of the light in which men and things appear when seen from a position in the midst of them; but the deliberate judgment formed at a distance, and undisturbed by inequalities of perspective, is the most to be depended on, even for application to practice. Alternating between the two positions I combined the advantages of both. And, though the inspirer of my best thoughts was no longer with me, I was not alone: she had left a daughter – my stepdaughter, Miss Helen Taylor, the inheritor of much of her wisdom, and of all her nobleness of character, ‡ whose ever growing and ripening talents from that day to this have been devoted to the same great purposes, and have already made her name better and more widely known than was that of her mother, though far less so than I predict that if she lives, it is destined to become. Of the value of her direct cooperation with me, something will be said hereafter: of what I owe in the way of instruction to her great powers of original thought and soundness of practical judgment, it would be a vain attempt to give an adequate idea. ‡ Surely no one ever before was so fortunate, as, after such a loss as mine, to draw another such prize in the lottery of life – another companion, stimulator, adviser, and instructor of the rarest quality. ‡ Whoever, either now or hereafter, may think of me and of the work I have done, must never forget that it is the product not of one intellect and conscience but of three, the least considerable of whom, and above all the least original, is the one whose name is attached to it. ‡

The work of the years 1860 and 1861 consisted chiefly of two treatises, only one of which was intended for immediate publication. This was the *Considerations on Representative Government*, a connected exposition of what, by the thoughts of many years, I had come to regard as the best form of a popular constitution. Along with as much of the general theory of government as is necessary to support this particular portion of its practice, the volume contains my matured views of the principal questions which occupy the present age, within the province of purely organic institutions, and raises by anticipation some other questions to which growing necessities will sooner or later compel the attention both of theoretical and of practical politicians. The chief of these last is the distinction between the function of making laws, for which a numerous popular assembly is radically unfit, and that of getting good laws made, which is its proper duty, and cannot be satisfactorily fulfilled by any other authority: and the consequent need of a Legislative Commission, as a part of the constitution of a free country; consisting of a small number of highly trained political minds on whom, when Parliament has determined that a law shall be made, the task of making it should be devolved; Parliament retaining the power of passing or rejecting the bill when drawn up, but not of altering it otherwise than by sending proposed amendments to be dealt with by the Commission. The question here raised respecting the most important of all public functions, that of legislation, is a particular case of the great problem of modern political organization, stated I believe for the first time in its full extent by Bentham, though in my opinion not always satisfactorily resolved by him; the combination of complete popular control over public affairs, with the greatest attainable perfection of skilled agency.

The other treatise written at this time is the one which was published some years later under the title of *The Subjection of Women.*†
It was written at my daughter's suggestion‡ that there might, in any event, be in existence a written exposition of my opinions on that great question, as full and conclusive as I could make it. The intention was to keep this among other unpublished papers, improving it from time to time if I was able, and to publish it at the time when it should seem likely to be most useful. As ultimately published it was enriched with some important ideas of my daughter's, and passages of her writing. But‡ in what was of my own composition, all that is most striking and profound belongs to my wife; coming from the fund of thought which had been made common to us both, by our innumerable conversations and discussions on a topic which filled so large a place in our minds.

Soon after this time I took from their repository a portion of the unpublished papers which I had written during the last years of our married life, and shaped them, with some additional matter, into the little work entitled *Utilitarianism*; which was first published in three parts, in successive numbers of *Fraser's Magazine*, and afterwards reprinted in a volume.†

Before this however the state of public affairs had become extremely critical, by the commencement of the American civil war. My strongest feelings were engaged in this struggle, which, I felt from the beginning, was destined to be a turning point, for good or evil, of the course of human affairs for an indefinite duration. Having been a deeply interested observer of the Slavery quarrel in America, during the many years that preceded the open breach, I knew that it was in all its stages an aggressive enterprise of the slave owners to extend the territory of slavery; under the combined influences of pecuniary interest, domineering temper, and the fanaticism of a class for its class privileges, influences so fully and powerfully depicted in the admirable work of my friend Professor Cairnes, *The Slave Power*.† Their success, if they succeeded, would be a victory of the powers of evil which would give courage to the enemies of progress and damp the spirits of its friends all over the civilised world, while it would create a formidable military power grounded on the worst and most anti-social form of the tyranny of men over men, and by destroying for a long time the prestige of the great democratic republic would give to all the privileged classes of Europe a false confidence, probably only to be extinguished in blood. On the other hand, if the spirit of the North was sufficiently roused to carry the war to a successful termi-nation, and if that termination did not come too soon and too easily, I foresaw, from the laws of human nature and the experience of revo-lutions, that when it did come it would in all probability be thorough: that the bulk of the Northern population, whose conscience had as yet been awakened only to the point of resisting the further extension of slavery, but whose fidelity to the Constitution of the United States made them disapprove of any attempt by the Federal Government to interfere with slavery in the States where it already existed, would acquire feelings of another kind when the Constitution had been shaken off by armed rebellion, would determine to have done for ever with the accursed thing, and would join their banner with that of the noble body of Abolitionists, of whom Garrison† was the courageous and single minded apostle, Wendell Phillips† the eloquent orator, and John Brown† the voluntary martyr.[4] Then, too, the whole mind of the United States would be let loose from its bonds, no longer corrupted by the supposed necessity of apologising to foreigners for the most flagrant of all possible violations of the free principles of their Constitution, while the tendency of a fixed state of society to

---

[4] The saying of this true hero, after his capture, that he was worth more for hanging than for any other purpose, reminds one, by its combination of wit, wisdom, and self devotion, of Sir Thomas More.

stereotype a set of national opinions would be at least temporarily checked and the national mind would become more open to the recognition of whatever was bad in either the institutions or the customs of the people. These hopes, so far as related to Slavery, have been completely, and in other respects are in course of being progressively realized. Foreseeing from the first this double set of consequences from the success or failure of the rebellion, it may be imagined with what feelings I contemplated the rush of nearly the whole upper and middle classes of my own country, even those who passed for Liberals, into a furious pro-Southern partisanship: the working classes, and some of the literary and scientific men, being almost the sole exceptions to the general frenzy. I never before felt so keenly how little permanent improvement had reached the minds of our influential classes and of what small value were the liberal opinions they had got into the habit of professing. None of the Continental Liberals committed the same frightful mistake. But the generation which had extorted negro emancipation from our West India planters had passed away; another had succeeded which had not learnt by many years of discussion and exposure to feel strongly the enormities of slavery; and the inattention habitual with Englishmen to whatever is going on in the world outside their own island, made them profoundly ignorant of all the antecedents of the struggle, insomuch that it was not generally believed in England, for the first year or two of the war, that the quarrel was one of slavery. There were men of high principle and unquestionable liberality of opinion who thought it a dispute about tariffs, or assimilated it to the cases in which they were accustomed to sympathise, of a people struggling for independence.

It was my obvious duty to be one of the small minority who protested against this perverted state of public opinion. I was not the first to protest. It ought to be remembered to the honour of Mr. Hughes† and of Mr. Ludlow,† that they, by writings published at the very beginning of the struggle, began the protestation. Mr. Bright† followed in one of the most powerful of his speeches, followed by others not less striking. I was on the point of adding my words to theirs when there occurred, towards the end of 1861, the seizure of the Southern envoys on board a British vessel, by an officer of the United States.† Even English forgetfulness has not yet had time to lose all remembrance of the explosion of feeling in England which then burst forth, the expectation, prevailing for some weeks, of war with the United States, and the warlike preparations actually commenced on this side. While this state of things lasted there was no chance of a hearing for anything favourable to the American cause; and moreover I agreed with those who thought the act unjustifiable and such as to require that England should demand its disavowal. When the disavowal came, and the alarm of war was over, I wrote, in January 1862, the paper, in *Fraser's Magazine*, entitled 'The Contest in America.'[†] And I shall always feel grateful to my daughter that her urgency prevailed on me to write it when I did: for we were then on the point of setting out for a journey of some months in Greece and Turkey, and but for her, I should have deferred writing till our return.[‡] Written and published when it was, the paper helped to encourage those Liberals who had felt overborne by the tide of illiberal opinion, and to form in favour of the good cause a nucleus of opinion which increased gradually, and after the success of the North began to seem probable, rapidly. When we returned from our journey I wrote a second article, a review of Professor Cairnes' book published in the *Westminster Review*. England is paying the penalty, in many uncomfortable ways, of the durable resentment which her ruling classes stirred up in the United States by their ostentatious wishes for the ruin of America as a nation; they have reason to be thankful that a few, if only a few known writers and speakers, standing firmly by the Americans in the time of their greatest difficulty, effected a partial diversion of these bitter feelings, and made Great Britain not altogether odious to the Americans.

This duty having been performed, my principal occupation for the next two years was on subjects not political. The publication of Mr. Austin's *Lectures on Jurisprudence* after his decease, gave me an opportunity of paying a deserved tribute to his memory and at the same time expressing some thoughts on a subject on which, in my old days of Benthamism, I had bestowed much study.[†] But the chief product of those years was the *Examination of Sir William Hamilton's Philosophy*.[†] His *Lectures*, published in 1860 and 1861, I had read towards the end of the latter year, with a half formed intention of giving an account of them in a Review, but I soon found that this would be idle, and that justice could not be done to the subject in less than a volume. I had then to consider whether it would be advisable that I myself should attempt such a performance. On consideration, there seemed to be strong reasons for doing so. I was greatly disappointed with the *Lectures*. I read them, certainly, with no prejudice against Sir W. Hamilton. I had up to that time deferred the study of his Notes to Reid[†] on account of their unfinished state, but I had not neglected his *Discussions in Philosophy*;[†] and though I knew that his general mode of treating the facts of mental philosophy differed from that of which I most approved, yet his vigorous polemic against the later Transcendentalists, and his strenuous assertion of some important principles, especially the Relativity of human knowledge, gave me many points of sympathy with his opinions, and made me think that genuine psychology had considerably more to gain than to lose by his authority and reputation. His *Lectures* and the 'Dissertations on Reid' dispelled this illusion: and even the *Discussions*, read by the light which these threw on them, lose much of their value. I found that the points of apparent agreement between his opinions and mine were more verbal than real; that the important philosophical principles which I had thought he recognised, were so explained away by him as to mean little or nothing, or were continually lost sight of, and doctrines entirely inconsistent with them were taught in nearly every part of his philosophical writings. My estimation of him was therefore so far altered, that instead of regarding him as occupying a kind of intermediate position between the two rival philosophies, holding some of the principles of both, and supplying to both powerful weapons of attack and defence, I now looked upon him as one of the pillars, and in this country from his high philosophical reputation the chief pillar, of that one of the two which seemed to me to be erroneous.

Now, the difference between these two schools of philosophy, that of Intuition, and that of Experience and Association, is not a mere matter of abstract speculation; it is full of practical consequences, and lies at the foundation of all the greatest differences of practical opinion in an age of progress. The practical reformer has continually to demand that changes be made in things which are supported by powerful and widely spread feelings, or to question the apparent necessity and indefeasibleness of established facts; and it is often an indispensable part of his argument to shew, how those powerful feelings had their origin, and how those facts came to seem necessary and indefeasible. There is therefore a natural hostility between him and a philosophy which discourages the explanation of feelings and moral facts by circumstances and association, and prefers to treat them as ultimate elements of human nature; a philosophy which is addicted to holding up favourite doctrines as intuitive truths, and deems intuition to be the voice of Nature and of God, speaking with an authority higher than that of our reason. In particular, I have long felt that the prevailing tendency to regard all the marked distinctions of human character as innate, and in the main indelible, and to ignore

148

the irresistible proofs[†] that by far the greater part of those differences, whether between individuals, races, or sexes, are such as not only might but naturally would be produced by differences in circumstances, is one of the chief hindrances to the rational treatment of great social questions and one of the greatest stumbling blocks to human improvement. This tendency has its source in the intuitional metaphysics which characterized the reaction of the nineteenth century against the eighteenth, and it is a tendency so agreeable to human indolence, as well as to conservative interests generally, that unless attacked at the very root, it is sure to be carried to even a greater length than is really justified by the more moderate forms of the intuitional philosophy. That philosophy, not always in its moderate forms, had ruled the thought of Europe for the greater part of a century. My father's *Analysis of the Mind*, my own *Logic*, and Professor Bain's great treatise,[†] had attempted to reintroduce a better mode of philosophizing, latterly with quite as much success as could be expected; but I had for some time felt that the mere contrast of the two philosophies was not enough, that there ought to be a hand-to-hand fight between them, that controversial as well as expository writings were needed, and that the time was come when such controversy would be useful. Considering then the writings and fame of Sir W. Hamilton as the great fortress of the intuitional philosophy in this country, a fortress the more formidable from the imposing character, and the in many respects great personal merits and mental endowments, of the man, I thought it might be a real service to philosophy to attempt a thorough examination of all his most important doctrines, and an estimate of his general claims to eminence as a philosopher. And I was confirmed in this resolution by observing that in the writings of at least one, and him one of the ablest, of Sir W. Hamilton's followers,[†] his peculiar doctrines were made the justification of a view of religion which I hold to be profoundly immoral – that it is our duty to bow down in worship before a Being whose moral attributes are affirmed to be unknowable by us, and to be perhaps extremely different from those which, when we are speaking of our fellow-creatures, we call by the same names.[†]

As I advanced in my task, the damage to Sir W. Hamilton's reputation became greater than I at first expected, through the almost incredible multitude of inconsistencies which shewed themselves on comparing different passages with one another. It was my business however to shew things exactly as they were, and I did not flinch from it. I endeavoured always to treat the philosopher whom I criticized with the most scrupulous fairness; and I knew that he had abundance of disciples and admirers to correct me if I ever unintentionally did him injustice. Many of them accordingly have answered me, more or less elaborately; and they have pointed out oversights and misunderstandings, though few in number, and mostly very unimportant in substance. Such of those as had (to my knowledge) been pointed out before the publication of the latest edition (at present the third) have been corrected there, and the remainder of the criticisms have been, as far as seemed necessary, replied to. On the whole, the book has done its work: it has shewn the weak side of Sir W. Hamilton, and has reduced his too great philosophical reputation within more moderate bounds; and by some of its discussions, as well as by two expository chapters, on the notions of Matter and of Mind, it has perhaps thrown additional light on some of the disputed questions in the domain of psychology and metaphysics.

After the completion of the book on Hamilton, I applied myself to a task which a variety of reasons seemed to render specially incumbent upon me; that of giving an account, and forming an estimate, of the doctrines of Auguste Comte. I had contributed more than any one else to make his speculations known in England. In consequence chiefly of what I had said of him in my *Logic*, he had readers and admirers among thoughtful men on this side of the Channel at a time when his name had not yet, in France, emerged from obscurity. So unknown and unappreciated was he at the time when my *Logic* was written and published, that to criticise his weak points might well appear superfluous, while it was a duty to give as much publicity as one could to the important contributions he had made to philosophic thought. At the time however at which I have now arrived, this state of affairs had entirely changed. His name at least was known almost universally, and the general character of his doctrines very widely. He had taken his place, in the estimation both of friends and opponents, as one of the conspicuous figures in the thought of the age. The better parts of his speculations had made great progress in working their way into those minds, which by their previous culture and tendencies, were fitted to receive them: under cover of those better parts those of a worse character, greatly developed and added to in his later writings, had also made some way, having obtained active and enthusiastic adherents, some of them of no inconsiderable personal merit, in England, France, and other countries. These causes not only made it desirable that some one should undertake the task of sifting what is good from what is bad in M. Comte's speculations, but seemed to impose on myself in particular a special obligation to make the attempt. This I accordingly did in two Essays, published in successive numbers of the *Westminster Review*, and reprinted in a small volume under the title *Auguste Comte and Positivism*.[†]

The writings which I have now mentioned, together with a small number of papers in periodicals which I have not deemed worth preserving, were the whole of the products of my activity as a writer during the years from 1859 to 1865. In the early part of the last mentioned year, in compliance with a wish frequently expressed to me by working men, I published cheap People's Editions of those of my writings which seemed the most likely to find readers among the working classes; viz. *Principles of Political Economy*, *Liberty*, and *Representative Government*. This was a considerable sacrifice of my pecuniary interest, especially as I resigned all idea of deriving profit from the cheap editions, and after ascertaining from my publishers the lowest price which they thought would remunerate them on the usual terms of an equal division of profits, I gave up my half share to enable the price to be fixed still lower. To the credit of Messrs. Longman they fixed, unasked, a certain number of years after which the copyright and stereotype plates were to revert to me, and a certain number of copies after the sale of which I should receive half of any further profit. This number of copies (which in the case of the *Political Economy* was 10,000) has for some time been exceeded, and the People's Editions have begun to yield me a small but unexpected pecuniary return, though very far from an equivalent for the diminution of profit from the Library Editions.

In this summary of my outward life I have now arrived at the period at which my tranquil and retired existence as a writer of books was to be exchanged for the less congenial occupation of a member of the House of Commons. The proposal made to me, early in 1865, by some electors of Westminster, did not present the idea to me for the first time. It was not even the first offer I had received, for, more than ten years previous, in consequence of my opinions on the Irish Land question, Mr. Lucas[†] and Mr. Duffy,[†] in the name of the popular party in Ireland, offered to bring me into Parliament for an Irish County, which they could easily have done: but the incompatibility of a seat in Parliament with the office I then held in the India House, precluded even consideration of the proposal. After I had quitted the India House, several of my friends would gladly have seen me a member of Parliament; but there seemed no probability that the idea would ever take any practical shape. I was convinced that no numerous or influential portion of any electoral body, really wished to be represented by a person of my opinions; and that one who possessed no local connexion or popularity, and who did not choose to stand as the mere organ of a party, had small chance of being elected anywhere unless through the expenditure of money. Now it was, and is, my fixed conviction, that a candidate ought not to incur one farthing of expense for undertaking a public duty. Such of the lawful expenses of an election as have no special reference to any particular candidate ought to be borne as a public charge, either by the State or by the locality.† What has to be done by the supporters of each candidate in order to bring his claims properly before the constituency, should be done by unpaid agency, or by voluntary subscription. If members of the electoral body, or others, are willing to subscribe money of their own for the purpose of bringing by lawful means into Parliament some one who they think would be useful there, no one is entitled to object: but that the expense, or any part of it, should fall on the candidate, is fundamentally wrong; because it amounts, in reality, to buying his seat. Even on the most favourable supposition as to the mode in which the money is expended, there is a legitimate suspicion that any one who gives money for leave to undertake a public trust, has other than public ends to promote by it; and (a consideration of the greatest importance) the cost of elections, when borne by the candidates, deprives the nation of the services, as members of Parliament, of all who cannot or will not afford to incur a heavy expense. I do not say that, so long as there is scarcely a chance for an independent candidate to come into Parliament without complying with this vicious practice, it must always be morally wrong in him to spend money, provided that no part of it is either directly or indirectly employed in corruption. But, to justify it, he ought to be very certain that he can be of more use to his country as a member of Parliament than in any other mode which is open to him; and this assurance, in my own case, I did not feel. It was by no means clear to me that I could do more to advance the public objects which had a claim on my exertions from the benches of the House of Commons, than from the simple position of a writer. I felt, therefore, that I ought not to seek election to Parliament, much less to expend any money in procuring it.

But the conditions of the question were considerably altered when a body of electors sought me out, and spontaneously offered to bring me forward as their candidate. If it should appear, on explanation, that they persisted in this wish, knowing my opinions, and accepting the only conditions on which I could conscientiously serve, it was questionable whether this was not one of those calls upon a member of the community by his fellow citizens, which he was scarcely justified in rejecting. I therefore put their disposition to the proof by one of the frankest explanations ever tendered, I should think, to an electoral body by a candidate. I wrote in reply to the offer a letter for publication,† saying that I had no personal wish to be a member of parliament, that I thought a candidate ought neither to canvass nor to incur any expense, and that I could not consent to do either. I said further that if elected I could not undertake to give any of my time and labour to their local interests. With respect to general politics, I told them without reserve what I thought on a number of important subjects on which they had asked my opinion; and one of these being the suffrage, I made known to them, among other things, my conviction (as I was bound to do, since I intended, if elected, to act on it) that women were entitled to representation in Parliament on the same terms with men. It was the first time, doubtless, that such a doctrine had ever been mentioned to electors; and the fact that I was elected after proposing it, gave the start to the movement which has since become so vigorous, in favour of women's suffrage. Nothing, at the time, appeared more unlikely than that a candidate (if candidate I could be called) whose professions and conduct set so completely at defiance all ordinary notions of electioneering, should nevertheless be elected. A well known literary man, who was also a man of society, was heard to say, that the Almighty himself would have no chance of being elected on such a programme. I strictly adhered to it, neither spending money nor canvassing, nor did I take any personal part in the election until about a week preceding the day of nomination, when I attended a few public meetings to state my principles and give to any questions which the electors might exercise their just right of putting to me for their own guidance, answers as plain and unreserved as my Address. On one subject only, my religious opinions, I announced from the beginning that I would answer no questions; a determination which appeared to be completely approved by those who attended the meetings. My frankness on all other subjects on which I was interrogated, evidently, did me far more good than my answers, whatever they might be, did harm. Among the proofs I received of this, one is too remarkable not to be recorded. In the pamphlet *Thoughts on Parliamentary Reform* I had said, rather bluntly, that the working classes, though differing from those of some other countries in being ashamed of lying, are yet generally liars.† This passage some opponent got printed in a placard, which was handed to me at a meeting, chiefly composed of the working classes, and I was asked whether I had written and published it. I at once answered 'I did.' Scarcely were these two words out of my mouth, when vehement applause resounded through the whole meeting. It was evident that the working people were so accustomed to expect equivocation and evasion from those who sought their suffrages, that when they found, instead of that, a direct avowal of what was likely to be disagreeable to them, instead of being offended they concluded at once that this was a person whom they could trust. A more striking instance never came under my notice of what, I believe, is the experience of those who best know the working classes – that the most essential of all recommendations to their favour is that of complete straightforwardness; its presence outweighs in their minds very strong objections, while no amount of other qualities will make amends for its apparent absence. The first working man who spoke after the incident I have mentioned (it was Mr. Odger) said, that the working classes had no desire not to be told of their faults; they wanted friends, not flatterers, and felt under obligation to any one who told them of anything in themselves which he sincerely believed to require amendment. And to this the meeting heartily responded.†

Had I been defeated in the election, I should still have had no reason to regret the contact it had brought me into with large bodies of my countrymen; which not only gave me much new experience, but enabled me to scatter my political opinions rather widely, and by making me known in many quarters where I had never before been heard of, increased the number of my readers and the presumable influence of my writings. These latter effects were of course produced in a still greater degree, when, as much to my surprise as to that of any one, I was returned to Parliament by a majority of some hundreds over my Conservative competitor.†

I was a member of the House during the three sessions of the Parliament which passed the Reform Bill;† during which time Parliament was necessarily my main occupation, except during the recess. I was a tolerably frequent speaker, sometimes of prepared speeches, sometimes extemporaneously. But my choice of occasions was not such as I should have made if my leading object had been parliamentary influence. When I had gained the ear of the House, which I did by a successful speech on Mr. Gladstone's Reform Bill,† the idea I proceeded on was that when anything was likely to be as well done, or sufficiently well done, by other people, there was no necessity for me to meddle with it. As I therefore, in general, reserved myself for work which no others were likely to do, a great proportion of my appearances were on points on which the bulk of the Liberal party, even the advanced portion of it, either were of a different opinion from mine, or were comparatively indifferent. Several of my speeches, especially one against the motion for the abolition of capital punishment,[†] and another in favour of resuming the right of seizing enemies' goods in neutral vessels,[†] were opposed to what then was, and probably still is, regarded as the advanced liberal opinion. My advocacy of women's suffrage,[†] and of Personal Representation,[†] were at the time looked upon by many as whims of my own, but the great progress since made by those opinions, and especially the zealous response made from almost all parts of the kingdom to the demand for women's suffrage, fully justified the timeliness of those movements, and have made what was undertaken as a moral and social duty, a personal success. Another duty which was particularly incumbent on me as one of the Metropolitan Members, was the attempt to obtain a Municipal Government for the Metropolis: but on that subject the indifference of the House of Commons was such that I found hardly any help or support within its walls. On this subject, however, I was the organ of an active and intelligent body of persons outside, with whom and not with me the scheme originated, who carried on all the agitation on the subject and drew up the Bills. My part was to bring in Bills already prepared, and to sustain the discussion of them during the short time they were allowed to remain before the House; after having taken an active part in the work of a Committee presided over by Mr. Ayrton,[†] which sat through the greater part of the Session of 1866 to take evidence on the subject. The very different position in which the question now stands (1870) may justly be attributed to the preparation which went on during those years, and which produced but little visible effect at the time; but all questions on which there are strong private interests on one side, and only the public good on the other, have a similar period of incubation to go through.

The same idea, that the use of my being in Parliament was to do work which others were not able or not willing to do, made me think it my duty to come to the front in defence of advanced Liberalism on occasions when the obloquy to be encountered was such as most of the advanced Liberals in the House, preferred not to incur. My first vote in the House was in support of an amendment in favour of Ireland,[†] moved by an Irish member and for which only five English and Scotch votes were given, including my own: the other four were Mr. Bright, Mr McLaren,[†] Mr. T. B. Potter,[†] and Mr. Hadfield.[†] And the second speech I delivered[5] was on the bill to prolong the suspension of the Habeas Corpus in Ireland.† In denouncing, on this occasion, the English mode of governing Ireland, I did no more than the general opinion of England now admits to have been just; but the anger against Fenianism† was then in all its freshness; any attack on what Fenians attacked was looked upon as an apology for them; and I was so unfavourably received by the House, that more than one of my friends advised me (and my own judgment agreed with the advice) to wait, before speaking again, for the favourable opportunity that would be given by the first great debate on the Reform Bill. During this silence, many flattered themselves that I had turned out a failure, and that they should not be troubled with me any more. Perhaps their uncomplimentary comments may, by the force of reaction, have helped to make my speech on the Reform Bill the success it was. My position in the House was further improved by a speech in which I insisted on the duty of paying off the National Debt before our coal supplies are exhausted,† and by an ironical reply to some of the Tory leaders who had quoted against me certain passages of my writings and called me to account for others, especially for one in my *Considerations on Representative Government* which said that the Conservative party was by the law of its composition the stupidest party.† They gained nothing by drawing attention to this passage, which up to that time had not excited any notice, but the *soubriquet* of 'the stupid party' stuck to them for a considerable time afterwards. Having now no longer any apprehension of not being listened to, I confined myself, as I have since thought, too much, to occasions on which my services seemed specially needed, and abstained more than enough from speaking on the great party questions. With the exception of Irish questions, and those which concerned the working classes, a single speech on Mr. Disraeli's Reform Bill† was nearly all that I contributed to the great decisive debates of the last two of my three sessions.

I have, however, much satisfaction in looking back to the part I took on the two classes of subjects just mentioned. With regard to the working classes, the chief topic of my speech on Mr. Gladstone's

---

[5] The first was in answer to Mr. Lowe's reply to Mr Bright on the Cattle Plague Bill, and was thought at the time to have helped to get rid of a provision in the Government measure which would have given to landholders a second indemnity, after they had already been once indemnified for the loss of some of their cattle by the increased selling price of the remainder.

Reform Bill was the assertion of their claims to the suffrage. A little later, after the resignation of Lord Russell's ministry and the succession of a Tory Government, came the attempt of the working classes to hold a meeting in Hyde Park, their exclusion by the police, and the breaking down of the park railing by the crowd.[†] Though Mr. Beales[†] and the leaders of the working men had retired under protest before this took place, a scuffle ensued in which many innocent persons were maltreated by the police, and the exasperation of the working men was extreme. They shewed a determination to make another attempt at a meeting in the Park, to which many of them would probably have come armed; the Government made military preparations to resist the attempt, and something very serious seemed impending. At this crisis I really believe that I was the means of preventing much mischief. I had in my place in Parliament taken the side of the working men, and strongly censured the conduct of the Government. I was invited, with several other Radical members, to a conference with the leading members of the Council of the Reform League; and the task fell chiefly upon myself of persuading them to give up the Hyde Park project, and hold their meeting elsewhere. It was not Mr. Beales and Colonel Dickson who needed persuading; on the contrary, it was evident that those gentlemen had already exerted their influence in the same direction, thus far without success. It was the working men who held out: and so bent were they on their original scheme that I was obliged to have recourse to *les grands moyens*. I told them that a proceeding which would certainly produce a collision with the military, could only be justifiable on two conditions: if the position of affairs had become such that a revolution was desirable, and if they thought themselves able to accomplish one. To this argument after considerable discussion they at last yielded: and I was able to inform Mr. Walpole[†] that their intention was given up. I shall never forget the depth of his relief or the warmth of his expressions of gratitude. After the working men had conceded so much to me, I felt bound to comply with their request that I would attend and speak at their meeting at the Agricultural Hall: the only meeting called by the Reform League which I ever attended.[†] I had always declined being a member of the League, on the avowed ground that I did not agree in its programme of manhood suffrage[†] and the ballot:[†] from the ballot I dissented entirely; and I could not consent to hoist the flag of manhood suffrage, even on the assurance that the exclusion of women was not intended to be implied; since if one goes beyond what can be immediately carried and professes to take one's stand on a principle, one should go

157

the whole length of the principle. I have entered thus particularly into this matter because my conduct on this occasion gave great displeasure to the Tory and Tory-Liberal press, who have charged me ever since with having shewn myself, in the trials of public life, intemperate and passionate. I do not know what they expected from me; but they had reason to be thankful to me if they knew from what I had in all probability preserved them. And I do not believe it could have been done, at that particular juncture, by any one else. No other person, I believe, had at that moment the necessary influence for restraining the working classes, except Mr. Gladstone and Mr. Bright, neither of whom was available: Mr. Gladstone, for obvious reasons; Mr. Bright, because he was out of town.

When, some time later, the Tory Government brought in a bill to prevent public meetings in the Parks, I not only spoke strongly in opposition to it, but formed one of a number of advanced Liberals, who, aided by the very late period of the Session, succeeded in defeating‡ the Bill by what is called talking it out.† It has not since been renewed.

On Irish affairs also I felt bound to take a decided part. I was one of the foremost in the deputation of Members of Parliament who prevailed on Lord Derby† to spare the life of the condemned Fenian insurgent, General Burke.† The Church question was so vigorously handled by the leaders of the party, in the session of 1868, as to require no more from me than an emphatic adhesion; but the land question was by no means in so advanced a position: the superstitions of landlordism had up to that time been little challenged, especially in Parliament, and the backward state of the question, so far as concerned the Parliamentary mind, was evidenced by the extremely mild measure brought in by Lord Russell's Government in 1866, which nevertheless could not be carried.† On that bill I delivered one of my most careful speeches,† in which I attempted to lay down some of the principles of the subject, in a manner calculated less to stimulate friends, than to conciliate and convince opponents. The engrossing subject of Parliamentary Reform prevented either this bill, or one of a similar character brought in by Lord Derby's Government,† from being carried through. They never got beyond the second reading. Meanwhile the signs of Irish disaffection had become much more decided; the demand for complete separation between the two countries had assumed a menacing aspect,† and there were few who did not feel that if there was still any chance of reconciling Ireland to British connexion, it could only be by the adoption of much more thorough reforms in the territorial and social relations of the country, than had yet been contemplated. The time seemed to me to have come when it would be useful to speak out my whole mind; and the result was my pamphlet *England and Ireland*,[†] which was written in the winter of 1867, and published shortly before the commencement of the session of 1868. The leading features of the pamphlet were on the one hand an argument to shew the undesirableness, for Ireland as well as England, of separation between the countries, and on the other, a proposal for settling the land question by giving to the existing tenants a permanent tenure at a fixed rent, to be assessed after due enquiry by the State.

The pamphlet was not popular, except in Ireland, as I did not expect it to be. But, if no measure short of that which I proposed would do full justice to Ireland, or afford a prospect of conciliating the mass of the Irish people, the duty of proposing it was imperative; while if on the other hand, there was any intermediate course which had a claim to a trial, I well knew that to propose something which would be called extreme was the true way not to impede but to facilitate a more moderate experiment. It is most improbable that a measure conceding so much to the tenantry as Mr. Gladstone's Irish Land Bill,[†] would have been proposed by a Government, or could have been carried through Parliament, unless the British public had been led to perceive that a case might be made, and perhaps a party formed, for a measure considerably stronger. It is the character of the British people, or at least of the higher and middle classes who pass muster for the British people, that to induce them to approve of any change it is necessary that they should look upon it as a middle course: they think every proposal extreme and violent unless they hear of some other proposal going still farther, upon which their antipathy to extreme views may discharge itself. So it proved in the present instance; my proposal was condemned, but any scheme of Irish Land reform, short of mine, came to be thought moderate by comparison. I may observe that the attacks made on my plan usually gave a very incorrect idea of its nature. It was usually discussed as a proposal that the State should buy up the land and become the universal landlord; though in fact it only offered to each individual landlord this as an alternative, if he liked better to sell his estate than to retain it on the new conditions; and I fully anticipated that most landlords would continue to prefer the position of landowners to that of Government annuitants, and would retain their existing relation to their tenants, often on more indulgent terms than the full rents on which the compensation to be given them by Government would have been based. This and many other explanations I gave in a speech on Ireland, in the debate on Mr. Maguire's Resolution,[†] early in the session of 1868. A corrected report of this speech, together with my speech on Mr. Fortescue's Bill, has been published (not by me, but with my permission) in Ireland.

Another public duty, of a most serious kind, it was my lot to have to perform, both in and out of Parliament, during these years. A disturbance in Jamaica, provoked in the first instance by injustice, and exaggerated by rage and panic into a premeditated rebellion, had been the motive or excuse for taking hundreds of innocent lives by military violence or by sentence of what were called courts martial, continuing for weeks after the brief disturbance had been put down; with many added atrocities of destruction of property, flogging women as well as men, and a great display of the brutal recklessness which generally prevails when fire and sword are let loose. The perpetrators of these deeds were defended and applauded in England by the same kind of people who had so long upheld negro slavery:[†] and it seemed at first as if the British nation was about to incur the disgrace of letting pass without even a protest, excesses of authority as revolting as any of those for which, when perpetrated by the instruments of other governments, Englishmen can hardly find terms sufficient to express their abhorrence. After a short time, however, an indignant feeling was roused; a voluntary Association formed itself under the name of the Jamaica Committee, to take such deliberation and action as the case might admit of, and adhesions poured in from all parts of the country. I was abroad at the time but I sent in my name to the Committee as soon as I heard of it, and took an active part in the proceedings from the time of my return. There was much more at stake than only justice to the Negroes, imperative as was that consideration. The question was, whether the British dependencies, and eventually perhaps Great Britain itself, were to be under the government of law, or of military license; whether the lives and persons of British subjects are at the mercy of any two or three officers however raw and inexperienced or reckless and brutal, whom a panic-stricken Governor or other functionary may assume the right to constitute into a so-called Court Martial. This question could only be decided by an appeal to the tribunals; and such an appeal the Committee determined to make. Their determination led to a change in the Chairmanship of the Committee, as the Chairman, Mr. Charles Buxton,[†] thought it not unjust indeed, but inexpedient, to prosecute Governor Eyre and his principal subordinates in a criminal court: but a numerously attended General meeting of the Association having decided this point against him, Mr. Buxton withdrew from the Committee, though continuing to work in the cause, and I was, quite unexpectedly on my own part, proposed and elected Chairman. It became, in consequence, my duty to represent the Committee in the House of Commons, sometimes by putting questions to the Government, sometimes as the recipient of questions more or less provocative, addressed by individual members to myself; but especially as speaker in the important debate originated in the session of 1866 by Mr. Buxton: and the speech I then delivered is that which I should probably select as the best of my speeches[†] in Parliament.[6] For more than two years we carried on the combat, trying every avenue legally open to us, to the courts of criminal justice. A bench of magistrates in one of the most Tory counties in England dismissed our case: we were more successful before the magistrates at Bow Street;[†] which gave an opportunity to the Lord Chief Justice of the Queen's Bench, Sir Alexander Cockburn,[†] for delivering his celebrated charge, which settled the law of the question in favour of liberty, as far as it is in the power of a judge's charge to settle it. There, however, our success ended, for the Old Bailey[†] Grand Jury by throwing out our bill prevented the case from coming to trial. It was clear that to bring English functionaries to the bar of a criminal court for abuses of power committed against negroes and mulattoes, was not a popular proceeding with the English middle classes. We had however redeemed, so far as lay in us, the character of our country, by shewing that there was at any rate a body of persons determined to use all the means which the law afforded to obtain justice for the injured. We had elicited from the highest criminal judge in the nation an authoritative declaration that the law was what we maintained it to be; and we had given an emphatic warning to those who might be tempted to similar guilt hereafter, that though they might escape the actual sentence of a criminal tribunal, they were not safe against being put to some trouble and expense in order to avoid it. Colonial Governors and other persons in authority will have a considerable motive to stop short of such extremities in future.

---

[6] Among the most active members of the Committee were Mr. P. A. Taylor, M.P., always faithful and energetic in every assertion of the principles of liberty; Mr. Goldwin Smith, Mr. Frederick Harrison, Mr. Slack, Mr. Chamerovzow, Mr. Shaen, and Mr. Chesson, the Honorary Secretary of the Association.

As a matter of curiosity I kept some specimens of the abusive letters, almost all of them anonymous, which I received while these proceedings were going on. They are evidence of the sympathy felt with the brutalities in Jamaica by the brutal part of the population at home. They graduated from coarse jokes, verbal and pictorial, up to threats of assassination.[†]

Among other matters of importance in which I took an active part, but which excited little interest in the public, two deserve particular mention. I joined with several other independent Liberals in defeating an Extradition Bill, introduced at the very end of the session of 1866 and by which, though surrender avowedly for political offences was not authorised, political refugees, if charged by a foreign Government with acts which are necessarily incident to all attempts at insurrection, would have been surrendered to be dealt with by the criminal courts of the government against which they had rebelled: thus making the British Government an accomplice in the vengeance of foreign despotisms.[†] The defeat of this proposal led to the appointment of a Select Committee (in which I was included) to examine and report on the whole subject of Extradition Treaties; and the result was that in the Extradition Act, which passed through Parliament after I had ceased to be a member, opportunity is given to any one whose extradition is demanded, of being heard before an English court of justice to prove that the offence with which he is charged is really political.[†] The cause of European freedom has thus been saved from a serious misfortune, and our own country from a great iniquity. The other subject to be mentioned is the fight kept up by a body of advanced Liberals in the session of 1868, on the Bribery Bill of Mr. Disraeli's Government,[†] in which I took a very active part. I had taken council with several of those who had applied their minds most carefully to the details of the subject – Mr. W. D. Christie,[†] Serjeant Pulling,[†] Mr. Chadwick[†] – as well as bestowed much thought of my own, for the purpose of framing such amendments and additional clauses as might make the Bill really effective against the numerous modes of corruption, direct and indirect, which might otherwise, as there was much reason to fear, be increased instead of diminished by the Reform Act. We also aimed at engrafting on the Bill, measures for diminishing the mischievous burthen of what are called the legitimate expenses of elections. Among our many amendments was that of Mr. Fawcett[†] for making the returning officer's expenses a charge on the rates instead of on the candidates; another was the prohibition of paid canvassers, and the limitation of paid agents to one for each candidate; a third was the extension of the precautions and penalties against bribery, to municipal elections, which are well known to be not only a preparatory school for bribery at parliamentary elections, but an habitual cover for it. The Conservative Government, however, when once they had carried the leading provision of their Bill (for which I voted and spoke),[†] the transfer of the jurisdiction in elections from the House of Commons to the Judges,[†] made a determined resistance to all other improvements; and after one of our most important proposals, that of Mr. Fawcett, had actually obtained a majority, they summoned the strength of their party and threw out the clause in a subsequent stage. The Liberal party in the House was greatly dishonoured by the conduct of many of its members in giving no help whatever to this attempt to secure the necessary conditions of an honest representation of the people. With their large majority in the House they could have carried all the amendments, or better ones if they had better to propose. But it was late in the Session; members were eager to set about their preparations for the impending General Election:[†] and while some (such as Sir Robert Anstruther)[†] honourably remained at their post, though rival candidates were already canvassing their constituency, a much greater number placed their electioneering interests before their public duty. Many Liberals also looked with indifference on legislation against bribery, thinking that it merely diverted public interest from the Ballot, which they considered, very mistakenly as I expect it will turn out, to be a sufficient, and the only, remedy.[†] From these causes our fight, though kept up with great vigour for several nights, was wholly unsuccessful, and the practices which we sought to render more difficult, prevailed more widely than ever in the first General Election held under the new electoral law.

In the general debates on Mr. Disraeli's Reform Bill, my participation was limited to the one speech already mentioned; but I made the Bill an occasion for bringing the two greatest improvements which remain to be made in representative government formally before the House and the nation. One of them was Personal, or, as it is called with equal propriety, Proportional Representation. I brought this under the consideration of the House, by an expository and argumentative speech on Mr. Hare's plan; and subsequently I was active in support of the very imperfect substitute for that plan, which, in a small number of constituencies, Parliament was induced to adopt.[†] This poor makeshift had scarcely any recommendation, except that it was a partial recognition of the evil which it did so little to remedy: as such however it was attacked by the same fallacies, and required to be defended on the same principles, as a really good measure; and its adoption in a few parliamentary elections, as well as the subsequent introduction of what is called the Cumulative Vote in the elections for the London School Board,† have had the good effect of converting the equal claim of all electors to a proportional share in the representation, from a subject of merely speculative discussion, into a question of practical politics, much sooner than would otherwise have been the case.

This assertion of my opinions on Personal Representation cannot be credited with any considerable or visible amount of practical result. It was otherwise with the other motion which I made in the form of an amendment to the Reform Bill, and which was by far the most important, perhaps the only really important public service I performed in the capacity of a Member of Parliament: a motion to strike out the words which were understood to limit the electoral franchise to males, thereby admitting to the suffrage all women who as householders or otherwise possess the qualification required of male electors. For women not to make their claim to the suffrage at the time when the elective franchise was being largely extended, would have been to abjure the claim altogether; and a movement on the subject was begun in 1866, when I presented a petition for the suffrage signed by a considerable number of distinguished women.† But it was as yet uncertain whether the proposal would obtain more than a few stray votes in the House: and when, after a debate in which the speakers on the contrary side were conspicuous by their feebleness, the votes recorded in favour of the motion amounted to 73 – made up by pairs and tellers to above 80 – the surprise was general and the encouragement great: the greater too because one of those who voted for the motion was Mr. Bright, a fact which could only be attributed to the impression made on him by the debate, as he had previously made no secret of his non-concurrence in the proposal.‡ The time appeared to my daughter, Miss Helen Taylor, to have come for forming a Society for the extension of the suffrage to women. The existence of the Society is due to my daughter's initiative; its constitution was planned entirely by her, and she was the soul of the movement during its first years, though delicate health and superabundant occupation made her decline to be a member of the Executive Committee. Many distinguished members of parliament, professors, and others, and some of the most eminent women of whom the country can boast, became members of the

Society, a large proportion either directly or indirectly through my daughter's influence, she having written the greater number, and all the best, of the letters by which adhesion was obtained, even when those letters bore my signature. In two remarkable instances, those of Miss Nightingale and Miss Mary Carpenter,[†] the reluctance those ladies had at first felt to come forward (for it was not on their part difference of opinion) was overcome by appeals written by my daughter though signed by me. Associations for the same object were formed in various local centres, Manchester, Edinburgh, Birmingham, Bristol, Glasgow, and others which have done much valuable work for the cause. All the Societies take the title of branches of the National Society for Women's Suffrage; but each has its own governing body, and acts in complete independence of the others.

I believe I have mentioned all that is worth remembering of my proceedings in the House. But their enumeration, even if complete, would give but an inadequate idea of my occupations during that period, and especially of the time taken up by correspondence. For many years before my election to Parliament I had been continually receiving letters from strangers, mostly addressed to me as a writer on philosophy, and either propounding difficulties or communicating thoughts on subjects connected with logic or political economy. In common, I suppose, with all who are known as political economists, I was a recipient of all the shallow theories and absurd proposals by which people are perpetually endeavouring to shew the way to universal wealth and happiness by some artful reorganisation of the currency. When there were signs of sufficient intelligence in the writers to make it worth while attempting to put them right, I took the trouble to point out their errors, until the growth of my correspondence made it necessary to dismiss such persons with very brief answers. Many, however, of the communications I received were more worthy of attention than these, and in some, oversights of detail were pointed out in my writings, which I was thus enabled to correct. Correspondence of this sort naturally multiplied with the multiplication of the subjects on which I wrote, especially those of a metaphysical character. But when I became a member of parliament I began to receive letters on private grievances and on every imaginable subject that related to any kind of public affairs, however remote from my knowledge or pursuits. It was not my constituents in Westminster who laid this burthen on me: they kept with remarkable fidelity to the understanding on which I had consented to serve. I received indeed now and then an application from some ingenuous youth to procure for him a small government appointment; but these were few, and how simple and ignorant the writers were, was shewn by the fact that the applications came in about equally whichever party was in power. My invariable answer was, that it was contrary to the principles on which I was elected to ask favours of any Government. But on the whole hardly any part of the country gave me less trouble than my own constituents. The general mass of correspondence, however, swelled into an oppressive burthen.‡ At this time, and thenceforth, a great proportion of all my letters (including many which found their way into the newspapers)[7] were not written by me but by my daughter; at first merely from her willingness to help in disposing of a mass of letters greater than I could get through without assistance, but afterwards because I thought the letters she wrote superior to mine, and more so in proportion to the difficulty and importance of the occasion. Even those I wrote myself were generally much improved by her, as is also the case with all the more recent of my prepared speeches, of which, and of some of my published writings, not a few passages, and those the most successful, were hers.

While I remained in Parliament my work as an author was unavoidably limited to the recess. During that time I wrote (besides the pamphlet on Ireland already mentioned) the Essay on Plato† published in the *Edinburgh Review* and reprinted in the third volume of *Dissertations and Discussions*; and the Address which conformably to custom I delivered to the University of St. Andrews, whose students had done me the honour of electing me to the office of Rector.† In this Discourse I gave expression to many thoughts and opinions which had been accumulating in me through life respecting the various studies which belong to a liberal education, their uses and influences, and the mode in which they should be pursued to render their influences most beneficial. The position I took up, vindicating the high educational value alike of the old classic and the new scientific studies, on even stronger grounds than are urged by most of their

---

[7] One which deserves particular mention is a letter respecting the Habitual Criminals Act [1869] and the functions of a police generally, written in answer to a private application for my opinion, but which got into the newspapers and excited some notice. [*Morning Star*, 23 December 1868] This letter which was full of original and valuable thoughts was entirely my daughter's. The fertility and aptness which distinguishes her practical conceptions of the adaptation of means to ends is such as I can never hope to rival.

advocates, and insisting that it is only the stupid inefficiency of the usual teaching which makes those studies be regarded as competitors instead of allies, was, I think, calculated, not only to aid and stimulate the improvement which has happily commenced in the national institutions for higher education, but to diffuse juster ideas than we often find even in highly educated men on the conditions of the highest mental cultivation.

During this period also I commenced (and completed soon after I had left Parliament) the performance of a duty to philosophy and to the memory of my father, by preparing and publishing an edition of the *Analysis of the Phenomena of the Human Mind*[1] with notes bringing up the doctrines of that admirable book to the latest improvements in science and in speculation. This was a joint undertaking: the psychological notes being furnished in about equal proportions by Mr. Bain and myself, while Mr. Grote supplied some valuable contributions on points in the history of philosophy incidentally raised, and Dr. Andrew Findlater[†] supplied the deficiencies in the book which had been occasioned by the imperfect philological knowledge of the time when it was written. Having been originally published at a time when the current of metaphysical speculation ran in a quite opposite direction to the psychology of Experience and Association, the *Analysis* had not obtained the amount of immediate success which it deserved, though it had made a deep impression on many individual minds, and had largely contributed, through those minds, to create that more favourable atmosphere for the Association Psychology of which we now have the benefit. Admirably adapted for a class-book of the Experience Metaphysics, it only required to be enriched, and in some cases corrected, by the results of more recent labours in the same school of thought, to stand, as it now does, in company with Mr. Bain's treatises, at the head of the systematic works on Analytic psychology.

In the autumn of 1868 the Parliament which passed the Reform Act was dissolved, and at the new election for Westminster I was thrown out;[†] not to my surprise, nor, I believe, to that of my principal supporters, though in the few days preceding the election they had become more sanguine than before. That I should not have been elected at all would not have required any explanation; what excites curiosity is that I should have been elected the first time, or, having been elected then, should have been defeated afterwards. But the efforts made to defeat me were far greater on the second occasion than on the first. For one thing, the Tory Government was now struggling for existence, and success in any contest was of more importance to them. Then, too, all persons of Tory feelings were far more embittered against me individually than on the previous occasion; many who had at first been either favourable or indifferent, were vehemently opposed to my reelection. As I had shewn in my political writings that I was aware of the weak points in democratic opinions, some Conservatives, it seems, had not been without hopes of finding me an opponent of democracy: as I was able to see the Conservative side of the question, they presumed that, like them, I could not see any other side. Yet if they had really read my writings, they would have known that after giving full weight to all that appeared to me well grounded in the arguments against democracy, I unhesitatingly decided in its favour, while recommending that it should be accompanied by such institutions as were consistent with its principle and calculated to ward off its inconveniences: one of the chief of these remedies being Proportional Representation, on which scarcely any of the Conservatives gave me any support. Some Tory expectations appear to have been founded on the approbation I had expressed of plural voting, under certain conditions: and it has been surmised that the suggestion of this sort made in one of the Resolutions which Mr. Disraeli introduced into the House preparatory to his Reform Bill† (a suggestion which meeting with no favour he did not press) may have been occasioned by what I had written on the point: but if so, it was forgotten that I had made it an express condition that the privilege of a plurality of votes should be annexed to education, not to property, and even so, had approved of it only on the supposition of universal suffrage.† How utterly inadmissible such plural voting would be under the suffrage given by the present Reform Act, is proved, to any who could otherwise doubt it, by the very small weight which the working classes are found to possess in elections even under the law which gives no more votes to any one elector than to any other.

While I thus was far more obnoxious to the Tory interest, and to many Conservative Liberals than I had formerly been, the course I pursued in Parliament had by no means been such as to make Liberals generally at all enthusiastic in my support. It has already been mentioned, how large a proportion of my prominent appearances had been on questions on which I differed from most of the Liberal party, or about which they cared little, and how few occasions there had been on which the line I took was such as could lead them to attach any great value to me as an organ of their opinions. I had moreover done things which had excited, in many minds, a personal prejudice against me. Many were offended by what they called the persecution of Mr. Eyre: and still greater offence was taken at my sending a subscription to the election expenses of Mr. Bradlaugh.† Having refused to be at any expense for my own election, and having had all its expenses defrayed by others, I felt under a peculiar obligation to subscribe in my turn where funds were deficient for candidates whose election was desirable. I accordingly sent subscriptions to nearly all the working class candidates, and among others to Mr. Bradlaugh. He had the support of the working classes; having heard him speak I knew him to be a man of ability, and he had proved that he was the reverse of a demagogue by placing himself in strong opposition to the prevailing opinion of the democratic party on two such important subjects as Malthusianism and Personal Representation. Men of this sort, who while sharing the democratic feelings of the working classes, judged political questions for themselves, and had courage to assert their individual convictions against popular opposition, were needed, as it seemed to me, in Parliament, and I did not think that Mr. Bradlaugh's anti-religious opinions (even though he had been intemperate in the expression of them) ought to exclude him. In subscribing, however, to his election, I did what would have been highly imprudent if I had been at liberty to consider only the interests of my own reelection; and, as might be expected, the utmost possible use, both fair and unfair, was made of this act of mine, to stir up the electors of Westminster against me. To these various causes, combined with an unscrupulous use of the usual pecuniary and other influences on the side of my Tory competitor† while none were used on my side, it is to be ascribed that I failed at my second election after having succeeded at the first. No sooner was the result of the election known than I received three or four invitations to become a candidate for other constituencies, chiefly counties; but even if success could have been expected, and this without expense, I was not disposed to deny myself the relief of returning to private life. I had no cause to feel humiliated at my rejection by the electors; and if I had, the feeling would have been far outweighed by the numerous expressions of regret which I received from all sorts of persons and places, and in a most marked degree from those members of the liberal party in Parliament with whom I had been accustomed to act.

Since that time little has occurred which there is need to commemorate in this place. I returned to my old pursuits and to the enjoyment of a country life in the South of Europe; alternating twice a year with a residence of some weeks or months in the neighbourhood of London. I have written various articles in periodicals (chiefly in my friend Mr. Morley's *Fortnightly Review*),[†] have made a small number of speeches on public occasions,[‡] especially at the meetings of the Women's Suffrage Society, have published *The Subjection of Women*, written some years before, with some additions by my daughter and myself,[‡] and have commenced the preparation of matter for future books, of which it will be time to speak more particularly if I live to finish them.[†] Here therefore, for the present, this Memoir may close.

Speech on
The Utility of Knowledge

Delivered at the Mutual Improvement Society 1823 [†‡]

❦

The beneficial effects produced upon the human mind and upon the structure of society by the revival of science and by the cessation of feudal darkness have been so obvious that there is scarcely room for the smallest discussion. No one, I apprehend, would insult the understanding of this Society by reviving the ascetic sophistry of the fanatic Rousseau [†] by maintaining that what are called the comforts and conveniences of life are in fact neither comforts nor conveniences, and add not the smallest particle to human happiness; that the progress of civilization is in fact the progress of barbarism and that the Hurons and the Iroquois [†] are the happiest and the most enlightened of mankind. Were such a reasoner to arise I should ask him by what authority he claims to know better than A, B, and C what constitutes the happiness of A, B, and C. I should maintain that what all men have uniformly considered as comforts and conveniences cannot be otherwise than comforts and conveniences, and I should require him who considers knowledge as standing in the way of happiness to go and legislate for those savages upon whose blissful state of ignorance he would have an opportunity of trying his skill without those obstacles which he finds in the knowledge of this comparatively enlightened country.

Such doctrines are scarcely worthy of a serious reply, but as the refutation may be made remarkably pointed and concise, it may be better to give it. In reasoning on these general questions a want of precision in the use of language is the principal engine of sophistry. Here the confusion lies in the word *knowledge*, a word so vague and indefinite as to be an easy instrument in the hands of *mala fide* [†] arguers, being capable of signifying just as much or as little as they please. It is not this kind of knowledge which is of such extensive importance. The only useful knowledge is that which teaches us how to seek what is good and avoid what is evil; in short, how to increase the sum of human happiness. [†] This is the great end: it may be well or ill pursued, but to say that knowledge can be an enemy to happiness is to say that men will enjoy less happiness, when they know how to seek it, than when they do not. This reasoning is on a par with that of anyone who should refuse when asked to point out

171

the road to York, saying that his inquirer would have a much better chance of reaching York without direction than with it.† It is impossible then to suppose that anyone should get up in this Society and maintain that knowledge in the abstract is mischievous. Arguments may indeed be directed against much of what passes current under the name of knowledge to show that it is not really knowledge but prejudice, and is therefore not favourable but unfavourable to happiness. But this is one of those cases where the reason of the exception proves the truth of the general rule. It is precisely because knowledge is useful that prejudice is mischievous.

The question, simple in itself, is in some degree confused by the manner in which it is worded, and which, with deference to the worthy proposer, might, I conceive, have been made more clearly expressive of his meaning. If asked whether the revival of letters has tended to promote happiness I know what to say, and by what arguments to support it; but if I am asked whether it tends to refine or to corrupt manners I confess myself at a stand. The three words, *manners, corrupt*, and *refine*, are to me in the sense here bestowed upon them equally enigmatical. If by refinement of manners is meant that ceremonious politeness in intercourse between the higher orders, and that assiduous gallantry towards the fair sex which were the distinguishing characteristics of the old feudal aristocracy, then I should say that manners had not gained but lost by the revival of letters: but far from lamenting I should rejoice in the change, as I do in everything which turns the attention of mankind from the frivolous details of a petty and ceremonious trifling to the concerns which interest their real and substantial welfare. But if the intention of the proposer was to inquire into the effect of increased civilization in promoting genuine morality, then although on a general view of the question all will probably agree with me that this effect has been highly beneficial, it will be no loss of time to examine in detail from how dreadful a state of misery the human race has been elevated by knowledge into a state where they have at least the hope, the speedy hope, of establishing a better state of things.

The revival of art and science has contributed to promote morality in two ways; by the increase of wealth and by the diffusion of information. The discoveries in chemical and mechanical philosophy – should I not rather say the creation of these branches of knowledge? – has enabled the human race to provide themselves abundantly at little expense of labour with those necessaries and comforts which formerly they either could not procure at all, or if at all, only in a very small amount and with very great labour. This increase of wealth must have contributed greatly to the improvement of morality. I would not be understood as affirming that the rich are more moral than the poor. As far as general reasoning and my own particular experience can lead me I should rather adopt the contrary

172

conclusion. But when the augmentation of wealth is not, by being confined in the hands of a few, reduced to be but one expedient more for the oppression of the many; when I say instead of being exclusively devoted to the enjoyment of a few the increase of wealth is generally and equally diffused throughout the whole community; then by conferring upon the working classes the inestimable benefit of leisure, it forces them to seek society, it forces them to seek education. Each working man becomes himself better qualified to distinguish right from wrong, while each knows that he is under the constant surveillance of hundreds and thousands equally instructed with himself. Thus does the improvement of the physical sciences, by increasing and diffusing wealth, indirectly tend to promote morality.

But the evils which man is doomed to suffer from the hands of nature are nothing when compared to those which man frequently suffers from man. Communities have been known to flourish in spots which Nature seems to have selected for the sepulchre of the universe; but there is no country, however favoured by nature, which superstition and misgovernment do not suffice to ruin. Let us therefore take a general view of the situation of our ancestors with respect to these two main points, religion and government.

And first as to their government: he must be an adept in the art of rendering mankind miserable who could devise anything more destructive of all happiness. It was not here the common vice of a rude government, where each man has not yet learned to trust his neighbour, and where no one will as yet renounce the privilege of protecting himself. These are imperfect governments for they afford imperfect securities for happiness, but they are not in every sense as execrable as the feudal system. Imagine a tribe with a government such as that to which I have alluded spreading itself by conquest over a large portion of the globe, and reducing the native population to the state of domestic cattle! Each chief absolute master of thousands of human beings, and himself acknowledging no regular government, but striving to retain his pristine independency! Not only is no one secure from the arbitrary will of a master; even that master cannot afford him protection against other despots and slaves! It has frequently been made a question whether despotism or anarchy is worst; but this is not the question here, for the feudal system united the evils of both. The laws were openly and flagrantly violated, and the violations remained unpunished. Judge of the security which the administration of justice could afford when the trial by battle was the best expedient which could be devised to ensure the purity of judicature, and where it was usual for the party who was cast in a lawsuit to challenge his judge to mortal combat.

The religion of our ancestors is next to be considered, and here I shall begin by laying down a principle of which the ordinary reasoners on these

173

subjects have usually lost sight.[†] It is not indeed extremely recondite for it is no other than this, that priests are men. They are usually considered as partaking of that perfect goodness and wisdom which they verbally attribute to the Great Master whom they profess to serve, although the actions and precepts which they ascribe to Him partake but too often of a contrary character.

From the principle that priests are men I draw the inference that in those cases which very frequently occur, and in which their individual interest is opposed to the interest of mankind, they will act as other men would act in similar circumstances; they would pursue their own interest to the detriment of mankind. Now if all men agree to believe whatever they say, they have a decided interest in making them believe everything which is likely to make them venerate and worship their spiritual guides; and if true opinions on the subject of religion are not of a nature calculated to inspire the requisite degree of veneration, it would be unfair to expect that these irresponsible directors of the public mind should confine themselves strictly to what is true; and we might indeed predict with tolerable certainty that they would not fail to intermingle much of what is utterly false, the more so as they may do this without the slightest insincerity. There is no fact better ascertained than the facility with which men are persuaded to believe what they wish. It is only necessary that there should be someone, who may be either a knave or a madman, to start a falsehood; if it is unfavourable to the clergy he will be hunted down as a heretic, but if it is favourable to them it will not be long before he finds many sincere disciples among the clergy themselves, who of course propagate it among the laity. It is in this way that the Catholic priesthood added to their religion the profitable doctrine of purgatory and masses for the dead, the crime-promoting doctrine of indulgences, and above all the terrific engines of auricular confession and absolution, the concentration of which, and particularly of the former, in the hands of the clergy, make it astonishing that mankind should ever have emancipated themselves from the terrific sway of priests and their coadjutors, aristocracies and kings.[†] If at this day we rarely hear of murders perpetrated in the name of religion, still more rarely of those terrible persecutions which once disgraced every nation in Europe, we owe this to the revival of letters and the consequent diffusion of knowledge.

Such a government and such a religion as our ancestors had the happiness to enjoy afford us in some degree the means of appreciating that ancestorial wisdom which is even now held up to us as a model for imitation. In the nineteenth century we are not infrequently called upon to pursue the course which was followed by those sages, our ancestors, in the eleventh and twelfth. But this appeal from the age of civilization to the age of barbarism is made, we may observe, by those and by those alone who now, as then, would wish to see the great mass of mankind subject to the despotic sway of nobles, priests, and kings. But although it is in one respect true that the aristocracy of wealth and rank has given place to the democracy of intellect, I would not insinuate that the evils of feudal despotism and superstition are altogether eradicated even from this enlightened country. Knowledge has done much, but it has not yet done all. We are still subject to a constitution which is at best a shattered fragment of the feudal system; we are still subject to a priesthood† who do whatever is yet in their power to excite a spirit of religious intolerance and to support the domination of a despotic aristocracy. We cannot therefore be surprised that those who are interested in misgovernment should raise a cry against the diffusion of knowledge on the ground that it renders the people dissatisfied with their institutions. When despotism and superstition were in their greatest vigour the same cry was raised, and for the same reason. Knowledge has triumphed. It has worked the downfall of much that is mischievous. It is in vain to suppose that it will pass by and spare any institution the existence of which is pernicious to mankind.

Speech on
The British Constitution

Delivered at the London Debating Society 1826‡

By the word Constitution, Sir, I understand the institutions which exist for the purpose or with the supposed effect of affording securities for good government. The question, therefore, concerning the goodness of our Constitution, is the question whether, in so far as depends upon institutions, good government is practically attained. It will I think be allowed that as long as we suffer under any evil of which government is the cause, good government in the practical sense of the word is not attained. The first question, therefore, is, Do any evils exist; the second, are any of them to be imputed to our government.

To most persons it would appear very unnecessary to prove that evils of some sort or another do exist, and impossible to suppose the contrary opinion capable of being entertained by any rational being. So much language has however been held which if it has not this meaning has none at all, that I am compelled to regard even this point as not out of the reach of controversy. If we believe some gentlemen, England is a perfect Utopia.† The happiness of the golden age† was nothing to that we enjoy. Luxury pervades the upper classes, comfort and knowledge diffuse themselves among the middle, competence and contentment among the lower. We are great in war, honoured and powerful in peace, no man in his senses *could* hope for any thing better, and no honest man *would*. If this be true, it certainly puts an end to the question. If no evils exist, none, it is evident, can be occasioned by our practical Constitution. If we are already enjoying the whole of the happiness which we are to look for in this world, it is very obvious that we have nothing better to do than just to remain as we are. I must confess however that my aspirations do not stop at that degree of felicity to which we have at present attained, and that rather a higher standard of competence and contentment than six shillings a week will afford, seems to me greatly to be desired for our agricultural population. Prosperity, Sir, is the test of good government, but the prosperity must first be proved.

We have flourished under the Constitution. Who has flourished under the Constitution? These gentlemen are apt to fall into the mistake, a very natural one I admit, of supposing that all the world has flourished because they have. Do they mean to allege that the great body of the people has flourished? But the people is not a word in their vocabulary. Instead of the people, they talk of the country: the wealth power and glory of the country: by which is to be understood the wealth power and glory of one man in a hundred, and the misery of the remaining 99. By this word country, they always mean the aristocracy. Whenever they talk of the prosperity of the country, it is the prosperity of the aristocracy that is meant. When they say country read aristocracy, and you will never be far from the truth. They tell you that the Constitution has worked well: you ask them particulars, and they answer that it has brought us a great deal of money and a great deal of glory: So much the better for those who have got it, I am sure we have got none: They may talk as they please about our being the richest nation in the world. The richest nation, in one sense of the word, we certainly are, but then it is like Mr. Alexander Baring† and me: between us, we certainly have a very handsome fortune. But what illustrates more than any thing else the peculiar view which they take of national prosperity, is their talk about military and naval renown. They have particularly selected as a proof of good government exactly what I should have chosen as a specimen of bad. I have as little respect, Sir, for a fighting nation as I have for a fighting individual, and I am by no means anxious that my country should be considered the Tom Cribb† of Europe.

They talk of the last war, and seem to think it highly honourable to our Constitution that having first got us into what they call an arduous struggle, it afterwards at the expense of many myriads of lives got us out again. But let me ask, what was gained by the last war, and who gained it? We knocked down one despot, and set up a score;† this was their concern not ours. Then as to the substantial part of the gain, the money and glory. The generals and admirals and colonels and lieutenant-colonels and all the rest of them got money, and most of them a little glory, some a great deal. The poor privates who took the disagreeable part of the business, and who were sent home when it was over to loiter about Chelsea hospital† with one leg or follow the plough with two, they got no glory; any more than those at home who paid the piper. The contractors who had the fingering of the loans got no glory, but they got what was much better, many millions of pounds sterling which made them very comfortable at our expense. Sir, I grudge nobody his glory, if he would pay for it himself. I have a great respect for Sir Arthur Wellesley,† and *ceteris paribus*† I would much rather that he should be, as he is, a hero and a duke, than not: but when I consider that every feather in his cap has cost the nation more than he and his whole lineage would fetch if they were sold for lumber, I own that I much regret the solid pudding which we threw away in order that he might obtain empty praise.

Those who have called in question the goodness our Constitution never thought of denying that it was good for some persons. The British

Constitution is the Constitution of the rich. It has made this country the paradise of the wealthy. It has annexed to wealth a greater share of political power, and a greater command over the minds of men, than were ever possessed by it elsewhere. It has given us rich merchants, and extensive landholders. It has given to those who have money already, great facilities for making it more. It has produced a fine breed of country gentlemen, and to support the breed it has charged us with an additional 3d. on the quartern loaf.† All this, Sir, is very fine, but I cannot help reflecting that the peasant of Languedoc† eats his three meals of meat a day and cultivates his vineyard, he has cheap justice at his doors, he may go where he pleases, engage in any trade that he pleases, and tread upon as many partridge eggs as he pleases, and need not fear to find himself next day on the treadmill, a victim of the unpaid patriotism of a game-eating squire. We are a free country, Sir, but it is as Sparta was free:† the Helots are overlooked.

Whenever the honourable opener sees so much as a scrap of good, he gives the credit of it to the Constitution. By this rule, we ought to impute to it our evils likewise. I might say that our manufacturers are starving by reason of the Constitution. I might say that our peasantry is the poorest in Europe, because our Constitution is the worst. I believe a greater number of individuals suffer capital punishment in this country than in all the rest of Europe put together, and I might thence infer that our Constitution is a complication of all the vices of all the Governments in Europe. But I do not think myself justified in reasoning unfairly because the honourable opener has set me the example. I impute to the Constitution no evils which do not naturally follow from the interests to which it has given birth. But when there is an obvious connexion between the evil suffered, and the interests of the governors, I think it reasonable to place the evil to the account of the Constitution, because it is the Constitution which suffers the interests of the governors to be paramount to those of the governed. Such is the case with those evils which were depicted in perhaps more unmeasured language than was necessary by my honourable friend opposite on a former evening and if I were to swell the list as I might do I should perhaps be betrayed into language still more intemperate than his. But as this part of our case has already been so well stated, I shall allow it to rest upon his statements and proceed to another.

I thought, Sir, that the question related to the practice of the Constitution, but the defenders of the Constitution have thought otherwise: they seem determined to prove *à priori* the goodness of the Constitution, finding themselves unable to prove it *à posteriori*: and they have been good enough to reveal to us their several theories of the Constitution, with the view as I suppose of convincing us that if we are not very well off, yet upon correct principles we ought to be. Now though I myself care very little by what machinery my pocket is picked, the beauty of the machinery has sometimes the effect of persuading people that their pocket is not picked when in fact it is: it may therefore conduce somewhat to the understanding of the question if their theories be cleared away. The commonplace theories have all had their supporters in the Society. We are told by one, that our Constitution is a balance, by another that it is a representation of classes, by a third that it is an aristocratical republic, sufficiently checked by public opinion. To this I will add my theory, that it is an aristocratical republic, insufficiently checked by public opinion. If I seem to dismiss these theories in a summary manner, want of time must be my apology.

The class representation theory requires most words, as it is the most modern, and the most plausible. It has been very fully, though not very distinctly, stated this evening, and amounts to this, that if the landed interest, the mercantile interest, the army, the law, the manufacturing interest, and all the other great interests are represented, and the people represented, enough is done for good government, and that under our Constitution this is actually the case.

Now it seems to be forgotten in this view of the subject, that every one of these classes has two interests, its separate interest and its share of the general interest. That which ought to be represented is the latter. What really is represented is the former. Most true it is that the separate interests of a great number of classes are represented in the House of Commons: and so perfectly is the system adapted to ensure the predominance of these interests, that there is hardly any class of plunderers (pickpockets and highwaymen excepted) which has not a greater number of representatives in the House of Commons than the whole body of the plundered. The consequence is that there is hardly ever a job proposed for the benefit of any set of persons at the expense of the community, which does not find in that assembly somebody or other who is interested in supporting it; and as there is a natural alliance among jobs of every description, one *interest* plays into the hands of another, *hodie mihi cras tibi*† is the word, and the upshot of it is, that taking the great jobs with the little ones there is not on the face of God's earth such another jobbing assembly as the House of Commons. Sir, this is the very thing we complain of. The amount of misrule is not diminished by the multitude of the sharers. According to our notions, the House of Commons should represent only one interest – the general interest. As for these particular interests which are opposed to the general one, as nobody ought to attend to them, I suppose nobody need represent them.

Fable, Sir, as we are taught by the ancients, sometimes throws light upon truth. I will tell you a fable and you shall judge for yourself whether or not it is in point.

Once upon a time there happened an insurrection among the beasts. The little beasts grew tired of being eaten by the great ones. The swinish,

179

goatish and sheepish multitude grew weary of the sway of the intellectual and virtuous. They demanded to be governed by just and equal laws and as a security for these laws, to be subject to a representative government. The Lion, finding himself hard-pressed, called together the aristocracy of the forest, and they jointly offered a rich reward to whoever could devise a scheme for extricating them from their embarrassment. The Fox offered himself, and his offer being accepted, went forth to the assembled multitude, and addressed them thus. 'Surely my friends, you would not deny to others the advantage which you seek to partake of yourselves. The only true representation is representation by classes. The tigrish interest should be represented, the wolfish interest should be represented, all the other interests should be represented, and the great body of the beasts should be represented. My royal master has an objection to anarchy, but he is no enemy to a rational and well-regulated Freedom: any other sort of representation he never will agree to, but a class representation he consents to grant.' The people, delighted to have got the name of a representation, quietly dispersed, and writs were issued to the different interests to chuse their representatives. The tigers chose six tigers, the panthers six panthers, the hyaenas six hyaenas, and the wolves six wolves. The remaining beasts, who were only allowed to chuse six, chose by common consent six dogs. The parliament was opened by a speech from the Lion, recommending unanimity. When this was concluded, the Jackal, who was Chancellor of the Exchequer, introduced the subject of the Civil List: † and after a long panegyric on the royal virtues, proposed a grant, for the support of those virtues, of 1,000 sheep a year. The proposition was received with acclamations from the ministerial benches. The Tiger, happening to be in the opposition, made an eloquent speech, in which he enlarged much upon the necessity of economy, inveighed bitterly against the profusion of ministers, and ended by moving that His Majesty must be humbly requested to content himself with 999.† The Dogs declared that as kings must eat, they had no objection to His Majesty devouring as many dead sheep as he pleased; but solemnly protested against his consuming any of their constituents alive. This remonstrance had its natural effect. The first impulse of the representatives of the aristocracy was to fall tooth and nail upon the representatives of the people. The Lion however representing that such conduct would be dishonourable, and the Fox that it might provoke a renewal of the insurrection, they abandoned the intention of worrying these demagogues, and contented themselves with always outvoting them. The sequel may be guessed. The Lion got his thousand sheep; the Fox his pension of 100 ducks a year, and the Panthers, Wolves, and the other members of the aristocracy got as many kids and lambs in a quiet way, as they could devour.

With this allegory, which is worth a thousand syllogisms, I shall dismiss the subject of the class representation.

The gentleman who first propounded to us the theory of the balance, will forgive me for saying that he seems to have studied the Constitution chiefly in the writings of its panegyrists. The balance of King Lords and Commons I have met with in books, and it has a very pretty appearance upon paper: but even those who maintain that it existed once acknowledge that it has no existence now: the Commons, it is allowed, have complete possession of the Government, and the only balance now contended for, is a balance in the House of Commons itself. That there is such a balance, I do not deny, since a balance is still a balance, although the weights may be unequal. But if anybody maintains that the weights are equal, he should first find means of explaining away the fact, that the aristocracy alone commands twice as many members of parliament as the King and the people together. The parliament is just as effectual an instrument of the aristocracy, if they have a majority of the votes, as it would be if they had the whole. With the fact that the parliament is made by the aristocracy staring us in the face, it would be useless to enter into the speculative question whether the balance is possible, or whether, if possible, it would be good. Possible or not, at any rate it does not exist. If there be any counterpoise to the power of the Aristocracy, it cannot come from within the House of Commons, it must come from without.

With that class of the defenders of our Constitution who consider public opinion as expressed by petitions, public meetings, and a free press, as the one and sufficient check, I am less widely at issue. The question between us is merely a question of degree. We both allow that the House of Commons requires a check, we both agree that public opinion is the proper check. They think that the check is sufficient if the public are allowed to speak freely, I think that it is not sufficient unless they are allowed to act as well as speak. Now I do not see how the question between us can be tried, except by looking about us and seeing what this free speaking has done. That it has done much I allow. It is probably the cause that we are not at this moment the slaves of a military despotism. But has it abolished the Corn Laws? Has it abolished the Game Laws?[†] Did it prevent the Six Acts?[†] Did it prevent the Manchester Massacre[†] – or did it prevent the House of Commons from approving of it? Has it cut down our civil, military, and naval establishments? Has it reformed the Magistracy, the Church, and the Law? It has been said by the gentleman who started this theory, that the laws of England are deserving of absolute condemnation. If this be true, what a satire is it upon the Constitution which he applauded! For my part, I do not think the laws of England deserving of absolute condemnation, but I think that they require many and great ameliorations; ameliorations which I am persuaded that none but a reformed parliament will have the courage, I will not say the inclination, to make.

181

What is the influence of public opinion? Nothing at bottom, but the influence of fear. Of what consequence is it to a minister what the public say so long as they content themselves with saying? When it comes to blows it becomes a serious matter. I do not deny the influence of character, of the opinion of others, even independently of fear. The opinion of others is a peaceful check upon every man, but then it must be the opinion of his own class. Experience has shewn that there is no action so wicked that even an honest man will not do, if he is borne out by the opinion of those with whom he habitually associates. Was there ever a more unpopular minister than Lord Castlereagh?[†] Was there ever a minister who cared so little about it? The reason was that although he had the people against him, the predominant portion of the aristocracy was for him, and all his concern about public dissatisfaction was to keep it below the point of a general insurrection. Things are a little better now, because we accidentally have a ministry who knowing themselves to be no favourites with the bulk of the aristocracy, and feeling that to use a homely expression it is touch and go with their places, court the people as a sort of makeweight, though an inconsiderable one, to that portion of the aristocracy who are on their side. But should they be turned out and should we for our sins be visited with another Castlereagh, we shall be governed by the new one exactly as we were governed by the old, in spite of the public opinion check, the dread of insurrection, which it seems we have, and which the Turks have likewise. The Constitution of Turkey may be defined to be the fear of the bowstring: and the constitution of Great Britain it seems according to this view of it, may be defined to be the fear of the guillotine.[†] Let who will be satisfied with this check: I, for one, have a most decided objection to it.

I fear that my observations on the theories of the Constitution have been dull: but I must crave the indulgence of the Society for a short time longer. There is another subject which must not be altogether passed over. Gentlemen have not merely enlarged upon the goodness of our Constitution, they have expatiated upon the exceeding badness of every other. More especially a popular government has been the theme of their invectives, nor have they by any means spared the people themselves. This, Sir, is the way with them. If we believe some people, the many who are interested in good government are the determined enemies of good government, and the only persons who are its friends are the few, who are interested against it. They are always fearing evil to the many from the many, never from the few. Now I beg you to remark how many advantages these gentlemen have over me. We are always ready to believe what we fear. The orator who has the fears of his audience on his side, has only to awaken the emotion by a few frightful words, and persuasion follows of itself. Very different is the task of him who has the fear of his audience against him. Having to work conviction by means of evidence, in minds ill prepared to receive it, to have any chance of success he must heap proof upon proof – he must add argument to argument – his discourse lengthens into prolixity, he has wearied the patience of his audience before he has triumphed over their apprehensions, and to the misfortune of failing in his object, he adds that of being voted a bore. Sir, it is among the disadvantages of my present situation, that I am compelled to be prolix. Misrepresentation is always beautifully brief; refutation always tediously long. There are single sentences in the speech of the honourable opener, each containing half a score of assumptions, each assumption requiring a long detail of facts or train of reasoning to refute it.[‡]

Speech on Perfectibility

Delivered at the London Debating Society 1828‡

Mr. President, if I had much anxiety to save my credit as a wise and practical person, I should not venture to stand forth in defence of the progressiveness of the human mind. I know that among all that class of persons who consider themselves to be *par excellence*, the wise and the practical, it is esteemed a proof of consummate judgment, to despair of doing good. I know that it is thought essential to a man who has any knowledge of the world, to have an extremely bad opinion of it: and that whenever there are two ways of explaining any fact, wise and practical people always take that way which attributes most folly, or most immorality, to the mass of mankind. Sir, it is not for me to dispute the palm of practicality with these sage and cautious persons. Howsoever it may be with all other aberrations of the human intellect, there is one description of errors from which it would be uncandid to deny that they are wholly free, viz. all those which arise from immoderate benevolence, or ill-regulated philanthropy. It behoves those who have discarded errors so pleasing, so encouraging, so ennobling to every virtuous mind, to be very certain that they have discarded them in favour of truth. Those who have stripped themselves so philosophically of every prejudice which acts as a stimulus to our duty, should be very sure that they have left no other prejudices of a more discreditable description behind. They may be assured that the errors of benevolence are by no means those from which human prosperity has most to apprehend, and however desirable it may be for the good of mankind that the love of virtue should never rise above temperate, we must be careful not to go on cooling it till it sinks to the freezing point. Sir, I do not feel my virtue to be of so warm and impetuous a character as to need any cooling, neither have I that confidence in my own judgement which would induce me to set up my opinion of truth in opposition to hopes and feelings which at least serve as a counteracting force against hopes and feelings far less pure, and I cannot but think far more pernicious. If we must err, at least let our errors not be on the side of selfishness; it is not that part, that element of the human constitution, which needs strengthening; there is not the slightest danger that it should ever be weaker than the good of human society requires.

But is it indeed an error to suppose mankind capable of great improvement? And is it really a mark of wisdom, to deride all grand schemes of human amelioration as visionary? I can assure honourable gentlemen that so far from being a proof of any wisdom it is what any fool can do as well as themselves, and I believe it is the fools principally, who have attached to that mode of proceeding the reputation of wisdom. For as I have observed that if there is a man in public or private life who is so impenetrably dull that reason and argument never make the slightest impression upon him, the dull people immediately set him down as a man of excellent judgement and strong sense, as if because men of talent and genius are sometimes deficient in judgement, it followed that it was only necessary to be without one spark of talent or genius in order to be a man of consummate judgement, because people are sometimes deceived by rash hopes in the same manner. I think I have observed that not the man who hopes when others despair, but the man who despairs when others hope, is admired by a large class of persons as a sage, and wisdom is supposed to consist not in seeing further than other people, but in not seeing so far. I mean no disrespect to some highly estimable persons, who are of a different opinion from myself on this question, but I am persuaded that a vast majority of those who laugh at the hopes of those who think that man can be raised to any higher rank as a moral and intellectual being, do so from a principle very different from wisdom or knowledge of the world. I believe that the great majority of those who speak of perfectibility as a dream do so because they feel that it is one which would afford them no pleasure if it were realised. I believe that they hold the progressiveness of the human mind to be chimerical, because they are conscious that they themselves are doing nothing to forward it and are anxious to believe that great work impossible in which if it were possible they know it would be their duty to assist. I believe that there is something else which powerfully helps many persons to the same conclusion, a consciousness that they do not wish to get rid of their own imperfections, and a consequent unwillingness to believe it practicable that others should throw off theirs. I believe that if persons ignorant of the world sometimes miscalculate from expecting to find mankind wiser and better than they are, those persons who most affect to know the world are incessantly miscalculating the opposite way, and confidently reckoning upon a greater degree of knavery and folly among mankind than really exists. These last indeed differ from the others in not being so ready to correct their error, since the same utter incapacity of taking any generous and enlarged views which caused their mistake, prevents them from discovering it, and makes them impute those effects of the better part of man's nature which they did not calculate upon, only to a different species of selfishness. I will even say, that so far from its being a mark of wisdom to despair of human improvement there is no more certain

185

indication of narrow views and a limited understanding, and that the wisest men of all political and religious opinions, from Condorcet to Mr. Coleridge, have been something nearly approaching to perfectibilians. Nay further, that the anti perfectibility doctrine, far from having the sanction of experience, is brought forward in opposition to one of the clearest cases of experience which human affairs present, and that by all just rules of induction we ought to conclude that an extremely high degree of moral and intellectual excellence may be made to prevail among mankind at large, since causes exist which have confessedly been found adequate to produce it in many particular instances.

In the little which I intend to say, I shall attempt little more than to expand and develope this last remark. There are others in this Society far more competent than myself to discuss in detail the past progress of the human mind, and the stages through which it is likely to pass in the road to further improvement. I leave it to them to point out how the difficulties are to be struggled with – it is enough for me if I can establish on the ground of solid experience, that these difficulties may be overcome.

I shall confine myself in the first instance to the question of moral improvement. I shall not ask you, Sir, to expect among mankind any degree of moral excellence that is without parallel. My standard shall be one which we all know, which we all believe in, with which we are all familiar in our own experience. I suppose it will not be denied that there are and have been persons who have possessed a very high degree of virtue. Now here I take my stand: there have been such persons. I do not care how many; nor who they were. If I were to name any person, any historical character, to whom I think the designation applicable, without doubt that person might be cavilled at and something raked up to throw a doubt upon his virtue, for it is difficult to adduce evidence on such a point that shall leave no possibility of cavil; but will those persons who say that this man or that man was not virtuous go farther and say that nobody was ever virtuous? I should think not. All they can say is that in the most virtuous there has been some frailty, some fault or weakness which has rendered even the best of them less than perfect. Certainly all this may be safely admitted. I shall not affirm that men in general can be made better than the best men whom the human race has hitherto produced.

Well then, here is a fact: there have been virtuous men: Now, what made them virtuous? I call upon the gentlemen on the other side to answer this question, for if it should turn out that those who are virtuous are so from causes which though they now act only upon a few, can be made to act upon all mankind, or the greater part, it is within the power of human exertion to make all or most men as virtuous as those are. I therefore challenge the honourable gentlemen to say to what they attribute the superior moral excellence of some persons. If they do not answer, I will. It is to the original influence of good moral education in their early years, and the insensible influence of the world, of society, of public opinion, upon their habits and associations in after life. Here then is specific experience. It is distinctly proved that these two forces, education and public opinion,[†] when they are both of them brought fairly into play, and made to act in harmony with one another, are capable of producing high moral excellence. And yet the greater part of the arguments which have been advanced against us this evening are intended to prove that moral education and public opinion are *not* capable of producing these effects.

Why then have these causes not produced the same effects upon all, which they have upon some? Why but because they have not acted upon all. No pains have been taken with the moral education of mankind in general. The great business of moral education, to form virtuous habits of mind, is I may say entirely neglected: the child is indeed punished for certain immoral acts, but as for going to the root of the evil, and correcting the dispositions in which these acts originate, the thing is never thought of, or if it is thought of, nothing can be more ridiculously inefficacious than the means which are taken to effect it. And all this from sheer ignorance: for it is not that people do not set a sufficient value upon those habits of mind which lead to good habits of conduct; it is that they really do not know how such habits are generated, what they depend upon, and what mode of education favours or counteracts them. While that education which is called education is in this deplorable state, that insensible education which is not called education is still worse, for almost every where the great objects of ambition, those which ought to be the rewards of high intellectual and moral excellence, are the rewards either of wealth, as in this country, or of private favour, as in most others; and it is an established fact in the nature of man that whatever are the means by which the great recompenses of ambition are to be obtained, the person who possesses these means and can therefore pretend to these recompenses, is the person who exercises influence over the public mind; he is the person whose favour is courted, whose actions are imitated, whose opinions are adopted, and the contagion of whose feelings is caught by the mass of mankind.

It is a very poor and ill divided public opinion, which can be formed out of an aggregate so ill composed. And yet that public opinion which is the result of so bad a moral education, is sufficient whenever it is combined with a better moral education to produce all the virtue which we see realized in some individuals of mankind as they now are.

It will of course be said that although good moral education and the operation of public opinion produce so much excellence in some persons, it does not follow that they can in all. I maintain on the contrary, that there is much less difficulty in producing it in all than there has been to produce it in some. Whatever of moral excellence now exists, has been produced in spite of a thousand obstacles: in spite of systems of education which if the names were altered and they were reported to us as existing in some far distant country would be considered incredible from the absolute fatuity, the utter abnegation of intellect which they exhibit; in spite of laws which in a hundred ways inflict evil upon one man for the benefit of another, and generate a spirit of domination and oppression on one side, of cringing and servility, mixed with bitter and vindictive resentment on the other; in spite of systems of judicial procedure which seem devised on purpose to give right and wrong an equal chance, and in which every possible encouragement is held out to the vice of insincerity – in spite of political institutions which in this at least, the most civilized country in the world, render wealth the only acquisition which is desired, poverty almost the only evil that is dreaded.† All these evils might be remedied by the hand of God. If notwithstanding all these things the best moral education which the present circumstances of mankind admit of has produced, in those to whom it is given, so much excellence, what may not be expected if we remove these obstacles, and when they are taken away, give even as good a moral education to the greater portion of mankind – why not to all mankind: for moral excellence does not suppose a high order of intellectual cultivation, since it is often found in greatest perfection in the rudest minds.

With respect to such doctrines as have been advanced this evening on the other side, some of them I must confess have surprised me. We have been told that it is impossible to diminish the amount of vice, because vice arises from the passions, and it is impossible to vanquish the passions. Now, Sir, I demur to this, first, that it is taking a very narrow view of the principles of morals and the nature of the human mind to suppose that it is necessary for any good purpose to vanquish the passions. There is not one of the passions which by a well regulated education may not be converted into an auxiliary of the moral principle: there is not one of the passions which may not be as fully and much more permanently gratified, by a course of virtuous conduct than by vice. And if this be the case, surely it would be the worst of policy even looking to moral excellence without regarding happiness in the least, to eradicate the passions, because it is they which furnish the active principle, the moving force; the passions are the spring, the moral principle only the regulator of human life.

But further, this very assertion that the passions cannot be vanquished may be taken as a specimen of the shallow philosophy of these gentlemen and their very superficial experience of mankind. They who profess to know human nature so well, seem to be very little aware what it is capable of. Have we not seen that men have lain for their whole lives upon beds of spikes; that they have stood all their lives upon the tops of pillars; that they have remained all their lives without stirring for one moment from a certain posture because they have willed it? Have they not swung by hooks drawn through their backs, and suffered themselves to be crushed by chariot wheels, and laid themselves voluntarily on funeral piles to be burned? Have not these things been done not by heroes and philosophers, but thousands and millions of common men, commonly educated? And then let gentlemen come and give us arguments which, if they prove any thing, prove the impossibility of all this. We could do none of these things: why? because we have never been accustomed to fix our imaginations on these things long enough for our first horror of them to wear off: but what caused these surprising achievements? It must have been either religion, conscience, or public opinion; gentlemen may choose, it shall be any one of the three: we have heard the force of each of the three separately explained away, and very plausible arguments adduced to prove that no one of them is strong enough to produce these effects. And yet the effects are produced. And let me ask these gentlemen the reason why? I will give up any two of the forces to them, but they must grant me the third. If they ask, my own opinion is that all helped, but that the proximate motive had most influence, that derived from public opinion: and some honourable gentlemen who have sometimes wondered at hearing public opinion spoken of in this Society as the immense force that it is, may perhaps now see from these instances why it is so spoken of. (Introduce a passage from Combe.) †

But if such is the force of public opinion, what is wanting to produce that high state of general morality which we aspire to? Simply that public opinion should be well directed in respect of morality: that such a system of education should exist, as will give to the mass of mankind, not learning but commonsense – practical judgement in ordinary affairs, and shall enable them to see that a thing is wrong when it is wrong, as shall make them despise humbug and see through casuistry and imposture, not to accept subterfuges and excuses for neglecting a duty, and not think the same thing laudable under a fine name and blamable under a vulgar one, for instance, not to think, like some persons in this room, that giving a man money, or money's worth, for voting against his conviction, is criminal when called bribery, but laudable when called legitimate influence of property: to judge of men by the manner in which they act, not by the manner in which they talk; not to estimate a man's moral excellence by the quantity of grimace which he exhibits in his own person, or by the quantity of hypocrisy which he exacts from his family and dependants; not to give men any credit for making great sacrifices at other people's expense, or for being philanthropic at a distance and prudent at home; not to think that charity consists in making laws to take away bread from the poor, and subscribing a few pounds annually to some institution for giving it to them; and in short not to see a great many other nice distinctions which the refined and cultivated people of the present day are able to see, and very ready to act upon. And there is another thing that is requisite – to take men out of the sphere of the opinion of their separate and private coteries, and make them amenable to the general tribunal of the public at large – to leave no class possessed of power sufficient to protect one another in defying public opinion, and to manufacture a separate code of morality for their private guidance; and so to organize the political institutions of a country that no one could possess any power save what might be given to him by the favourable sentiments, not of any separate class with a separate interest, but of the people.

Notes of my
Speech against Sterling

Delivered at the London Debating Society 1829[‡]

Before I commence, it is proper to explain to those who were not present at the last debate, the reasons which will induce me to occupy their attention with other topics and in another manner than what the terms of the question would suggest, or perhaps, in most cases, justify.

An honourable gentleman who spoke towards the conclusion of the previous debate, and whose speech, I imagine, most of those who heard it will not easily forget, has thought proper to ground his defence of the merits of Montesquieu[†] chiefly upon the demerits of those who have adopted a method of philosophizing opposite to that of Montesquieu in politics and legislation. Whether this be the proper basis to rest the discussion upon, is a question which will probably be answered differently by different persons: at all events I do not mean to contend that it is not, as it is my intention to imitate the honourable gentleman in making this, whether it be a branch of the subject or a digression from it, the principal topic of my speech. I am impelled to this by what, indeed, forms my only motive for troubling the Society at all on this question, and especially for undertaking the task, for which I feel myself wholly unfit, of opening the debate: I mean the desire of taking with as little delay as possible what appears to me the proper notice of the fierce attack which the honourable gentleman was pleased to make upon the principles and practice of those who think as I do on this question. The honourable gentleman was not content with stigmatizing their opinions as false. He ascribed to those opinions, all manner of demoralizing effects – there was no end to the expressions which he heaped, indicative of the odious or disagreeable habits of mind, which were connected with those opinions, and of which, as he told us, the character and lives of the persons who held them were a practical illustration. The persons of whom these things were alleged were generally all those the current of whose speculations on government and laws runs in a different channel from that in which he tells us, Montesquieu's did; but more particularly those, who profess the principles of Mr. Bentham. Sir, I do not profess to be a follower of Mr. Bentham; partly because no person, who thinks for himself, will ever call himself the follower of any one, and partly because I altogether dissent

191

from many of the opinions which those, who are ignorant enough to fancy that there is a Benthamite sect, are also ignorant enough to suppose to be the opinions of that sect.[†] And I believe, that of the far too great numbers of speeches which the indulgence of this Society has permitted me to make during this and the last two years, a majority would be found to have been made in opposition to some one or other of what are vulgarly considered to be the Benthamite doctrines. In those opinions of Mr. Bentham, however, which have been the object of the honourable gentleman's invective as in most of the opinions really professed by that great man, I have the misfortune to agree; and I consequently feel myself a party concerned in the honourable gentleman's denunciations, and as such, I do not feel disposed to sit down quietly under them. I am far from denying that among the countless aberrations of the human understanding it is possible that a person might think all which the honourable gentleman has said, and might think that it was his duty to say it. I take it however for granted that in resorting to this mode of controversy, the honourable gentleman did not reckon upon having the use of it entirely to himself. I conclude, that in dealing with his opponents after this fashion, he was alive to the possibility that those whom he attacked might one day come to the conclusion that the employment of this description of weapons on his part, justified a recourse to it on theirs. They have indeed hitherto remained tolerably passive under the animadversions which the honourable gentleman is in the habit of pouring forth against them, for various reasons, and among others probably because they did not consider it very dignified to evince an overanxiety to stand forth in defence of themselves on slight occasions. But they have entered into no compact with the honourable gentleman that he shall fight with daggers and they with foils: and they will probably think that it is now time for the honourable gentleman to be reminded that the censorial authority which he has assumed over us is one to which he has no title but by his own election of himself to that office. On the contrary I believe that the sense of the Society will go along with me when I say, that while we do justice to the honourable gentleman's talents, and are ready to submit to any moderate pretensions which he may set up to authority among us on that ground we yet do not recognize in him any such vast and immeasurable superiority to ourselves, as should *entitle* him to pronounce dictatorially upon the moral tendency of our principles and of our minds. Above all, we do not discern in him that calmness of temperament, that impartiality in collecting and care in weighing evidence, that power of representing to himself the feelings and the ideas of other men, or that accurate knowledge of the systems and opinions that he condemns which are necessary for executing so high a judicial office faithfully.

I believe the honourable gentleman does not seek to conceal, that he once held the opinions, which he now so strongly censures. Now I by no means wish to insinuate, that these opinions, as they existed in his mind, may not have been attended with every absurd and every immoral consequence which he deduces from them. From the apparent incapacity of the honourable gentleman to rest anywhere but in extremes, that was probably the case. But I would beg the honourable gentleman to remember that if in his mind, these opinions were really as absurd and as immoral as he represents them, the case is far otherwise in ours; and that we do not think it absolutely necessary that we should be bound by his inferences from our opinions: nay more: that we think ourselves fully as well qualified to judge what are the legitimate consequences deduceable from our principles as he is, having probably considered them much more; and that we do not precisely see why our morality should be made responsible for the errors of his logic. It has probably never entered into the mind of the honourable gentleman to reflect what a large assumption in favour of his own discernment is involved in the assertion that any set of philosophical opinions have a demoralizing tendency. For my part, I do not profess to understand all the bearings of an opinion, better than those who hold the opinion, and who have therefore so much stronger an interest than I have in discovering to what conclusions it leads. I know that those immoral consequences which may appear to me to follow from an opinion, may not follow from it considered in itself, but only when combined with some other erroneous opinion of my own. I know that there is no principle whatever which being conjoined with a sufficient number of sufficiently important errors of fact will not lead to immoral consequences. I know, that no conclusion can ever follow from a single premise; that two at least are requisite, and that very probably those to whom I am opposed may not acknowledge that other premise which is necessary to make the immoral consequence follow; that very possibly it is one which no rational person would acknowledge; and so the whole scheme of imaginary immorality may be futile. But though there is so much assumption in pronouncing any opinions to be essentially attended with immoral consequences, there is no assumption at all in supposing that an individual may have afforded ample evidence, with what consequences they are attended in his mind. And I will tell the honourable gentleman that if we are to judge what his opinions lead to, or what would result from them in a mind of a more austere or supercillious disposition, by the effect they seem to have produced even on a mind so much the opposite of those bad qualities as his own, principles more calculated to make men bigots and fanatics, and amidst the greatest external contempt for sects, to foster a spirit of mere exclusive sectarianism, never were promulgated among men. The honourable gentleman may think this very extraordinary; but what is a bigot, or what is a sectarian, except a person who is incapable of being just to men or opinions out of a certain pale, and who is perpetually ascribing evil qualities to them without ground? I am well aware that we are not entitled to impute these consequences to the honourable gentleman's opinions, which may be very true and very useful notwithstanding: and that all opinions have in themselves a certain tendency to sectarianism. But yet, it does appear to me that if there be any difference according to the nature of the opinion, that tendency must belong in rather a superior degree to those opinions, be they true or false, which elevate and swell men with the idea that they possess a superfine, a double-distilled virtue unknown to others, which teaches them, let us understand, not to detest the vices of other people but to despise their virtues as not being sufficiently lofty and refined. Enthusiasm we know is a powerful principle: And Vanity also is a powerful principle: but when Enthusiasm and Vanity are combined there is no limit to the lengths to which men are hurried, or to that injustice which they are capable of doing to other people.

I imagine that it will hardly be required of me by the Society that I should enter very particularly into the details of the honourable gentleman's charges of immorality, but I shall advert to one of the most curious of them, not assuredly with any purpose of repelling it, but because it illustrates a little of the nature of the honourable gentleman's own ideals of virtue, and renders it pretty easy to see what cause is likely hereafter to have the benefit of his support. He asserted with great emphasis that there is hardly any thing which has so corrupting an effect upon the mind as to be always looking with impatience and anxiety for some external change, and to be unquiet and uneasy because it does not happen. Now he cannot mean, that at no time, and in no place, and in no state of things is any external change necessary. I should suppose even the honourable gentleman's ardent optimism, his fervent liberality, will not carry him thus far: and indeed it does appear to me that when people are without bread they are likely enough to imagine that they would be the better for some external change which should feed them, and that when men are in the dungeons of the Bastille or of the Inquisition it is not unreasonable to suppose that they would be benefitted by any external change which should have the effect of letting them out. We must therefore conclude that in the honourable gentleman's opinion men may be suffering every extremity of misery for want of some external changes, but that nothing can be more degrading or more contrary to true virtue than to be rendered at all uneasy by the contemplation of this misery. It is not the man who causes the misery, upon whom the honourable gentleman's wrath is poured forth: *he* is protected by the honourable gentleman's reverence for whatever is hoary and venerable, and ancient of days, and there is nothing so ancient, nothing so hoary, and therefore I suppose nothing so venerable as sin: accordingly it is not the sin which calls forth the honourable gentleman's indignation, but the avenger. If this is to be the upshot of the honourable gentleman's supersublimated virtue, if it is to render men indifferent spectators of other men's misfortunes – if by its influence they shall not suffer with those whom they see suffer, if the spectacle of men bowed down by tyranny or worn out by privation is to give them no uneasiness and to inspire them with no desire to behold the tyranny overthrown and the privations alleviated, then it is impossible to conceive any system of morals more admirably adapted to serve as a cover and an apology for the vilest of selfishness. This is at least a new view of the nature of virtue, which places those who have too much feeling for other people in the foremost rank of vice. It is most true that any more than ordinary sensibility to the evils of others, or any very impatient anxiety for the amendment of the world is sufficiently apt to sour the temper and embitter the existence of the disappointed philanthropist, and that those who have spent their lives in protecting the feeble and righting the wronged have commonly enough a thankless office: but it is something new to hear them openly stigmatized as immoral themselves and the causes of immorality in others. I shall not stop to enquire how far this is consistent with the doctrines of One whom the honourable gentleman professes to reverence, of Jesus Christ, nor whether it was under the influence of such opinions as these that Howard spent his life in effecting external changes in the prisons of Europe and Hampden and Sidney met their death by endeavouring to effect them in the government of England. I shall bring the honourable gentleman to a less high standard by comparing him with himself. The time certainly was, nor is that time long gone by, when the honourable gentleman thought that great external changes were necessary. Does the Society remember the debate on the disfranchisement of Penryn? Does it remember the honourable gentleman's memorable peroration in which he described to us one after another in sounding sentences and with the most emphatic delivery, the great and crying evils of the external order of things in this country, and closed each successive article of the long catalogue by contemptuously declaring, that as a cure for these evils, the government would disfranchise Penryn? Nay, even the miserable contrivance of a ballot box did not in those days seem to the honourable gentleman a security absolutely to be despised. Let me ask, then, was it precisely from the honourable gentleman that those who held these same opinions were to expect a strain of intemperate abuse, on the same topics precisely which are employed against them by the most vulgar hirelings of the Tory faction? Those who think that the social arrangements of this country contain much requiring amendment are well aware that they have to reckon upon the bitter and unscrupulous hostility of all who make the vulgar objects of a low selfishness the end of their lives, from the prime minister down to him who furnishes penny a line slanders to the *Age* newspaper. But how happens it that for some time past the only persons towards whom the honourable gentleman has seemed to feel with any bitterness are those who pursue the same ends with himself for different reasons? What means this coalition in which he whose head rises so far above the clouds that whatever he may perceive that is to us invisible of the pure resplendent aether beyond, his vision as respects the affairs of this world seems to be sufficiently dim and misty, is side by side and arm in arm with the reptiles who grovel upon the earth? Is it the alliance – unnatural as some may esteem it, but as it appears to me the most natural and legitimate alliance that ever existed, between the extreme of spirituality and the extreme of worldlinesss, a virtue of pure speculation being the only one which is compatible with the very furthest extremity of practical vice? Or is it because one whose forte lies in invective and declamation is in the long run almost always found on the side of vulgar antipathy, because it is on that side chiefly and almost entirely that invective or declamation tells? Or is it, as I fear it is, because the pure light of transcendentalism, which had only dawned upon him when he made his peroration on Penryn, having since illuminated his mind with its meridian splendour, he has now become convinced that those external changes which he formerly wished for are not necessary? If so, keenly as we must regret the loss of the honourable gentleman's support to our cause, we perhaps ought to congratulate him in a worldly point of view, that he no longer holds any opinions which need at all stand in the way of his temporal advancement: that while his premises have been constantly receding farther and farther from vulgar apprehension, his conclusions, like the other pole of the needle have all the time been veering round in the opposite direction, and that he now sees all practical questions with the same eyes as the persons who have nothing but the light of their own self-interest to guide them. It is true, that of the many points on which the honourable gentleman once differed from that description of persons, he still differs from them on one. He still thinks that Manchester and Leeds ought to be represented, that is to say the property and intelligence of those places, words which he habitually joins together, as if there were any connexion between the two; as if intelligence, and what he calls property, that is to say large property, were not much oftener found apart, than in combination. Now as I am sincerely desirous of the honourable gentleman's worldly welfare, which even this solitary relic of his former radical opinions may materially impede, perhaps he will permit me to suggest to him that having proceeded thus far, he may just as well go one step farther. It has been again and again unanswerably urged by Mr. Canning that the property of Manchester and Leeds does not need representation; it is already virtually represented, a phrase which here at least involves no imposture. The men of property in Leeds are represented by the representatives of the men of property elsewhere between whose interest and theirs there is the most perfect identity. Have we not the men of greatest wealth in

Leeds and Manchester already in Parliament for other places? Who ever heard that the interests of Manchester had been sacrificed to those of Liverpool, or that Manchester, meaning thereby the men of property in Manchester, had ever suffered in the most minute particular for want of a representative? All descriptions of property are abundantly, and more than abundantly represented in the legislature, they have not only full protection for themselves but a great deal of undue power over other people. It is the men of no property as they are called who are not represented: it is the body of the people who are the owners of the small masses of property which being nothing to their superiors, and supposed to be nothing to them and who are not represented either actually or virtually in the House of Commons, while all the interests most decidedly opposed to them are. But it is not this portion of the inhabitants of Manchester and Leeds, that the honourable gentleman would admit to the benefits of a representation. I trust therefore that on further reflexion he will see, that he and his Tory allies are now quarrelling about a trifle, and that it is a pity such good friends should be divided by a hair's breadth and that he will be induced by what I have now said to review and alter this only survivor of his old opinions. He will then be fully qualified as a candidate for that bad eminence which Burke attained towards the end of his career when after having talked sense and virtue all his life to the powerful classes with as little effect as sense and virtue usually have upon the possessors of power, he all at once became their idol by furnishing them with a theory to their practice, with a philosophy to the measure of their inclinations by urging them for the love of virtue to do all manner of injury to those whom they hated for the sake of vice, by giving them fine new reasons why they ought to do those things to which they were already urged by every selfish and every malignant passion in their nature. Such is likely to be the fate of the honourable gentleman. He will never carry any person with him, but when he is attacking those whom his audience have far more substantial reasons than any he gives them, to dislike.

With respect to the merits of Montesquieu, the honourable gentleman has told us very little about them. But it appeared that the historical school of jurists, of which he told us that Montesquieu was the founder, stood very high in his estimation; not so much however for any thing which they did, but for something which they have not done: they did not fall into the error, which he says has been committed by Mr. Bentham, of imagining that there is a universal science of politics, applicable with certain modifications to all countries. They think on the contrary that every country ought to have its separate science of politics, founded on an attentive consideration of its history, and in which the conservation of all the principal institutions of that country and of all the habits and feelings of its people should be received as a fundamental axiom.

Now, Sir, these may be the honourable gentleman's opinions but it is altogether a mistake to suppose that they were Montesquieu's. Montesquieu did not undertake to treat of the science of politics or of legislation. It is only incidentally that we learn from his book any of his opinions on these subjects. Montesquieu's book is essentially a treatise on a branch of the philosophy of history: he treated of l'esprit des lois; i.e. the pervading principle of the laws of any country: his object was to enquire what are the circumstances which give to the whole body of the institutions of any country that peculiar character, which distinguishes them from the institutions of other countries. In doing this he of course had frequent occasion to shew not only why an institution had been established, but why it should be by adducing the reasons of expediency which had led to its establishment in different states: but what I wish to point out is that by the very nature of his design he was confined to the circumstances of difference in the situation of different nations, from which it by no means follows that he was insensible to the more numerous and far more important circumstances of agreement. Although his notions unquestionably were very often obscure and confused on various topics of what may be termed the metaphysics of law, I believe him to have been altogether guiltless of the absurdities to which the honourable gentleman, his defender, lays claim on his behalf. Doctrines which when we come to analyse them, amount to this, that there are no tendencies which are common to all mankind. For if there are any tendencies, common to all mankind and in particular if all the stronger tendencies of human nature are such, both those which require to be regulated and those whose agency you must employ to regulate them, it surely is not an irrational subject of enquiry, what are the laws and other social arrangements which would be desirable, if no other tendencies than these universal tendencies of human nature existed. And this, when ascertained, merely constitutes *pro tanto* a universal science of politics, although before we apply it to any particular nation we must also ascertain what are the tendencies peculiar to that nation, and correct the abstract principles of the science by the modifications which those tendencies introduce.

I was surprised at first to find that the honourable gentleman, professing to discuss the merits of two opposite schools of law, one of which was that of Mr. Bentham, should have adverted only to Mr. Bentham's opinions on constitutional legislation, omitting his much more original and valuable labours in other branches of the field of law: but the fact is that if the honourable gentleman had not acted in that manner, he would not have found any thing to differ from Mr. Bentham upon. Nobody ever supposed that the detailed provisions of the civil and penal code were to be the same for any two countries, or for the same country at different periods of its history. What is universal in this branch of the science

198

consists chiefly in what I have already termed the metaphysics of law, which belongs equally to all nations because it is in truth nothing more than the explication of the fundamental ideas which are involved in the very conception of a law, or a body of laws of whatever description. And this of which Montesquieu was absolutely ignorant, to which the Roman jurists made but a very distant approximation, and which by the way it would do the honourable gentleman no harm to study, is a branch of science which we owe entirely to Mr. Bentham and to those who have followed in his footsteps.

The honourable gentleman, however, confined his animadversions to Mr. Bentham's opinions on constitutional law; of which he seems to have formed rather a curious idea. He says that a tribe of North American Indians is the exact type and representation of Mr. Bentham's republic – for there we may see universal suffrage, daily parliaments, and the total absence of all such pernicious institutions as a church or an aristocracy, to which Mr. Bentham ascribes all the evils which exist. Now I really do not know that the honourable gentleman in the days of his radicalism may not have had the egregious folly to think, that a good government might be constructed out of negatives: but of this he may perfectly assure himself that Mr. Bentham does not: that in Mr. Bentham's estimation, there go some positive conditions to the making up of a good state of society as well as some negative ones, and that the negative conditions are only required in order to give to the positive conditions full effect. In order that the honourable gentleman may be enabled better to comprehend the nature of the blunder which he has been committing, I will beg him to suppose that he were a writer on medicine, of which I dare say that he knows a great deal more than he does of Mr. Bentham's philosophy; and that in this character he had composed and given to the world a treatise on poisons: and suppose that having read this book, I were to walk up to the honourable gentleman, present him with a bag of sawdust and to say, 'Look here. Behold the type, the *beau idéal* of your system of diet. Observe this sawdust: there is no arsenic in it, no verdigris, not one particle of corrosive sublimate is here, you are bound to give this to all your patients and make it their daily food.' Let the honourable gentleman consider what answer he would give to a person who should thus address him, and suppose himself answered in the same way.

With respect to universal suffrage and short parliaments which the honourable gentleman has most unaccountably found among a people who have no parliaments and no representative system at all, I will tell the honourable gentleman that he has himself done precisely what when it is done by any other person makes him so excessively indignant. He has taken the mere *accidents* of Dr. Bentham's system, those very parts of it which Mr. Bentham himself would allow ought to vary with difference of circumstances, and has insisted upon judging of the whole system by those accidents, keeping its great and leading principle wholly out of view. Universal suffrage and annual parliaments, let me tell the honourable gentleman, are in Mr. Bentham's apprehension nothing more than a particular set of means for giving effect to his system. The one great principle of Mr. Bentham's system is, that that body which like the House of Commons in this country, holds substantially in its own hands the governing power, should be chosen by, and accountable to, some portion or other of the people whose interest is not materially different from that of the whole. Now this, I am ready to maintain in the face of the honourable gentleman, is a universal principle in politics, a principle which he may add if he pleases to the two other principles respecting slavery and Christianity, which he says are not inconsistent with any form of government which ought to exist. And Mr. Bentham, of whose pretended universal science of politics the honourable gentleman has such a horror, gives so moderate an extent to that science, that he does not require the honourable gentleman to do more than add a third universal proposition to the two which he has already conceded; for wherever this one principle is in operation, there is Mr. Bentham's system: and in all the other parts of the social system the honourable gentleman is perfectly at liberty as far as Mr. Bentham is concerned, to determine himself by circumstances. Whether this principle is or is not in operation among the North American Indians I am not sufficiently conversant with that people to know. The honourable gentleman however might have found another people in North America, on the banks of the Ohio, and likewise a people on the other side of the British Channel, in both of which, by various means, and among others by the miserable contrivance of a ballot box, this sole principle of Mr. Bentham's system has been brought happily into operation; and either of which, I can assure the honourable gentleman is a much nearer approximation to the beau idéal of Mr. Bentham's republic, than the example which he suggested to us. And I am perfectly willing that the merits of Mr. Bentham's system should be tried by the effects with which it is attended in either of these cases, being persuaded, that these two nations considered as entire nations, are by many degrees the happiest and the most virtuous nations on the face of the earth: † and that although the form of their government would not of itself have sufficed to make them so, yet if it had not been for the form of their government those other circumstances which have so cooperated in producing the effect would many of them never have had existence, and such as did exist being entirely controlled and stripped of their beneficial effect might as well, for the happiness and virtue of the people, have likewise been nonexistent.

Speech on
The Church

Delivered at the London Debating Society 1828‡

My honourable friend the proposer of the question has observed in his speech, that it is difficult to speak against the church, because men will not listen to the evidence. The experience of the preceding evening has shewn that there is another difficulty, viz. that when they do listen to it, they are very much disposed to fritter it away. It would indeed be difficult to compose a speech on any subject that would stand the test which these gentlemen seemed disposed to apply to it. If you rest your case upon the universal principles of human nature, and shew that from the situation in which the Church of England is placed, certain actions are the natural consequences, this is called declamation and assumption, and you are asked for facts: when, in obedience to this demand, you bring forward facts, drawn from different periods of church history, these facts are exhibited singly, and you are triumphantly informed that each one, if there were only that one, might be a singular instance and was no proof of a general rule. If you allude to persecuting statutes enacted long ago, you are told that they were evidence of a spirit which no longer exists: if to shew that the spirit survives you observe that the laws still subsist even although it is not possible to execute them, you are told by way of reply that as the spirit is not strong enough to surmount an impossibility, no such spirit exists. If you cite a flagrant instance of direct persecution in what are considered by churchmen to be the best times of the church, you are told with much indignation that the church has changed. If you quote a modern instance, which fortunately happens to be universally known, they then at last stand at bay, drop all artifice and evasion, turn round upon the man who dares to condemn the persecution, and accuse him of sympathizing with the impious. And here, Sir, I cannot help blaming my honourable friend, not indeed for the warmth with which he repelled this accusation, for most assuredly if it was a charge to be repelled at all, it was a charge to be repelled warmly. But I blame him because the accusation, coming from the quarter it did and on the occasion on which it did, was one which he had reason to be proud of. I am thankful to the honourable gentleman for the term – I invite the honourable gentleman to apply it to me – I should blush to be that which

201

the honourable gentleman would not call a friend of the impious. I thank heaven that my heart is not so hardened by bigotry nor my understanding so perverted by lawyercraft but that I can sympathize with an oppressed man, whatever may be his religious opinions. The man, be he Christian or Atheist who endures torture and ignominy because he will not swerve from his convictions is to me a martyr, and I should detest myself if I could not venerate him as he deserves. What is it to me if Mr. Carlile† is not a good reasoner? I never thought him a good reasoner: but he is what I respect infinitely more, he is a man of principle, and a man who will stand to his principles though he should stand alone, and though to be merely supposed to sympathize with him is tantamount to an accusation of impiety, shall I, because this man is not a good logician, – a man who is as ready to die at the stake for what he thinks the truth, as any clergyman of the Church of England can be ready for what he thinks the truth to conduct him thither, – shall I knowing how few such men there are and how much is due to those few when they arise, be deterred from expressing my disapprobation of their persecutors by a cry of impiety? Let the honourable gentleman keep such stuff for the House of Commons: there he will find in hundreds of bosoms a chord which will respond to that which vibrates in his own: but I much mistake the tone of feeling in this Society, if it contains one man, Tory or Churchman though he be, to whom such feelings as the honourable gentleman gave utterance to, on the preceding evening, are not entirely unknown.

With regard to the question in hand, it would certainly be a waste of words to discuss, whether or not the Church of England is a persecuting church, with a gentleman who thinks that to immure Mr. Carlile and about twenty of his coadjutors in dungeons for terms of two, three, and five years is not persecution. If a man squares his conscience by what the church does to him of course the church can never be in the wrong; and if the good old practice of burning heretics were revived, no doubt some persons would be still found who would maintain that even this was not persecution. But my honourable friend who spoke fourth on the preceding evening is not of this stamp, and to him a somewhat different answer is due. He had discretion enough to admit the iniquity of these persecutions but affirmed that they are not imputable to the clergy of the Church of England. I am glad, Sir, that this is the line of defence now resorted to by the more able advocates of the Church of England because, in the first place, it shews that in their opinion the time is now come when such proceedings as those which have taken place against Mr. Carlile no longer admit of being openly defended: but further, I rejoice to learn that these are the sentiments of my honourable friend, because as he seems on this occasion to exculpate the church, not because such proceedings are defensible, but because the church has no share in them, I am led to conclude that if it could be proved to his satisfaction that these persecutions *are* in any degree imputable to the church, he would no longer consider the church capable of being defended on this ground. Now I shall easily be able to adduce evidence, which will satisfy even my honourable friend's scepticism on this point. I do not pretend that the church alone is to blame; there is enough of religious bigotry, God knows, both in other professions and in other sects, although the existence of a powerful body who are bound by interest to work up that baneful spirit, to the highest pitch cannot have much tendency to mitigate it, at least: But there is a good deal to be said in respect to the part which the Church of England has actually taken in the persecution. My honourable friend in speaking on this subject, has shewn (to parody an expression of Mr. Sheridan)[†] a very pious ignorance on some topics: he has buried all transactions of this description, anterior to the late prosecution of the Rev. R. Taylor, in discreet oblivion. In that proceeding he says that Dissenters were the chief agents, and seems not to be aware that the prime mover in the affair, Mr. Alderman Atkins, is no Dissenter but a most orthodox highchurchman. Although, however, my honourable friend cannot carry his recollection any further back I can, and I can state for the benefit of his rather short memories, that more than one-half of the prosecutions of Mr. Carlile, his family and his coadjutors, were at the prosecution of the Society for the Suppression of Vice.[†] Now although I give my honourable friend credit for a very considerable degree of ingenuity, I do not suppose him to possess so great a share of it as to be able to explain away the list of subscribers to that Society: a list comprising nearly as great a number of bishops, and dignitaries of the church as subscribed to that other creditable establishment, the Bridge Street Association, which last attempt to revive the execrable tyranny over political opinion, the good sense and virtue of this country crushed in the bud. As I have alluded to this final ebullition of feelings which, though as far as ever from being extinguished, no man now dares avow, I cannot help saying, that I find it difficult to decide which aspect of the affair tells most against the reverend subscribers; the odiousness of the design, or the contemptible imbecility of the execution. The whole funds of that Association sufficed only for, I believe, nine prosecutions – and these in every, or almost every instance, directed against mere accessories and not principals in what they pretended to call an offence. But the Association is gone, where all such Associations ought to go – gone, I should say for ever, were it not that clergymen, who according to the well-known remark of Lord Clarendon,[†] understand the least and take the worst measure of human affairs, of all men who can read or write, are likely enough to suffer themselves to be hoaxed out of a little more of their money by some cunning attorney, who if he can succeed in persuading them that his object in asking for it is to make use of it for the purpose of helping to degrade the human mind, can make himself sure of raising, among a large portion of them at least enough to make his own fortune by law expences, which is generally the purpose of the more prominent agents in such transactions.

But if this institution is now no more, the Vice Society still exists; and by this Society were most of the prosecutions against Carlile and his followers instituted. Here introduce the gloating.

My honourable friend has told me that the clergy gloated over his sufferings: this was perhaps going a little too far since there are persons to be found, and very likely some of them may be subscribers to the Vice Society, who, as is reported on one occasion of Napoleon, can with maudlin sensibility weep for the evils they inflict. This however is small consolation to the sufferer. The very fact, that such proceedings could emanate from a Society so named, is a pregnant proof of the spirit which prevails among its lay and clerical members. Suppression of opinions they term suppression of vice: the honest promulgation of doctrines different from what they consider right they have the audacity to term a vice, an act of immorality: I do not affect surprise at this; it is far better to say plainly that he who does not believe as they do, is *ipso facto*† a vicious and profligate man, than to impute all manner of other vices to him, as they have almost invariably done. The common vice of partisans, that of heaping calumnies upon the head of an opponent, is one by which it is matter of common observation that priests of all religions whether from blind credulity or from a still worse principle have been distinguished beyond all other men. The clergy of the Church of England have not, it is true, come quite up to the mark of the Roman Catholic clergy in this respect, because they have never had so much power of making false statements uncontradicted; but they have carried the practice of defamation as far as it could with safety be carried, and have by their calumnies embittered the lives of men among the brightest ornaments of human nature.

If my honourable friend has made so lame a defence of the church on the subject of religious prosecutions, his coadjutor has made a still more feeble one on the subject of those badges of a more widely spreading spirit of persecution which exist on our statute book under the name of the Test and Corporation Acts.† The honourable gentleman says that those Acts were not intended for the support of the church: The honourable gentleman is a good lawyer; but Blackstone was a better; and if the honourable gentleman is right, Blackstone is wrong; for Blackstone says expressly that these Acts exist for the support of the church. But, when I find the honourable gentleman ignorant of the tricks by which the Protestant Dissenters were persuaded not to oppose these Acts, under the pretence that they would not be enforced against them, tricks which are wittily typified by Arbuthnot† under the emblem of Don Diego persuading Jack to hang himself, under pretence that Sir Roger would cut

204

him down; when I likewise find the honourable gentleman ignorant, at least apparently so, of the too celebrated Act of Uniformity;[†] when I find him equally ignorant of the equally celebrated statute termed the Occasional Conformity Act[†] passed to keep out those who, although Dissenters, yet not considering the service of the Church of England to be profane or idolatrous, thought that they could conscientiously attend it occasionally and thereby escape the disabilities of the law – when I see all this and when I find him absolutely astonished that Hume should be considered a good witness against the church, a man who sold his conscience for them, a writer who violated every law of historical veracity in order to screen the church   I am tempted to ask, under what High Church parson, in what obscure corner of the kingdom remote from all access of books and converse of men, the honourable gentleman imbibed his knowledge of history. The battle of the church really is not to be thus fought – we all know how great allowances ought to be made for an extemporaneous effusion but it really is a fact, that some knowledge of the subject is necessary even to make a defender of the church; and until the honourable gentleman shall have acquired such knowledge or at least shall have it more under his command than he appeared to have on the former evening, it would be much wiser in him were he to leave the cause of the church in the hands of my honourable friend who so ably followed on the same side.

I have now concluded by far the greater part of what I intend to trouble the Society with on this evening. It was in fact only in order to support and vindicate my friend the proposer of the question, that I felt desirous of taking any part whatever in the discussion, since I do not consider the question to be one which admits of being discussed with much prospect of advantage in a debate, at least if the end in view be mutual persuasion. The difference between us is too deeply rooted, and is connected on both sides with too great a number of extensive and important principles, each of them far more than sufficient to form in itself the subject of an animated and protracted discussion. How, for instance, can we agree in our estimation of the church in respect of the support which it lends to the aristocratic institutions of this country, so long as there is one portion among us who disapprove of these institutions, and think that every support which they possess is one too many, while the remainder so far from thinking that any support should be taken away, are of opinion that those institutions require, and ought to have still stronger supports than they possess? Or how again can two of the ablest speakers on the last evening, agree in their estimate of Hume's argument in favour of a church establishment, that it diminishes the activity of the clergy; when the one is a warm admirer and partaker of religious enthusiasm, and the other condemns it under the name of fanaticism? There is a great deal more involved in this question than can be stated in a debate, and I should despise the man who, having previously been of a different opinion, could be convinced in an evening by my honourable friend's arguments or by mine. I believe it is perfectly well understood between my other honourable friend and me, that his opinion is the legitimate consequence of his principles, and my opinion of mine. I do not however think that a discussion of this sort is wholly useless. Though it does not enable us to compare our several views, it enables all of us to know what they are; which I cannot but consider as a point gained in favor of truth and fair dealing, since I think I have observed that much of the misrepresentation and misunderstanding which take place both in public and in private life, and very serious impediment to the fair and legitimate collision of opinion arises from real *bona fide* ignorance on one side, of the views and principles of the other. It is so important, that a perfect mutual understanding should exist on this point, that I think I shall be justified in occupying five minutes more of the Society's time for that purpose. As my object is only that gentlemen should know the reasons, not that they should be convinced by them, five minutes will suffice for that purpose as well as an hour. My honourable friend has given us an able statement of *his* reasons, and I freely admit that several of them are deserving of grave consideration. I do not at present intend to contest those reasons; I have only to state my own; and I shall be satisfied with one grand one, but that indeed may be said in a certain sense to include all the rest. I am an enemy to church establishments because an established clergy must be enemies to the progressiveness of the human mind.

I hold, that it is of the nature of the human mind to be progressive. But stop: I must not forget that there are persons in this country, and for aught I know in this Society, to whom the march of intellect, which is another word for the progressiveness of the human mind, is a subject of laughter and derision.[†] I know indeed that this feigned laughter is in reality a cloak for the most abject fear, and that it would be a most delightful relief to the minds of many of these laughers if they could really feel towards the march of intellect all the contempt they express. Still, however, since there are such persons, I think it advisable not to use any expression at which they are likely to cavil. I hold then, that it is of the nature of the human mind to profit by experience. As the aggregate of our experience is every day increasing, this of itself has a tendency to render the species progressive: but besides this we become better qualified to profit by experience in proportion to the culture of our intellectual faculties, and of that culture there are two great instruments, education and discussion. I hold that wherever mankind have been qualified to profit by experience, by possessing even in a moderate degree, these two great instruments, they have, as the mass of experience has increased, constantly grown wiser and better; and that this progressive advancement has never been interrupted but when these two means of instruction have been prevented from existing by despotism as in the Roman Empire, by anarchy as in feudal Europe, or by superstition and priestcraft as in Spain and Portugal. I further hold, that from the present state and future prospects of Great Britain, France, and North America, there is humanly speaking, no probability that these causes of retrogression should ever again recur, and that from the increasing diffusion and growing power of the two great instruments, education and discussion, it is to be expected that the human mind in these countries will continue to advance, not only with an unretarded, but as it has done during the last twenty years, with a rapidly increasing pace.

Now it is to this great tendency of the human mind, and to education and discussion as the promoters of it, that in my view of the matter, an established clergy by a sort of moral necessity must be, and at any rate always is, the bitter enemy. When I say an established clergy I mean any clergy, which is paid on condition of teaching a particular creed, but more especially a clergy connected with the governing powers of the state, and bound by that connexion to the support of certain political tenets as well as religious ones.

If there were a corporate body of physicians or a corporate body of engineers paid by the state, rewarded with honours and wealth, on condition that they should always teach a certain set of doctrines in physic or mechanics, it can scarcely be doubted that such a body would be interested in preventing all improvement in physic or mechanics, lest the public should get beyond their particular tenets, and having done so should cease to regard these their teachers with due veneration. Happily this is not the case. Neither the physician nor the engineer is bound down to a particular set of opinions in their respective sciences; the clergyman is. Wherever there is a hierarchy – wherever there is such a thing as church government, adherence to certain tenets is the condition on which he holds both his emoluments and his power. If there be not only a hierarchy but a hierarchy connected with the ruling powers in the state, it becomes the interest of its members to uphold the existing government with all the political and moral, as well as religious prejudices, which may conduce to their holding that government in veneration. It will perhaps be said, that these opinions are the right opinions. This may be true; but it likewise may be false. It would be a considerable stretch of arrogance in mankind to suppose that they had already attained the pinnacle of knowledge either in religion or politics; it is highly probable that there is still room for improvement in both: I am sure there is much need at least so long as our perfect government finds it very difficult to prevent half our population from dying of hunger and our perfect religion has not yet found the means of preventing our jails from being constantly full. I shall not however chuse to rest my case upon any argument which implies that it is possible for an established opinion to be wrong. I will suppose that our clergy teach no opinions but such as are right, either in religion or politics. It is not the less true that in the progress of human improvement, every one of these opinions comes to be questioned. The good of mankind requires that it should be so. The good of mankind requires that nothing should be believed until the question be first asked, what evidence there is for it. The very idea of progressiveness implies not indeed the rejection, but the questioning of all established opinions. The human intellect is then only in its right state when it has searched all things, in order that it may hold fast by that which is good. Now when this spirit of universal enquiry arises, it must extend to those two most important subjects: the experience of all ages warrants the assertion that when the human mind once begins to improve, men will discuss religion and politics and no force, which does not go the length of crushing the spirit of improvement altogether, can prevent it. In consequence of this discussion persons are sure to arise who dispute the established opinions. These persons are listened to, they are allowed at least a patient hearing. This the clergy will never voluntarily allow. It is of no use to say that the clergy may defend their opinions; so they may; and if the opinions be true, and be defended with as much ability as they are attacked, they will be defended successfully. But this would give an immensity of trouble. It is well known that richly endowed bodies are never very fond of trouble: it is allowed both by the friends and the enemies of opulent church establishments, that the love of ease is always their predominant infirmity. Besides the trouble there is moreover always a lurking apprehension, lest after all their endeavours to keep the people in the right path should not succeed, or if it should, people should no longer duly venerate their pastors for communicating to them truths which, as they had examined into the evidence, they would seem to owe to their own understanding alone. How much easier and how much safer would it be, if they could be prevented from enquiring at all, if they could be made to regard the very act of enquiry, nay the very thought of questioning an established opinion, as involving the deepest guilt. It is true that they will not then hold these opinions like rational creatures, but it is of no consequence to the clergy that they should hold them like rational beings, provided they only hold them strongly enough: and no opinions are held so strongly as those which we are taught that it is impious even to demand a reason for.

Such are the motives which induce an endowed clergy to be the enemies of discussion, and as discussion always accompanies improvement they are the enemies of improvement. In order to prevent discussion, they have not scrupled, wherever they had the power to debase the human mind down to the level of the brutes. In all countries where they could get the civil power to side with them, that is in almost all the Catholic countries of Europe, they have succeeded in their nefarious purpose, and mankind are still grovelling at their feet. It is very idle to say that these are Catholic priests, and therefore not to be quoted against the Church of England. That the Catholic priests perpetrated these things is not owing to any peculiar perversity in the nature of the men, it is owing to their interests as priests, aided by a religion which gave them more power to effect their purposes, but did not give them a stronger motive. In England at the reformation it became the interest of the civil power to raise public feeling against the church, and the latter consequently had no longer much power either moral or political of effecting its ends, but as soon as, under Charles I, it found the civil power ready to renew the alliance, it recommenced its war against the progress of the human mind, and nearly succeeded in throwing us back to the condition of France and Spain. Fortunately the habit of free inquiry had in the preceding years been too strong to be checked, and we were saved by a revolution from the double consummation of civil and ecclesiastical tyranny. Though this grand conspiracy had failed the Church of England has never ceased its resistance in the detail. Not one step has been made from persecution to religious liberty but in the teeth of their most strenuous opposition; never have they suffered one particle of discussion in religion and politics which it was in their power to prevent; not a step has been taken with their good will for the diffusion of education. I speak of them as a body. They have never originated any one plan for spreading or improving it – and whatever plans have been prepared by others, from the Lancastrian and Infant Schools up to the University of London† they have, as a body most violently opposed except that in most of these instances when they at last found that the thing would go on in spite of their opposition, they have, as the next best thing to preventing the improvement altogether, attempted to keep it in their own hands for sectarian purposes. As people would read, they might read the Bible and the Prayerbook: but as for reading the Bible without the Prayerbook, No, no, that was not to be endured. Their only doubt was whether the persons who proposed it were Atheists, Deists, or Dissenters. The word of God was not fit to be read, unless that of man was administered along with it: and their account of what God said, or what in their opinion he should have said, was to be forced down the throats of babes and sucklings avowedly on the ground that unless a belief in it were firmly fixed in the mind at an age previous to that at which the reasoning faculty begins to operate, in all probability the habit would never establish itself at all. But I have exceeded the time which I allowed myself for stating the grounds of my disapprobation of the church. I have stated them sufficiently for purposes of information. It was not my object to state them for purposes of argument – Here therefore I shall stop.

209

Speech on
Secular Education

Date and occasion unknown (after 4 November 1850) ‡

Sir, the commencement at Manchester of a movement for a national education not under the control or management of either established or non-established clergy has already, it would seem, made no inconsiderable impression on the public, or else *The Times* has made a false move and miscalculated the signs of the coming public opinion; for already at the very beginning of the agitation that journal has discovered, what it did not find out in the case of the Corn Law League† until the fourth or fifth year of its existence, that the thing is not merely a good thing, but what is so much better in the estimation of *The Times*,† a thing destined to succeed. The promoters doubtless thought no less, but they probably did not expect so early a recognition of their prospects. How much then it is to be lamented that an enterprise of so much promise should have been inaugurated by an act of truckling and compromise; that for the sake of conciliating people who are not to be conciliated and whom it ought not to have been an object to conciliate, the Association should have let itself be persuaded by Mr. Cobden,† aided by some dissenting ministers, to sacrifice its distinctive flag, and instead of calling itself an Association for secular education should have sheltered its timidity under the ambiguous designation of *unsectarian*.

If this is only a change in words and means nothing it deserves no better name than that of deception; if it does mean anything, if by *unsectarian* is to be understood something different from secular education, the broad principle of religious freedom which was to be the foundation of this great educational movement is abandoned.

In the debates of the Conference there was a good deal of misunderstanding, some of it I fear rather wilful on the part of Mr. Cobden and his supporters respecting the import of the word *secular*. There is no uncertainty about it. There is not a better defined word in the English language. *Secular* is whatever has reference to this life. Secular instruction is instruction respecting the concerns of this life. Secular subjects therefore are all subjects except religion. All the arts and sciences are secular knowledge. To say that *secular* means irreligious implies that all the arts and sciences are irreligious, and is very like saying that all professions except that of the law are illegal. There is a difference between irreligious and not religious, however it may suit the purposes of many persons to confound it. Now on the principles of religious freedom which we were led to believe that it was the purpose of this Association to accept, instruction on subjects not religious is as much the right of those who will not accept religious instruction as of those who will. To know the laws of the physical world, the properties of their own bodies and minds, the past history of their species, is as much a benefit to the Jew, the Mussulman, the Deist, the Atheist, as to the orthodox churchman; and it is as iniquitous to withhold it from them. Education provided by the public must be education for all, and to be education for all it must be purely secular education.

When, then, the Association refuses to say that their education is secular but are willing to say that it shall be unsectarian, what do they mean? Doubtless that it is still to be exclusive, though in a minor degree. That religion is to be taught, but not sectarian religion. That they are not to have Church of England teaching, or Catholic teaching, or Baptist, or Methodist, or Unitarian teaching, but I suppose Christian teaching; that is, whatever common elements of Christianity are supposed to be found in all these sects alike. How far this is likely to conciliate the various classes of sectarians the Association will probably hear loudly enough from the sectarians themselves. I am much mistaken if they will be at all thankful for any religious teaching which expresses no opinion on a subject on which Christians differ in opinion, or if the substratum of universal Christianity which it is proposed to teach will appear to them at all different from Deism. But this is their concern. I take higher ground. I maintain that if you could carry all the sects with you by your compromise you would have effected nothing but a compact among the more powerful bodies to cease fighting among themselves and join in trampling on the weaker. You would have contrived a national education not for all, but for believers in the New Testament. The Jew and the unbeliever would be excluded from it though they would not the less be required to pay for it. I do not hear that their money is to be refused, that they are to be exempted from the school rate. Religious exclusion and inequality are as odious when practised towards minorities as majorities. I thought the principle of the Association had been that of justice, but I find it is that of being unjust to those alone who are not numerous enough to resist.

I cannot help remarking how much less confidence professed Christians appear to have in the truth and power of their principles than infidels generally have in theirs. Disbelievers in Christianity almost always hail the advance of public intelligence as favourable to them; the more informed and exercised a mind is, the more likely they account it to adopt their opinions: but I cannot find a trace of similar confidence in most of the professedly religious. If they hold their belief with the same full assurance as the others their disbelief, surely infidels and the children of infidels are those to whom, even more than to any others, they would be eager to give all instruction which could render their minds more capable of pursuing and recognising truth. A person is without religious belief, or in other words is in their estimation in a state of the most pitiable, the most calamitous ignorance by which anyone can possibly be afflicted, and for this reason they refuse him instruction, they refuse him knowledge and the cultivation and discipline of the intellect as if they thought that mental cultivation could not possibly be favourable to Christianity, unless the mind is first strongly prepossessed on its behalf. Such sentiments as these are not complimentary to Christianity nor to the sincerity of their belief in it. Its greatest enemy could say nothing worse of it than that either ignorance or early prejudice is the soil it must have to flourish in, and that to instruct unbelievers, to make them rational and thinking beings, is but to confirm them in unbelief. I hoped that the founders of the Lancaster Association had been persons who thought that mental cultivation opens the mind to all truth, whether expressly taught or not. Let us hope that this conviction is still theirs and will guide and animate their labours; but they have missed through pusillanimity a splendid opportunity for inscribing it on their banner and proclaiming it in the face of the world.

Textual Notes

The works contained in this volume are the same as those of the *Autobiography* which Harold Laski edited for the World's Classics in 1924. The six speeches were then published for the first time. The substantive imperfections and omissions in both this and the First Edition of the *Autobiography* have been corrected here, and Mill's spelling and punctuation followed in large part. The textual history of the *Autobiography* itself is complex, and for a detailed study of all variants the reader is referred to the definitive work: *Collected Works of John Stuart Mill*, Vol I, *Autobiography and Literary Essays*, edited by John M. Robson and Jack Stillinger, University of Toronto Press 1981. Noticed here will be (1) text omitted from the First Edition; (2) passages in early drafts omitted in the final draft where these are of substantial import. For the speeches, see the textual notes below and *Collected Works of John Stuart Mill*, Vols XXVI and XXVIII.

Omissions from the First Edition

When Mill died on 7 May 1873, his will, dated 14 February 1872, named his step-daughter Helen Taylor his literary executor. She was given authority to publish the *Autobiography* or not at her will. When the book was published at price 7s 6d by Longmans, Green, Reader, and Dyer on 17 October 1873, Helen Taylor had excised ten short passages, totalling 563 words in all. The reason was the same in each case: they were passages referring to herself, mostly in terms of high praise. Also omitted was the first paragraph of the section which Mill wrote last.

Passages in early drafts later omitted

Mill's wife, Harriet Taylor, read and marked extensively Mill's first draft. In response to her marking, Mill made numerous alterations. In the words of Robson and Stillinger (op. cit. p.xxv) he 'suppressed personal and family details that, had they been retained, would have made the *Autobiography* a warmer, if often more critical document'. She also caused him to tone down his account of his own practical deficiencies, and some, though by no means all, of the passages praising herself.

The first draft was composed in the early months of 1854, when Mill supposed his own death to be imminent, and assumed that his wife would survive him, and probably edit and publish his text. In 1861, two or three years after his wife's death, he returned to the work. Where he is covering the same ground as in the early draft, he is in general more detached. He omits all reference to his mother. In the early draft he had spoken of his father's 'ill-assorted marriage' and of the lack of 'kindred intellect, tastes or pursuits'. It is not clear whether omissions are made out of kindness, or because he simply did not wish to mention at all the mother whom he supposed to have gravely offended him by lack of attention to his wife. He also toned down some references to his father's severity and ill-temper. He omitted hostile or cool character sketches of acquaintances such as Roebuck and Maurice. The last part of the text was written in the winter of 1869–70. Here the picture is more general, years pass more rapidly, and a general impression is left (not one shared by those who encountered Mill in the 1860s) that he was living out an unimportant extra bit of life after its *raison d'être* had departed with Harriet's death in 1858. The existing texts are:

(1) Early Draft. Acquired by University of Illinois in 1958, it consists of 169 leaves, 139 forming the first version of the book with 30 rejected leaves.

(2) Columbia MS. Purchased by Professor J.J. Coss for Columbia University Library in 1923. A revision and continuation of the Early Draft, this is the only draft of the whole work and, as Mill's final version, the authoritative copy-text. Its existence seems to have been unknown to Laski when he edited the World's Classics edition.

(3) Rylands Transcript. A transcript of the final version, mostly in the hand of Helen Taylor, including the passages suppressed by asterisks in the First Edition. It consists of 282 leaves. A substantial number of the errors it contains were corrected against the final version before the First Edition was printed. It came to light in 1959, and was acquired at Sotheby's by the John Rylands Library, Manchester.

(4) Yale Fragment. A short passage of about four pages in Mill's own hand, probably written after 1861, which covers, in a form later enlarged, the time immediately following his wife's death, with reflections on her collaboration in his writings.

Abbreviations for the following notes:
ED = Early Draft
C = Columbia MS
Y = Yale fragment
HT = marginal note to ED in handwriting
     of Harriet Taylor (Mrs. Mill)

Page 2, l.19   ED has, after 'upheld':
and to which he had not, and never could have supposed that he had, the inducements of kindred intellect, tastes, or pursuits.
Page 6, l.41   After 'continually' a cancelled passage in ED has:
no book ever delighted me more.
Page 9, l.34   After 'experiment', a cancelled passage in ED has:
This was a very easy and pleasant part of my mental education and by no means the least valuable part of it.
Page 13, l.11   After 'shape', ED has:
My private exercises in composition during my thirteenth and fourteenth year changed from historical to dramatic; though indeed they were

historical still, for my dramatic attempts were on historical subjects. Like most youthful writers I wrote tragedies: the first was on the Roman emperor Otho, the attraction to me not being the character or fortunes of the hero, but the movement and bustle of that portion of Roman history, as related by Tacitus. I wrote a play on the story of the Danaides, and began two more, one on a subject from Tacitus, another from Thucydides. What kindled my dramatic aspirations was not so much Shakespeare as the plays of Joanna Baillie, among which *Constantine Paleologus* appeared to me one of the most glorious of human compositions. I have read it since and I still think it one of the best dramas of the last two centuries.

Page 14, l.29   A cancelled version of ED has in place of 'employment': occupation, relieving him from the necessity of writing for subsistence,

Page 16, l.24   After 'above par', a cancelled passage of ED has:
I am, as all are aware who have intimately and closely observed me, not only not above par, but decidedly and greatly below it
A later cancelled version has:
But in every one of these natural gifts, as all are aware who have intimately or closely observed me, I am, to say the least, rather below than above par
HT altered 'every one of' to 'all' and deleted 'as all are ... observed me' and 'to say the least'.

Page 16, l.32   After 'effected', cancelled passage in ED has:
I am satisfied also that it could be done without the very considerable drawbacks with which in my case it was accompanied and which have pursued me through life.
     One drawback, which if it had existed would have rendered the whole of the intellectual education worthless, did not exist in my case

Page 17, l.41   Cancelled passage in ED has after 'at all':
I have, however, since found that those who knew me in early boyhood thought me greatly and most disagreeably self-conceited; the reason of which was, that I was disputatious, and made no scruple to give contradictions to what was said on things which I knew nothing whatever about. How I came by this detestable [altered to: offensive] habit, I do not know. Probably from being on the one hand, accustomed to lay down the law to my younger sisters, and having no other companions to withstand me
HT deleted: on things which I knew nothing whatever about.

Page 18, l.13   After 'presence', cancelled passage in ED has:
My mother did tax me with it, but for her remonstrances I never had the slightest regard.

Page 26, l.26   Cancelled version in ED has:
the most fortunate human life very little worth having;
This is in place of 'human life ... best'.

Page 27, l.25   After 'mischievous', HT wrote:
It is indeed generally true that knaves do less mischief in the world than fools. A dishonest man stops when he has got what he wanted, a fool carries on his foolishness thro him on to his descendants.

215

Page 28, l.5   'possible'. In place of three lines after 'intolerant' ED has:
nor does he err because he judges them by his own standard, but because
his own standard is wholly or partially wrong; and because his
antagonism to the opinions he dislikes is a stronger principle than his
desire to enlarge and rectify his own doctrines.
A cancelled version of ED has:
an inquisitor judges a heretic to deserve the fire in this world and
damnation in the next. When my father erred it was where his standard
was too narrow, and omitted some of the elements of right judgment
which might have been found scattered among the judgments of those
whom he condemned.

Page 29, l.28   HT supplied: 'close … father', altering Mill's original
text: greater closeness of my father's connexion with him

Page 39, l.20   In ED, in place of 'if … realized', there is:
for if the world has a ruler, and but one ruler, that one is certainly far less
deserving of worship than the author of the Sermon on the Mount.
A cancelled passage of ED has in place of 'that … than':
the character of that one must be atrocious, and the worship of such a
Being more morally degrading, if not more intellectually contemptible,
than almost any adoration which is capable of being directed to [the
author of the Sermon on the Mount.]

Page 42, l.16   After 'associated', cancelled passage in ED has:
not even in my father; although my father was as high principled as Mr.
Austin and had a stronger will; but Mr. Austin was both a prouder man,
and more a man of feeling than my father

Page 42, l.23   After 'much', ED has (in earlier version):
and who indeed made a sort of companion of me, to a certain extent, for
the next year or two

Page 53, l.29   After 'blemishes of it', ED has:
there were two articles in particular which I individually took extremely to
heart. [Probably he refers to W.J. Fox 'Men and Things in 1823' and
T.S. Smith 'Education' (1824)].

Page 53, l.35   After 'improve it', cancelled passage in ED reads:
My first contribution to the review was in the second number. In my
father's article the detailed shew-up of the *Edinburgh Review* had been left
unfinished, and he wished me to attempt to finish it. I had one
qualification for doing so, a strong indignation at many of the articles
which I had read in the course of my reading and notetaking for my
father's use. But I can now see that there was something ridiculous in this
pretension of a youth, not yet eighteen, to sit in judgment on some of the
principal writers of the time. The thing however was written and
published, and what seems strange, many if not most of its readers did
not suspect that the continuation was by a different hand from the first
article. So incapable are most people, when the *fond* of the thoughts is the
same, and the manner imitated, to distinguish the borrowed from the
original. The article of course was not, and could not be, anything more
than a theme written on the ideas which had been instilled into me by my
teachers. The style was bony and wiry, very unlike the writing of a young

person, but with a certain degree of vigour and of polish. No one but myself wrote any part of it, or even corrected it; but it went through an incredible amount of elaboration from myself under my father's eye, he giving it back to me repeatedly part by part to be amended, or cancelled and begun again, either to throw in more and better thoughts or to bring them out more pointedly in the expression. I suppose there are few sentences that were not rewritten with great pains and effort nearly a dozen times. The article was worth little enough in any other respect but to me it was very valuable as practice in composition.

In the same number of the review there were also articles by Charles Austin and Ellis; and gradually most of the writing radicals of my father's or my acquaintance were brought into play

HT made numerous small alterations, before (probably) inducing Mill to omit it.

Page 54, l.17   After 'thirteen articles' cancelled passage reads:
These were on subjects much more level than my first with my acquirements and experience:

Page 56, l.3   ED has 'persuasion' instead of conviction, and a cancelled passage adds 'amounting to arrogance'.

Page 56, l.27   ED has a full stop after 'conversation', then:
But what was [cancelled addition: 'ludicrously'] false of Bentham was to some extent true of my father:
The continuation as in published text from: 'He *was* sought ...'

Page 57, l.4   After 'rarity' ED has 'especially in England'.

Page 58, l.40   Cancelled passage in ED has in place of 'an almost unbounded': a most exaggerated

Page 59, l.30   After 'several', ED has:
I have already spoken of his rejection of both Christianity and Deism, both of which he regarded not only as false but as morally mischievous.

Page 60, l.22   ED does not have 'No one ... time', but instead:
I even proposed to myself to chronicle our doings, from that early period, on the model of Grimm's *Correspondence*, and actually for some time kept a journal with that intention. Charles Austin had a project of a philosophical Dictionary, suggested by Voltaire's, in which everything was to be spoken out freely; I entered eagerly into it and sent three or four articles (the only ones, I believe, ever written) towards a commencement of it. My particular companions and Charles Austin's however did not much associate with one another: an attempt we made to bring them together periodically at his lodgings was soon given up, and he and I did not long travel in the same direction. The head quarters of me and my associates was not my father's house but Grote's, which I very much frequented. Every new proselyte and every one whom I hoped to make a proselyte, I took there to be indoctrinated. Grote's opinions were at that time very much the same both in their strong and their weak points as those of us younger people, but he was of course very much more formed, and incomparably the superior of all of us in knowledge and present abilities.

Page 60, l.38   Instead of 'ambition', this earlier version in ED was cancelled by HT:

As for myself most of those common objects were quite sufficiently attractive to me. Money, indeed, having no expensive tastes, I only wished for as a means of independence and of promoting public objects; but ambition …'

Page 61, l.33   After 'particular', cancelled text in ED has:
And therefore we had at this time no idea of real culture. In our schemes for improving human affairs we overlooked human beings.

Page 62, l.4   In place of 'for the … conduct', ED has:
for the regeneration of human life

Page 64, l.40   After 'Courier', ED has in cancelled version:
(whom as a writer my father placed almost at the head of modern literature)

Page 69, l.5   After 'above him', ED has:
I made an elaborate reply to him at the next meeting, but he was not there to hear it; and except a few words interchanged between us as soon as he had done speaking, of admiration on my side, and politeness on his, we remained strangers to each other until I met him at dinner at M. Guizot's in 1840.

Page 70, l.14   After 'time longer', ED has:
… and took their part well in several debates. Robert Hildyard, a clever and vehement speaker from the Cambridge Union, then a violent radical Benthamite, since a Tory and Protectionist writer in the *Morning Post* and now a silent Derbyite member of Parliament, spoke two or three times well, and some new men, among others Henry Taylor, Vernon Smith and his brother Leveson, occasionally took part. But in the main the debates during the whole season rested on me and Roebuck: and very uphill work it was in the latter part of it, even the Villiers and other founders of the society having ceased to attend. In the season following, 1826/27, we had acquired …

Page 70, l.40   After 'listened to' ED has:
… and I even acquired a certain readiness of extemporary speaking, on questions of pure argument, and could reply offhand, with some effect, to the speech of an opponent: but whenever I had an exposition to make in which from the feelings involved or from the nature of the ideas to be developed, expression seemed important …

Page 71, l.17   After 'original funds' ED has:
contributed by Bentham

Page 81, l.11   ED has after 'depression' cancelled passage:
About Midsummer of that same year 1828 I set out on a short walking tour: for months before I had been in my old state of gloomy dejection, though as I have already mentioned not so intense as at first; this continued the greater part of the first day, but the walk by the side of Thames from Reading to Pangbourne, in one of the loveliest of summer evenings with the western sky in its most splendid colouring before me, and the calm river, rich meadows and wooded hills encompassing me, insensibly changed my state, and except a short interval two days later I had no return of depression during that excursion nor for several months afterwards.

Page 81, l.31   After 'influence', ED has:

At present my estimate of Wordsworth as a poet is very far indeed below that which I then formed

where C has: 'There have ... than Wordsworth'.

Page 83, l.30   ED here has a long analysis of Roebuck's character.

Page 85, l.32   The preceding paragraph is a shortened version of an account of Sterling in ED.

Page 88, l.10   'definite'. A cancelled passage in ED has:

I did not at this time push my logical speculations any further.

This was not the only modification which was taking place in my old opinions in the political department of things. The early writings of the St. Simonian school, with which I had now become acquainted, were gradually opening my eyes to the very limited and temporary value of the old political economy, which assumes individual hereditary property as a necessary fact, and freedom of production and exchange as the dernier mot of social improvement.

Page 95, l.2   ED has note after 'altogether':

This was an error I frequently committed: for example, in the summer of 1832, when the country was preparing for the first elections after the passing of the Reform Bill, I wrote several articles in the *Examiner* in strong opposition to the exaction of pledges from representatives. ['Pledges', *Examiner*, 1 July 1832, pp.417–18 and 15 July 1832, pp.449–51]. The doctrine of these articles was right in itself, and very suitable to democratic institutions when firmly established and rooted in the habits of the people: then no doubt it would be wise in the electors to look out for the most honest and most instructed men whom they could induce to take the office of legislators, and refrain from binding them beforehand to any definite measures: but I did not sufficiently consider that the transition from bad to good institutions was only commencing. Like many other persons at the time, I thought that we had had our revolution; that the way was now smooth for the advance of democracy, that precautions were henceforth chiefly required against the evils which might come from the popular side; and I little anticipated that the coming years would require a long continuance of the struggle to give democracy even its due influence.

Page 97, l.28   Here ED has an acid analysis of Mrs. Austin's character, accusing her of professing maternal feelings for himself which were not genuine, and of aping opinions she did not sincerely hold.

Page 104, l.20   ED has here:

During the first years of our acquaintance the principal effect of her nature upon mine was to enlarge and exalt my conceptions of the highest worth of a human being. The poetic elements of her character, which were at that time the most ripened, were naturally those which impressed me first, and those years were, in respect of my own development, mainly years of poetic culture. My faculties became more attuned to the beautiful and elevated, in all kinds, and especially in human feeling and character, and more capable of vibrating in unison with it; and I required, in all those in whom I could take an interest, a strong taste for elevated and poetic feeling, if not the feeling itself. This however did not check, but gave additional animation to my activity in all the modes of exertion for public objects to which I had been accustomed. I retained unabated interest in radical politics, kept up my connexion with such of the rising or promising politicians on the radical side, as I was previously acquainted with, and even became more involved than before in political as well as literary relations.

Page 106, 1.35   ED has a dismissive account of Grote's ineffectiveness in Parliament.

Page 112, 1.23   Laski proposed 'reticences' for 'retinences'.

Page 124, 1.13   After 'its side', ED has a cancelled passage:

The success of the *Logic* led to the publication in 1844 of the Political Economy *Essays*, written as I have already mentioned in 1830 and 1831. With this terminates what may be termed the second period of my writings; reckoning the old *Westminster Review* period as the first. The *Principles of Political Economy* and all subsequent writings belong to a third and different stage of my mental progress, which was essentially characterized by the predominating influence of my wife's intellect and character. Up to this time I have spoken of my writings and opinions in the first person singular because the writings, though (after we became intimate) mostly revised by her, and freed by her judgment from much that was faulty, as well as enriched by her suggestions, were not, like the subsequent ones, largely and in their most important features the direct product of her own mind: and the opinions, though in a state of continued growth, were not generically different from those which I had gradually wrought out on emerging from the narrowness of my original Benthamism. But in the great advance which I have since made in opinion I was wholly her pupil. Her bolder and more powerful mind arrived before mine at every conclusion which was derived from a more thorough comprehension of the present and insight into the future; and but for her intellect and her high moral feelings leading me on, it is doubtful if I should ever have advanced much further than the point I had now reached.

HT marked this passage, apparently indicating that she wished part or all of it omitted.

Page 125, 1.30   ED has after 'on herself':

and we disdained, as every person not a slave of his animal appetites must do, the abject notion that the strongest and tenderest friendship cannot exist between a man and a woman without a sensual relation, or that any impulses of that lower character cannot be put aside when regard for the feelings of others, or even when only prudence and personal dignity require it.

A cancelled passage goes on:

Certain it is that our life, during those years, would have borne the strictest scrutiny, and though for the sake of others we not only made this sacrifice but the much greater one of not living together, we did not feel under an obligation of sacrificing that intimate friendship and frequent companionship which was the chief good of life and the principal object in it, to me, and, conscious as I am how little worthy I was of such regard, I may say also to her.

Page 126, l.27   In ED, after 'industrious', HT wrote in margin:
The voice of Society on the great fundamental questions of social and political morals should be the voice of all.

Page 131, l.11   In place of 'writing' ED has:
even writing

Page 131, l.18   ED ends here. The First Edition (and Laski) departed from C over the following ten paragraphs by omitting the fourth altogether (the transition paragraph 'In resuming my pen ...') and reordering the others as follows: 5, 6, 1, 2, 3, 10, 7, 8 and 9.

Page 132, l.33   This is the point where Mill finished writing by 1861. What follows was written in the winter of 1869–70.

Page 133, l.4   This and the following two paragraphs are an expanded version of Y (which is headed 'Note, to be expanded in a supplement to the biographical sketch, concerning the participation of my wife in my writings'.)

Page 135, footnote, l.9   Mill mistakenly wrote *Système*.

Page 137, l.31   Y ends here.

Page 139, l.31   The following five lines (paragraph 10 in the note to p.131, l.18 above) end the section where text is transposed in the First Edition.

Page 143, l.16   Helen T. excised:
Miss Helen Taylor, the inheritor of much of her wisdom, and of all her nobleness of character,

Page 143, l.24   Helen T. excised:
... and have already made her name better and more widely known than was that of her mother, though far less so than I predict that if she lives, it is destined to become. Of the value of her direct cooperation with me, something will be said hereafter: of what I owe in the way of instruction to her great powers of original thought and soundness of practical judgment, it would be a vain attempt to give an adequate idea.

Page 143, l.27   Helen T. excised:
another companion, stimulator, adviser, and instructor of the rarest quality.

Page 143, l.31   Helen T. excised:
the least considerable of whom, and above all the least original, is the one whose name is attached to it.

Page 144, l.21   After 'written', Helen T. excised:
at my daughter's suggestion

Page 144, l.28   After 'published', Helen T. excised:
it was enriched with some important ideas of my daughter's, and passages of her writing. But ...

Page 147, l.11   After 'Contest in America', Helen T. excised:
And I shall always feel grateful to my daughter that her urgency prevailed on me to write it when I did: for we were then on the point of setting out for a journey of some months in Greece and Turkey, and but for her, I should have deferred writing till our return.

Page 158, l.17   First Ed. has 'defending'. Laski emended correctly.

Page 164, l.33   After 'proposal', Helen T. excised:
The time appeared to my daughter ... complete independence of the others.

Page 166, l.8   After 'burthen', Helen T. excised:
At this time ... the most successful, were hers.

Page 170, l.5   After 'occasions', Helen T. excised:
especially at the meetings of the Women's Suffrage Society,

Page 170, l.8   After 'additions', Helen T. excised:
by my daughter and myself,

Page 171   Fabian Society typescript. The whereabouts of the MS is unknown. First published in Laski's edition of the *Autobiography* (as were the other speeches included in this volume).

Page 176   The MS is in the Mill-Taylor Collection.

Page 183   The MS ends here. A further ten paragraphs, based on typescripts, are printed in *Collected Works*, Vol XXVI, pp.380–5

Page 184   The MS is in the Mill-Taylor Collection.

Page 191   The title derives from Mill's own inscription on the MS in the Mill-Taylor Collection. The present text includes additional material from Fabian Society transcripts and a MS fragment in the University of Toronto Library. In *Collected Works*, Vol XXVI, the speech is entitled 'Montesquieu,' reflecting the motion for debate: 'Montesquieu as a political and philosophical writer is not worthy of the character he usually bears.'

Page 201   The MS is in the Mill-Taylor Collection. The Fabian Society typescripts include an additional fragment which is reproduced here.

Page 210   Fabian Society typescript.

Explanatory Notes

Chapter I

Page 1

History of British India. Published early in 1818. It is an entirely bureaucratic history, composed mainly from India Office files. James Mill showed little curiosity about the life, thoughts and feelings of actual Indians.

Page 2

India House. The East India Company comprised three divisions, the Secretary's, the Military Secretary's and the Examiner's. James Mill's appointment was in the first.

before or since. Mill exaggerates here. Bentham was a highly respected and very prosperous member of society, and the imaginative literature of the time was full of fundamental controversies.

Page 3

Æsop's Fables. Æsop was a slave on the island of Samos in early 6th century BC. The *Fables* were familiar to many English readers (including children) in translation.

Anabasis. Xenophon's account of return of Greek mercenaries to safety (401–399 BC) after employment by Persian king, Cyrus. Xenophon lived about 428–354 BC.

Herodotus. (?484–?420 BC), historian of early Greece, especially of war with Persia.

Cyropaedia. A historical novel, featuring Cyrus the Elder, king of Persia, written in opposition to the theories of Plato.

Memorials of Socrates. Written between 381 and 355, defending Socrates against charges brought in 399 BC.

Diogenes Laertius. Dates unknown, perhaps first half of 3rd century AD. Historian of ancient philosophy.

Lucian. (b. c. AD 120). Author of *Menippean Satires*, especially noted for ridicule of popular paganism.

Isocrates. Athenian Orator (436–338 BC).

six dialogues. i.e. *Euthyphron, Apology, Crito, Phaedo, Cratylus, Theaetetus*. Plato c.429–347 BC.

Greek and English lexicons. Reviewing *Autobiography* in *Contemporary Review*, December 1873, J. M. Capes pointed out that there was a Greek–English lexicon, and that it was characteristic of James Mill to refuse to use it, since it was designed for the elucidation of Biblical Greek.

Page 4

Newington Green. Part of Southwark, later overtaken by growth of London.

Hornsey. 4½ miles north of King's Cross, central London.

Robertson. William Robertson (1721–93), author of *History of Scotland* (1759), *Charles V* (1769) and *History of America* (1777).

Hume. David Hume (1711–76), historian and philosopher, author of *History of Great Britain* (1754–62).

Gibbon. Edward Gibbon (1737–94), author of *Decline and Fall of the Roman Empire* (1776–88).

Watson. Robert Watson (?1730–81), author of *History of Philip II of Spain* (1777). Engaged on Philip III at time of his death.

Hooke. Nathaniel Hooke (d. 1763), friend of Alexander Pope, author of *Roman History* (1738–71).

Rollin's Ancient History. 11 vols, 1734–7.

Plutarch. (c.50–120 AD). His *Lives* were sources for Shakespeare, Montaigne, Dryden and others.

Burnet. Gilbert Burnet (1643–1715), voluminous historian. *History of His Own Time* published posthumously 1724–34.

Bentham. First mention of his father's influental mentor and patron, Jeremy Bentham (1748–1832), legal theorist and utilitarian.

Frederic. Lived 1712–86, known as the Great.

Paoli. Lived 1725–1807, friend of Samuel Johnson and Boswell.

American war. War of Independence from Great Britain of 1770s and '80s.

Millar. John Millar (1735–1801) produced *Historical View* 1787.

Page 5

Mosheim. Johann Mosheim (1694–1755), Professor at Göttingen, published his Latin ecclesiastical history in 1726.

McCrie. His biography of John Knox, Scottish Protestant (1505–72), published 1813.

Sewell. Willem Sewel (1654–1720) published his history in Dutch 1717. English version 1722.

Rutty. John Rutty (1698–1775) published his history in Dublin 1751.

Beaver. William Beaver (1766–1813), naval officer, published *African Memoranda* 1805.

Collins. David Collins, (1756–1810), soldier and colonial governor, published an account of N.S.W. 1798–1802.

Anson. George Anson (1697–1762), circumnavigator. Account of voyages published in 1748.

Hawkesworth. John Hawkesworth (1715–73) published *Voyages* 1773.

Drake. Sir Francis Drake (?1540–96), circumnavigator and admiral, victor over Spanish Armada, 1588.

Cook. James Cook (1728–79), circumnavigator, discoverer of Australia.

Bougainville. Louis-Antoine Bougainville (1729–1814), French circumnavigator.

Robinson Crusoe. Published in 1719 by Daniel Defoe (1660–1731). Here, for once, Mill's taste was in tune with that of ordinary C19 boys.

Arabian Nights. Translated from Arabic anonymously 1705–8.

Cazotte. Jacques Cazotte (1719–92), French author.

Don Quixote. Published 1605–15 by Cervantes (1547–1616) in Spanish. Influential on Fielding and other C18 English writers.

Popular Tales. Published 1804 by Maria Edgeworth (1768–1849), Irish novelist.

Fool of Quality. Published in Dublin 1765–70 by Henry Brooke (1703–83).

Cornelius Nepos. (c.99–24 BC). The first surviving biographer in Latin.

Caesar's Commentaries. Julius Caesar (100–44 BC). *De Bello Gallico* and *De Bello Civili*, accounts of his own military exploits, published in 58–52 BC.

Iliad. Of Homer, the first major Greek poem. Date much disputed.

Page 6

translation. Alexander Pope (1688–1744) published his *Iliad* (1715–20).

Euclid. The most famous of Greek geometers (fl. 300 BC). Invariably used for teaching of geometry in C19 England.

Virgil. Virgil (70–19 BC) generally reckoned greatest of Roman poets. By *Bucolics* Mill probably means *Eclogues* and *Georgics.*

Æneid. Virgil's greatest epic of Rome.

Horace … Epodes. Horatius, Roman poet (65–8 BC). Best known for *Odes. Epodes* may have been omitted on grounds of indecency.

Phædrus. Thracian slave (c.15 BC–50 AD). His *Fables* are largely based on those of Æsop, mentioned earlier.

Livy. (?59 BC–17 AD), historian of early Rome.

Sallust (?86–35 BC), Roman historian.

Ovid. Roman poet (43 BC–17 AD) wrote *Metamorphoses* mainly from sources in Greek myth.

Terence. Roman playwright (?190–?159 BC), his comic and naturalistic plays were partly based on Greek of Menander.

Lucretius. Roman poet (?94–?55 BC), author of Epicurean poem, *De Rerum Natura.*

Cicero. Most famous of Roman orators (106–43 BC).

Atticus. Cicero's literary adviser and publisher (110–32 BC).

Odyssey. The other great work of Homer.

Sophocles. One of the greatest of Greek tragedians (496–406 BC).

Euripides. Greek tragedian (485–406 BC).

Aristophanes. Greek comic dramatist (?450–?385 BC).

Thucydides. Great historian of the Pelopennesian War (?460–?400 BC).

Hellenics. History of Greece from 411–362 BC.

Demosthenes. Athenian orator (384–322 BC).

Æschines. Athenian orator (397–322 BC).

Lysias. Athenian orator, though not an Athenian citizen (459–380 BC).

Theocritus. Pastoral poet (?300–260 BC), b. Syracuse.

Anacreon. Lyric poet (b. ?570 BC).

Anthology. Collection of short epigrammatic Greek poems.

Dionysius. Probably Dionysius of Halicarnassus, who wrote in Greek on Roman history, planning his work as a supplement to Livy. It began to appear about 7 BC.

Polybius. Greek historian of Rome (?200–118 BC).

Aristotle's Rhetoric. Aristotle, Greek philosopher (384–322 BC), published his *Rhetoric* about 362 BC.

Mitford's Greece. William Mitford (1744–1827) produced history of Greece to death of Alexander 1785–1810.

Page 7

Ferguson. Adam Ferguson (1723–1816) published *Roman Republic* in 1783.

Licinian Laws. Probably the *Liciniae Pompeiae* (70 BC) on restoration of tribunate and the *de provincia Caesaris* (55 BC) which prolonged Caesar's Gallic command.

Niebuhr. Great German historian of Rome, whom Thomas Arnold and other English historians regarded as their master.

Agrarian Laws. Probably those of the brothers Gracchus of 133 BC which distributed parts of large estates to the poor.

Page 8

Winter. One of the four blank-verse poems *The Seasons* published 1726–30 by James Thomson (1700–48).

Joanna Baillie (1762–1851), Scottish poet and dramatist. She published *Constantine Paleologus* in 1804.

Milton. John Milton (1608–74), English poet. Published *Paradise Lost* 1667.

Page 9

Goldsmith. Oliver Goldsmith (1728–74), Anglo-Irish poet, novelist and dramatist.

Burns. Robert Burns (1759–96). Scotland's national poet.

Gray's Bard. Thomas Gray (1716–71) published 'The Bard' in 1757.

Cowper. William Cowper (1731–1800).

Beattie. James Beattie (1735–1803), Scottish philosopher who wrote a poem called *The Minstrel*.

Spenser. Edmund Spenser (?1552–1599) left his great epic *The Faerie Queen* unfinished at his death.

Walter Scott. Walter Scott (1771–1832) acquired a reputation as a poet before he became a novelist.

Dryden. John Dryden (1631–1700). Published *Alexander's Feast* 1697.

Campbell. Thomas Campbell (1777–1844) produced *Gertrude of Wyoming* in 1809. 'Lochiel' and 'Hohenlinden' are war songs.

Joyce. Jeremiah Joyce (1763–1816) published *Scientific Dialogues* in 1807.

Thomson. Thomas Thomson (1773–1852), chemist, supporter of Dalton's atomic theory.

Organon. Logical treatise by Aristotle.

Page 10

scholastic logic. The work of the mediæval schoolmen, e.g. St Thomas Aquinas (c.1225–1274).

Hobbes. Thomas Hobbes, philosopher (1588–1679).

Bagshot Heath. A high tract of land in Surrey and Berkshire.

Sandhurst. College in Berkshire for training of military officers.

Page 11

Tacitus. Roman historian (?56–?115 AD).

Juvenal. Roman satirical poet, published early 2nd century AD.

Quintilian. Roman rhetorician and literary critic, born in Spain c.30 AD.

Gorgias. Dialogue on nature of justice.

Protagoras. Dialogue containing view that pleasure is only good.

Republic. Theory of ideal state.

Socratic method. Method of argument based on questioning opponent's assumptions.

Page 12

intellectus sibi permissus. Mind free to roam.

elenchus. Testing of general statements by examples.

vague generalities. This was a favourite phrase of Bentham, used to criticise all who spoke of ideas and feelings of which he was ignorant.

Page 13

East India Company. It is ironical that this organization which governed India until after Mill's own retirement, and provided father and son with their living, should have found in John Mill one of its last diehard defenders when the inevitable transfer to the Queen's government occurred under Lord Palmerston. See p.131 and note.

Page 14

Indian administration. A characteristic example of Mill's unreasoning adulation of his father. When he came to write *On Liberty* (1859), Mill seems to have realized that if his argument in that book was correct, then the principles of administrative despotism on which the government of India was conducted must have been wrong. He met the difficulty by saying that an Indian of eighty was, for political purposes, still a child.

Ricardo. David Ricardo (1772–1823). Jewish economic theorist, published his *Principles of Political Economy* in 1817. Before the attacks of Carlyle and Ruskin, its Free Trade doctrines were widely regarded as 'scientific'.

Page 15

Elements of Political Economy. Published by James Mill in 1821. John Mill thus became part author at the age of fifteen.

Adam Smith. Lived 1724–90. Generally regarded as the founder of modern economic theory.

Page 16

education. Here, as often, Mill is on the side of tradition. His assumption that no-one would prefer other kinds of education even if Latin and Greek were well-taught is perhaps characteristic.

cotemporaries. The charming exaggeration of this, which would, if interpreted literally, entail the consequence that Mill could have taken a

First in Greats before he was born, springs from genuine modesty, and a persistent unawareness of the intellectual gifts which all his contemporaries knew him to possess.

Chapter II

Page 21

Butler. Joseph Butler (1692–1752) published his *Analogy of Religion, Natural and Revealed*, in 1736.

Page 22

Sabæan. Literally worship of host of heaven. Here apparently used as equivalent to …

Manichæan. Manes, a 3rd century heretic, taught a dualism, possible derived from the Zoroastrian (mod. Parsi) religion. James Mill's toleration of this view is directly related to his encounter with Christianity being with a heretical Calvinist form, which seemed to him to make God directly responsible for evil.

Lucretius. Lucretius used the example of the mythical sacrifice of Iphigeneia by her father, Agamemnon, as an example of evils caused by superstition. (*Tantum religio potuit suadere malorum*).

ne plus ultra. Ultimate reach.

Christianity. Here Mill's attitude to his father's mistake in identifying the Calvinist heresy with Christianity is very characteristic. He does not say that his father is wrong, but instead gives Christians the credit for abandoning a doctrine that most of them, and all in the Catholic tradition, had never dreamed of holding.

Page 23

Reformation. We cannot tell whether Mill noticed his father's inconsistency here. Having attributed the doctrine of Calvinist reprobation, introduced into Scotland by the Protestant Reformation, to all those Christians who vehemently repudiate it, he then praises that same Reformation for introducing 'liberty of thought'.

Page 25

religious. Mill apparently means 'high-minded' or 'moral' or 'reverent' thus trying to avoid a contradiction in terms.

Memorabilia. Recollections of Socrates, published 381 BC onwards.

Choice of Hercules. Hercules (Gk. Heracles) was offered the choice between virtue and pleasure, and chose virtue which led to immortality.

Socratici viri. Followers of Socrates.

Page 26

Stoic. The philosophy was founded by Zeno about 300 BC according to which pleasure and pain were indifferent, and only virtue had value.

Epicurean. Epicurus (b. Samos 341 BC, d. Athens 270 BC) taught that happiness was the only end of life, and held a metaphysical materialism.

Cynic. Followers of Diogenes of Sinope, who rejected all conventions, and was indifferent to material possessions.

Page 28
disagreeable to them. A characteristically robust endorsement of discipline in
education.

Page 29
Hume. Joseph Hume (1777–1855).
Godstone. Near Reigate and Redhill, Surrey.

Page 30
Westminster. Central London.
middle class life. It is striking to find Mill sharing the 'medieval' sentiments
of Horace Walpole, Walter Scott and some romantic poets.
France. Mill's conviction of the superiority of French intellectual life to
English was life-long. But he does not speak of what was probably
equally important, that it was one of the few times before the latter's
death in 1836 that he was able to escape his father, not only the tyrant
at home, but his official superior at the India Office.
Sir Samuel Bentham. A much younger brother of Jeremy, Sir Samuel lived
1757–1831. Eminent naval architect and engineer.
Gosport. Near Portsmouth, Hampshire.
Edgeworth. The educational theories of R.L. Edgeworth, father of Maria,
the novelist, were regarded as 'progressive' because of the stress on
learning by free enquiry.
Pompignan. J.-J. Marquis de Pompignan, author of a satirical opera,
directed at Voltaire.
Pau. Pau, S.W. France, was known throughout C19 for its English colony.

Page 31
low and petty objects. Cf. note to *France,* p.30.

Page 32
M. Say. Jean-Baptiste Say (1767–1832).
Saint-Simon. Saint-Simon (1760–1825), French social philosopher, held
that scientific and industrial men should be the real rulers of society.

Page 33
old friend of my father's. Joseph Lowe.

Chapter III
Page 35
Political Economy. See note to *Elements* p.15.

Page 35
Cours d'Etudes. Etienne de Condillac (1715–80), friend of Diderot and
Helvetius, published *Traité des sensations* in 1754, *Cours d'études du
Prince de Parme* 1769–73.
French Revolution. A good example of Mill's comparative ignorance, in the
midst of his precocious erudition, of the literature of his youth.

Wordsworth, Coleridge, Scott, Hazlitt, Byron, Shelley and others, were always writing in the shadow of the Revolution. The word 'democracy' begs many questions, ignoring the Terror and the Napoleonic dictatorship.

Louis XIV and XV. Kings of France 1643–1715 and 1715–74.

death. Louis XVI reigned 1774–1792, executed 21 January 1793. His queen, Marie Antoinette, executed 16 October 1793.

Lavoisier. Antoine-Laurent Lavoisier (1743–94), famous French chemist.

Bonaparte. Napoleon Bonaparte, soldier, lawgiver and Emperor (1769–1821).

Girondist. Revolutionary party in France overthrown in June 1793. Most of the leaders were executed. Mill's dream of moderate Revolution seems to be a synthesis of Whiggish, progressive English traditions, and fervour derived from reading about French revolutionaries.

Austin. John Austin (1790–1859). Jurist, collaborator of Bentham.

Page 36

Blackstone. Sir William Blackstone (1723–80). His *Commentaries* (1765–1769) embodied the view of law as based on tradition and precedent which Bentham and James Mill attacked.

Traité de Législation. Much of Bentham's work was published earlier in France than in England, and may have had more influence there.

Page 37

corpus juris. Body of law.

Page 38

Locke's Essay. John Locke (1632–1704) published *Essay concerning Human Understanding* (1690). His theory of the mind as a blank page appealed to the utilitarians because it underrated the force of heredity, and seemed to show the unlimited possibilities of education. Mill's extreme modesty about his own gifts, and his refusal to acknowledge the obvious fact that he had inherited a powerful intelligence from his father show the influence of this theory combined with a self-effacement which was natural to him.

Helvetius. Claude-Adrien Helvetius (1715–71), one of the 'encyclopedistes', published *De l'esprit* 1758.

Hartley. David Hartley (1705–57). Published *Observations on Man* 1749. His doctrine of 'association of ideas' is in harmony with Locke's. Chiefly remembered for his early influence (later repudiated) on Coleridge.

Analysis of the Mind. Published 1829.

Page 39

Berkeley. George Berkeley (1685–1753), philosopher of mind, opponent of Locke's theories.

Essays. Hume's *Essays Moral and Political* 1741–2.

Reid. Thomas Reid (1710–96), philosopher of empirical school.

Dugald Stewart. Scottish philosopher (1753–1828), disciple of Reid.

230

Cause and Effect. Thomas Brown (1778–1820).

Philip Beauchamp. A pseudonym of George Grote (1794–1871), friend of
Bentham and the Mills, historian of Greece. Published *Analysis* in 1822.

universal. This eccentric judgement, showing ignorance of the power and
sincerity of Evangelical revival, Oxford Movement and Catholic Revival
well illustrates Mill's extraordinary insulation from the intellectual life of
those of his contemporaries not involved with the Benthamite school.

Deism. The remark about Deism is partly true of the time when his father
was young, but strikingly untrue of his own mature years, when Deism
had almost disappeared.

Page 40

Pericles. Pericles, (495–429 BC), Athenian statesman, is a heroic figure in
the early part of Thucydides's history. His naval strategy involved
allowing the Lacedemonian army to besiege Athens and its port, and
ravage the surrounding country. This passage shows how strongly Mill's
emotions could be aroused by learned and difficult historic works.

Attica. District in which Athens lies.

Grote. See note to *Beauchamp* p.39.

Mackintosh. Sir James Mackintosh (1765–1832), philosopher and Whig
politician and theorist.

Edinburgh Review. Influential Whig journal, and doughty opponent of the
utilitarian *Westminster Review.*

Page 41

Bentinck. (1774–1839), 2nd son of 3rd Duke of Portland.

Page 42

Coleridge. S. T. Coleridge (1772–1834), poet, theologian and philosopher,
fascinated Mill, who regarded him as the most profound of religious and
conservative opponents of his father's and his own ideas.

Austin. Charles Austin, lawyer (1799–1874).

Macaulay. T. B. Macaulay (1800–59), politician, Indian administrator and
historian. A leading Whig and writer for the *Edinburgh Review.*

Page 43

Hyde and Charles Villiers. Thomas Hyde Villiers (1801–32) and Charles
(1802–96).

Strutt. Edward Strutt (1801–80).

Romilly. Lord Romilly (1802–74).

haud passibus æquis. Without keeping pace.

Page 44

Utilitarian. A rare case of Mill claiming something to which he was not
entitled. Bentham had used the word before he was born.

Parish. John Galt (1779–1839) published *Annals of the Parish* 1821.
Perhaps the best known Scottish novelist between Walter Scott and
Stevenson.

amanuensis. This was Richard Doane, who, like Mill, had stayed in France with Sir Samuel Bentham.

Tooke. W.E. Tooke (1808–34).

Page 45

Ellis. William Ellis (1800–81).

Roebuck. John Arthur Roebuck (1801–79), radical politician and MP. Allied himself with O'Connell's Irish policy, and was an early advocate of the Ballot, which Mill later came to oppose.

May 1823. Mill was 17 on 20 May 1823. Thus he had gained four or five years over contemporaries who might have hoped for such an appointment after completing a conventional education.

Page 46

Parliament. This shows how early political ambition began. He was elected only in 1865.

friends. Journals of these walking tours exist in holograph MS.

Chapter IV

Page 49

Coulson. Walter Coulson (1794–1850), lawyer.

rejoined. The articles were: R. Torrens, 'Political Economy Club', *Traveller*, 2 December 1822; Mill, 'Exchangeable Value', ibid., 6 December 1822; Torrens, 'Exchangeable Value', ibid., 7 December 1822; Mill, 'Exchangeable Value', ibid., 13 December 1822.

Carlile. Richard Carlile (1790–1843) was imprisoned for a total of nine years four months, for publishing works held to be atheistic or subversive, and for failure or refusal to pay fines and Church rates.

Morning Chronicle. 'Free Discussion', *Morning Chronicle*, 28 January, 8 February and 12 February 1823.

Page 50

article. *Morning Chronicle*, 9 May 1823.

Perry. Sampson Perry (1747–1823).

Black. John Black (1783–1855).

Fonblanque. Albany Fonblanque (1793–1868).

Page 51

Brougham. Henry Brougham, Lord Vaux (1778–1868). Politician, publicist and Lord Chancellor.

Westminster Review. Founded as utilitarian organ 1823–4, largely financed by Bentham.

Quarterly. *Quarterly Review*, founded 1809 as Tory rival to the *Edinburgh*.

Bowring. Sir John Bowring (1792–1872), linguist and traveller.

number. James Mill, 'Periodical Literature', *Westminster*, 1 January 1824.

Page 53

Southern. Henry Southern (1799–1853).

appearance. Mill seems to have confused the first number of the magazine (January 1824) with his own first contribution in April.

Bingham. Peregrine Bingham (1788–1864).

Page 54

Book of the Church. Robert Southey (1774–1843) was in youth an enthusiast for the French Revolution, who later became a High Tory and Poet Laureate. Published *Book of the Church* in 1824.

twelfth. James Mill, *Westminster*, January 1825 and October 1826.

McCulloch. John Ramsey McCulloch (1789–1864) wrote article on bequests, *Edinburgh Review*, July 1824. Austin replied in *Westminster*, October 1824.

History of Greece. Published in 8 vols, 1846–56.

Mitford. Cf. note to p.6.

libel. Article on libel April 1825, game laws January 1826.

represent. Mill shows himself sensitive here to the often-repeated charge of belonging to a party who were only a corporate echo of Bentham's opinions.

Page 55

Alliance. League formed after fall of Napoleon in 1815 by Russia, Austria and Prussia.

Burdetts. Sir Francis Burdett (1770–1854), aristocratic radical.

Cobbetts. William Cobbett (1762–1835), voluminous self-educated author and political agitator, became an MP 1832. The odd plurals given by Mill to these two names may indicate contempt of 'philosophical radicals' for 'sentimental ones'. That it was fully reciprocated may be seen in Dickens's *Hard Times* (1854).

Six Acts. After Peterloo (1819) six acts were passed, restricting drilling, empowering magistrates to search for arms, and severely limiting freedom of the press.

Caroline. Caroline, Princess of Brunswick, estranged Queen of George IV (1768–1821). Her 'trial' was an action for divorce before the House of Lords in which Brougham appeared on her behalf.

Baring. Alexander Baring, 1st Lord Ashburton (1774–1848), one of a famous banking family.

Huskisson. William Huskisson (1770–1830).

Canning. George Canning, Prime Minister (1770–1827).

1846. Repeal of Corn Laws, protective duties on food imports in time of hunger in England and famine in Ireland.

1860. W. E. Gladstone (1809–98). Later Prime Minister, was Chancellor of the Exchequer in 1860.

Peel. Sir Robert Peel (1788–1850). Later Prime Minister.

Page 56

fui. Virgil, *Aeneid* II, 6. 'In which I played a large part'.

Mackintosh. James Mill, *A Fragment on Mackintosh*, 1835.

233

Page 57

Samuel. Sir Samuel Romilly (1757–1818). Law reformer.
Buller. Charles Buller (1806–48). Liberal politician.
Essay on Government. Published in *Encyclopaedia Britannica*, 1820.

Page 58

directed. This paragraph is important for two reasons: (1) It is a
comparatively rare instance of Mill's being able to articulate clearly,
without any of the fudging found in other cases, disagreement with his
father on a major practical issue; (2) It shows that, though Harriet
Taylor no doubt stimulated and intensified his feminism, she was
not its origin.
metaphysics. It is hard to know exactly what is meant here, as Mill would
certainly have rejected the religious basis of Hartley's system. Probably
the stress is on the denial of innate ideas, and the unlimited educability
of the young.
Malthus's population principle. T. R. Malthus (1766–1834) published his
Essay on the Principle of Population in 1793. It argued that population
(growing geometrically) would always tend to outrun food supplies. In a
second edition (1803) the stress was once more on sexual restraint and
the eschewing of early marriage, so that the poorer classes should not be
destitute. Like Ricardo, Malthus was interpreted by those who had not
studied either closely as a prophet of hard-headed fatalistic pessimism.
Writers like Cobbett and Hazlitt rejected him as heartless. One of the
clear dividing lines between 'philosophic' and 'sentimental' radicals is to
be found here.
numbers. This passage brings out very well the double-edged consequences
of Malthus's argument. 'Malthusian' was often used as a euphemism for
support of artificial means of birth control.

Page 59

minds of mankind. Mill's criticism of his father here is only implied, yet the
undercurrent is powerful, and it may be taken as a clear adumbration of
the great issue brought out later in the account of the crisis of 1826,
when Mill learnt by experience how much stronger feeling is than
reason in some areas.
corrupter-general. Bentham's view has not, on the whole, been followed by
later radicals, for whom sentiment and tradition have usually had more
weight than they had for Bentham.
freedom. James Mill showed by his attitude to his son's feeling for Harriet
Taylor, that he ascribed a far higher degree of sanctity to the marriage
bond than his son, or perhaps he himself, thought.

Page 60

human mind. What is important here is what is not said. Mill has recorded
earlier how his father begot a large family upon a woman he despised.
The unspoken question in Mill's mind must have been: 'had he any
right to belittle the strength of the sexual impulse?'

and since. Characteristically, Mill persists in hoping, against accumulating evidence, that his father may after all have been right. Before the *Autobiography* was published, writers like Francis Galton would produce powerful arguments for the importance of heredity in determining ability (e.g. *Hereditary Genius* (1869)).

Page 62

misrepresentation. This phrase alone is enough to show that Mill could never have been a whole-hearted disciple of Bentham. See his remarks about Wordsworth in Chapter V, and his ultra-romantic essay 'Thoughts on Poetry' (1833).

reasoner. Quoted from Bingham 'Moore's Fables for the Holy Alliance', *Westminster*, January 1824.

Essay on Man. Alexander Pope (1688–1744) published *Essay on Man*, the most philosopical of his works 1732–4.

Turgot. A. N. de Condorcet, French philosopher, wrote life of Turgot, economist (1724–81) in 1786.

Page 63

Bingham. Peregrine Bingham (1788–1864) published his edition of Bentham's book in 1824.

lacunæ. Gaps.

Page 64

forego. Mill edited Bentham's *Treatise upon Evidence* 1825–6.

Westminster Hall. Here represents the whole legal profession and its procedure. The Hall itself, built in 1097 by William Rufus, is the only surviving part of the original Palace of Westminster.

Fragment ... Establishment. Bentham's *Fragment on Government*, published anonymously in 1776, was an attack on Blackstone's *Commentaries*. *Plan for the Organisation of the Judicial Establishment in France* published 1790.

Goldsmith. See note p.9.

Fielding. Henry Fielding (1707–54), novelist.

Pascal. Blaise Pascal (1623–62), French religious philosopher.

Voltaire. French playwright and philosopher (1694–1778).

Courier. P. L. Courier (1772–1825), French pamphleteer.

Page 65

Fallacies. Bentham's *Book of Fallacies* published 1824.

Hansard. Official record of Parliamentary debates.

Review. The *Parliamentary Review* appeared from 1825 to 1828.

much in it. e.g. Bingham on 'Combination Laws', 'County Courts' and 'Licensing'; C. Austin on 'Corn laws'; James Mill on 'Conduct of Parliament'; Coulson on 'Game Laws'.

Disabilities. Mill wrote on 'Ireland', 'Paper Currency', 'Trade with India', and 'United States relation to West Indies'.

Page 66

Threadneedle Street. In London EC2, the street in which the Bank of England is situated.

Prescott. W.G. Prescott (1790–1864).

Ricardo's … Political Economy. Published in 1817.

Dissertation on Value. Samuel Bailey (1791–1870) published this book in 1825.

Essays on … Political Economy. Mill published this in 1844.

Page 67

Aldrich. Artis logicae compendium 1691.

Du Trieu. Phillipus Du Trieu published *Manductio ad Logicam* in 1662.

Whately's Logic. Richard Whately (1787–1863), fellow of Oriel, Oxford and later Anglican Archbishop of Dublin, published his *Logic* in 1826.

Hobbes. Thomas Hobbes (1588–1679) published *Computatio sive Logica* 1655.

Logic. Mill's *System of Logic* was published in 1843.

Priestley's edition. David Hartley (1705–57) published *Observations on Man* 1749. Priestley's abridgement was published 1775.

Page 68

Owenites. Followers of Robert Owen (1771–1858), factory owner and pioneer of socialism. Described by the Dictionary of National Biography as 'one of those intolerable bores who are the salt of the earth'.

Chancery Lane. London WC2, a road associated with legal practice.

Inns of Court. Lincoln's Inn, Middle Temple, Inner Temple and Gray's Inn. Legal societies to which London barristers belong.

Thompson. William Thomson (?1785–1833).

Thirlwall. Connop Thirlwall, Bishop of St David's (1797–1874). Published *History of Greece* in 8 vols, 1835–44.

Page 69

Horner. Francis Horner (1778–1817).

Freemason's Tavern. In Great Queen St., London WC2.

Praed. W.M. Praed (1802–39). Chiefly remembered for skill in comic verse.

Howick. Lord Howick, later 3rd Earl Grey (1802–94), Whig politician, opponent of slavery and of Crimean War.

Wilberforce. Samuel Wilberforce (1805–73), youngest son of William Wilberforce, Evangelical campaigner against slavery. High Church bishop of Oxford and Winchester. Generally known as 'soapy Sam'.

Thomson. Lord Sydenham (1799–1841).

Bulwer. Sir Edward, later 1st Lord Lytton (1803–73), novelist and politician, and Sir Henry, later Lord Dalling (1801–72).

member of parliament. This unnamed man was Donald McLean (1800–74), MP for Oxford 1835–47.

Page 70

debate. Cf. Speeches pp.171–212 of this vol.

Hayward, and Shee. Abraham Hayward (1801–84) and Sir William Shee (1804–68).

Cockburn. Sir Alexander Cockburn (1802–80).

Maurice. F.D. Maurice (1805–72). Disciple of Coleridge, Broad Church theologian and Christian Socialist.

Sterling. John Sterling (1806–44). Disciple of Coleridge. Remembered mainly because Thomas Carlyle wrote his life.

new generation. This is one of the passages where what Mill does not say is as interesting as what he does. Maurice, Sterling and others were almost exact contemporaries, and Mill himself was, in years, still a boy at this time. But the passage reveals a wistful awareness that the C18 enlightenment view of Bentham and his father was about to be superseded, and that, though he would hanker after it with one part of his complex split personality all his life, it would never return. His deeper meditations on the subject are to be found in his essays on Bentham and Coleridge.

Page 72

article. James Mill: 'The Ballot', *Westminster Review* July 1830.

Sir Walter Scott. Sir Walter Scott (1771–1832) published *Life of Napoleon*, 9 vols, 1827.

Carlyle. Carlyle's masterpiece *The French Revolution* was published 1837, after the first draft, lent to Mill, had been accidentally burnt by a servant. As Carlyle had no regular source of income, Mill offered him £200, of which Carlyle accepted half.

Chapter V

Page 74

Dejection. 'Dejection: an Ode'. The significance of Mill's turning, perhaps without conscious deliberation, to a poet whom he would identify as the arch-enemy of Bentham and his father, was no doubt due to his helpless sense that they knew nothing of the feelings he was experiencing, and little of human nature in general.

thoughts:
> 'Canst thou not minister to a mind diseas'd
> Pluck from the memory a rooted sorrow,
> Raze out the written troubles of the brain,
> And with some sweet oblivious antidote
> Cleanse the stuff'd bosom of that perilous stuff
> Which weighs upon the heart.' (*Macbeth* V, iii. 40–45).

It is significant again that Mill found the best account of his state in the poet whom only Bentham and his father failed to recognize as the greatest in England.

Page 77

cannot live. The last two lines of a short poem composed by Coleridge, 21 February 1825.

Marmontel's Memoirs. J.-F. Marmontel (1723–99). The obvious significance of the fact that reading about the death of a father was a source of recovery was never mentioned by Mill. It is actually possible that he never even thought it.

Page 78

Carlyle. Carlyle later described in *Sartor Resartus* (1833–4) a crisis in some respects similar to Mill's, and concluded that a man should do his duty without expecting to be happy.

Page 79

Weber's Oberon. K.M. Weber (1786–1826) produced *Oberon* in 1826.

Page 80

Mozart. Wolfgang Amadeus Mozart (1756–91), the great Austrian composer

Laputa. In the third book of *Gulliver's Travels* (1726) by Jonathan Swift (1667–1745). The 'philosophers' are what we should call scientific madmen.

1828. Mill must have been one of the last readers of high intellectual tastes to discover the poetry of William Wordsworth (1770–1850), whose great period was long past at this time; but it is not surprising given his father's preference for information and argument over imagination.

Byron. Lord Byron (1788–1824) also came very late to Mill's attention.

Harold. Childe Harold's Pilgrimage (1812–18).

Manfred. Manfred, a poetic drama (1817).

Giaours. The Giaour (1813).

Laras. Lara (1814).

Page 81

Excursion. Published by Wordsworth in 9 books 1814.

Immortality. Intimations of Immortality from Recollections of Early Childhood (1807). Mill's comment 'falsely called Platonic' is interesting (and puzzling). Plato's doctrine of 'anamnesis' is expounded in the *Meno* and the *Phaedo,* the dialogues designed to prove that the soul is immortal. Socrates proposes that we 'remember' things that happened before our birth. For Wordsworth, probably, this is a poetic image rather than a truth literally proposed. In any case, the poem's connection with Plato is indubitable. For Mill to wish to deny it perhaps shows a yearning for a more rationalist, less religious writer than the Plato of history.

Page 82

unpoetical natures. This judgement is directly opposite to the traditional one; it is due perhaps to Mill's comparative unawareness of his own imaginative and intensely emotional nature.

theory. The debate was on 30 January 1829.

Page 83

necessary evils. A strange judgement, probably attributable once again to his unusual disposition to regard Bentham and his father as more significant and more typical of English thought than they were.

laws and relations. Here Mill to some extent redresses the balance in this passage of eloquent praise of imagination.

Hare and Carlyle. J. C. Hare (1795–1855), archdeacon of Lewes, published his life of Sterling in 1848. Carlyle's came in 1851.

Page 84

Goethe. J. W. von Goethe (1749–1832), great German poet. Carlyle did much to make him known in England.

Thirty-nine articles. The articles to which Anglican clergymen are required to subscribe.

Page 85

Fortschreitung. Wonderful power of development.

Page 86

Bacon's principles. He refers to Bacon's advocacy of inductive reasoning, especially in *The Advancement of Learning* (1605).

Essay on Government. T. B. Macaulay's 'Mill's Essay on Government' (*Edinburgh*, March 1829) and Bentham's 'Defence of Mill' (ibid. June 1829). Characteristically by introducing the irrelevant examples of physical scientists into a strictly political discussion, Mill hides from himself the completeness of Macaulay's dialectical triumph over his father.

against reason. See *English Works of Thomas Hobbes*, Ed. W. Molesworth, 11 vols (1839–45), Vol. IV, p.xiii.

Page 88

Moral Sciences. In *System of Logic* Bk. VI.

Reviews. e.g. on Richter, *Edinburgh*, June 1927, on Werner, *Foreign Review*, January 1828.

Page 89

many-sidedness. See Sarah Austin, *Characteristics of Goethe*, I, pp.12–13.

Page 90

Present Age. J. G. Fichte *The Characteristics of the Present Age* (Tr. W. Smith 1847).

Auguste Comte. Auguste Comte (1798–1857), the founder of Positivism, claimed that his system, described by T. H. Huxley as 'Catholicism minus Christianity', was destined to supersede Christianity.

A positivist congregation lingered in London until living memory. (See T. R. Wright, *The Religion of Humanity*, Cambridge 1986.)

Page 91

Bazard and Enfantin. Amand Bazard (1791–1832) and Barthélemy Enfantin (1796–1864).

Fourier. Charles Fourier (1772–1837).

Page 92

Fox. Charles James Fox (1749–1806).

quoad. In respect of.

Page 93

Logic. Bk. VI, chap. ii.

the State. Mill means the remains of the C18 spoils system. As, during the first half of the nineteenth century, official corruption was reduced, so did Mill and others become more sympathetic to social and economic action by the state.

Page 94

July. The Revolution of 29 July 1830, which resulted in Louis Philippe becoming king.

Lafayette. Marquis de Lafayette (1757–1834) helped to put Louis Philippe on the throne.

Lord Grey. Charles Grey, 2nd Earl Grey (1764–1845). Prime Minister in 1832.

Reform Bill. Widening the franchise. Passed 7 June 1832.

Spirit of the Age. Articles in *The Examiner* among others. 9 January, 23 January, 6 February, 13 March, 15 and 29 May, 1831.

Page 95

Sartor Resartus. It was perhaps characteristic of Mill to prefer Carlyle's most personal work, an opinion few have shared.

mystic. For these letters of January 1834, see *Letters of T. and J. W. Carlyle*, VII, 72. Though we will probably reject Carlyle's view that Mill was a Mystic, as Mill himself did, yet it is a useful corrective to the view of some contemporaries that his father had succeeded into turning him into an unfeeling machine.

Page 96

poet. An interesting example of the influence upon Mill of ultra-romantic critical theory. Carlyle was, obviously, not a poet in a literal sense, since he wrote exclusively in prose. But Shelley and others had used the word 'poet' to mean something like 'prophet', and Mill is (unconsciously perhaps) echoing this use.

more a thinker than I. The first allusion to Harriet Taylor, with the characteristic exaggeration of her talents.

Lectures. Published as *The Province of Jurisprudence Determined* (Murray, 1832).

Page 97

human nature. See Mill's essay 'Civilization' in *Essays on Politics and Society*.

Page 98

fifth Essay. 'On the Definition of Political Economy', *London and Westminster Review*, October 1836.

Dugald Stewart. Dugald Stewart, *Elements of the Philosophy of the Human Mind*, II, 28–49

Page 99

Tait's Magazine. 'The Currency Jungle' and 'Writings of Junius Redivivus' (*Tait's*, January and June, 1833).

Jurist. 'Corporation and Church Property' (*Jurist*, February 1833).
Dissertations and Discussions. Published in 2 vols, Parker 1859. Hereafter
    D&D.

Chapter VI

Page 101
my wife. Harriet Taylor.

Page 102
deceased. Eliza Flower (1803–46).
Shelley. P.B. Shelley, poet (1792–1822).

Page 103
mala in se. Evils in themselves.
mala prohibita. Offences against convention.

Page 104
Representative Government. Published 1861.
Democracy in America. Published in French 1835–40 by Alexis de
    Tocqueville (1805–59).

Page 105
1835. *London Review*, October 1835, *Edinburgh Review*, October 1840.

Page 106
Poor Law Reform of 1834. 14 August 1834. This law, abolishing outdoor
    relief, and enforcing upon married paupers single sex residence in the
    workhouse, was illustrative of the great divide between *philosophic* and
    sentimental radicals. To the former it was a tidy improvement on lax C18
    ways. To the latter (cf. Dickens in *Oliver Twist*) it was a monstrous
    inhumanity perpetrated by soulless bureaucrats. Mill almost sounds like
    Bentham himself (somewhat untypically) when he dismisses feeling for
    the family affections and Dicken's white-hot anger as 'irrational
    clamour'.
Irish Coercion Bill and *Canada coercion*. Enacted 2 April 1833 and
    10 February 1838.
Hume and O'Connell. Joseph Hume (1777–1855) and Daniel O'Connell
    (1775–1847), 'the liberator', whose election for an Irish constituency
    led to Catholic emancipation (1829).

Page 107
Parliament. A characteristic misjudgement. It is hard to think of a man of
    ability more certain to be a political failure than James Mill.
Molesworth (1810–55). Wealthy radical politician, and financial benefactor
    of *Westminster Review*.

Page 108
Monthly Repository. March–September 1834.

Fox. W. J. Fox (1786–1864).

Dissertations. A conflation of earlier versions of this, one of the most revealing of Mill's works, was published as *Thoughts on Poetry and Its Varieties*, *D&D*, Vol. I.

1834. 'Notes on Some of the More Popular Dialogues of Plato.' *Monthly Repository*, February–March, June–September, October–December 1834. Also February–March 1835.

England and the English. By Edward Lytton Bulwer, 2 vols, 1833.

Page 109

other writers. James Mill contributed articles on State of the Nation, the Ballot, Church and its Reform, Law Reform, Aristocracy, Political Economy, Theory and Practice in 1835–6.

Professor Sedgwick. Adam Sedgwick (1785–1873), geologist.

Discourse on the Studies of Cambridge. Published in 1833.

Locke and Paley. For Locke see note to p.38. Archdeacon William Paley (1743–1805), author of *Evidences of Christianity*.

Page 110

Civilization. *D&D*, Vol. I.

Page 111

progress. A touching, though inept, piece of filial piety.

Romans. Shakespeare, *Julius Caesar* V, iii, 99.

nineteenth. An interesting glimpse; but Mill fails either to place himself in relation to these two periods, or to perceive the full implications of his own admission that his father was by now far out of date.

Page 112

India. This could only be true if the argument of *On Liberty* was totally false, or if human nature was simply a different thing in Europe and India, neither of which propositions Mill could have entertained for a moment.

women. Harriet Taylor, of course.

Robertson. John Robertson of Aberdeen.

Page 113

Whewell. William Whewell (1794–1866), Master of Trinity College, Cambridge, friend of Tennyson, published *History of the Inductive Sciences*, 3 vols, 1837.

Philosophy. Sir J. Herschel (1792–1871) published *Natural Philosophy* 1831. Reviewed by Mill *Examiner* March 1831.

Page 114

Review. 'Parties and the Ministry' and 'Armand Carrel', *London and Westminster*, October 1837.

Philosophie Positive. 6 vols, 1830–42.

Page 115

adverted. Comte *Système de Politique Positive*, 1824.

latter. Mill often said that he tended to sympathize with mediaeval Popes in their contests with Emperors and Kings. This opinion sets him apart from standard Enlightenment views, especially those of Voltaire.

Positive. A different work to that referred to above with the same main title. Published in 4 vols, 1851–4.

Loyola. St. Ignatius (1491–1556) founder and first general of Society of Jesus.

Page 117

Durham. John George Lambton, 1st Earl of Durham (1792–1840).

honour. Mill's article was published in *London and Westminster*, August 1838, 'Lord Durham and his Assailants.'

Page 118

Coleridge. The essays on Bentham and Coleridge were republished together with an introduction by F. R. Leavis (Chatto 1950).

Page 119

Hickson. W. E. Hickson (1803–70).

Chapter VII

Page 121

de novo. Afresh.

Page 122

Sciences. Cf. note to *Whewell* p.113.

Page 123

1850. Whewell *Of Induction, with Especial Reference to Mr. J. Stuart Mill's System of Logic* (1849). See preface to 3rd ed. of Mill's *Logic*.

Page 125

Taylor. John Taylor married Harriet 14 March 1826, and died 18 July 1849.

true one. This passage shows obvious embarrassment. We need not doubt the truth of what appears, in the circumlocutory phrases, to be asserted: that Mill and Harriet did not have carnal relations during John Taylor's life. But it is hardly true that the concealments and evasions practised gave *not the slightest ground for any other supposition*. See Introduction for fuller discussion.

Page 126

shall not eat. Cf. 2 Thessalonians Ch. iii, v. 10. It is perhaps characteristic that Mill is unwilling to give the Biblical source of his view here, so opposite to that of the classical civilization admired by his father.

Page 127

foster it. Here Mill raises the most fundamental of all political questions, oddly oblivious of doing so. The alternative view that it is the inherent selfishness of human beings which causes bad institutions or tends to the corruption of good ones, deserves, one would think, some consideration at least.

Page 128

third. 1st ed. 1848, 2nd 1849, 3rd 1852.

Ireland. A series of 43 leading articles, running from 5 October 1846–7 January 1847.

Poor Law. Enacted 8 June 1847.

Page 129

Horatian precept. To keep it nine years. *Nonumque prematur in annum* (*Ars Poetica* l.388).

December 1851. The extinction of the brief Second Republic in France, and the accession of the Emperor Napoleon III.

Page 131

Politicians. The extraordinary bitterness of tone in this paragraph (unparalleled probably in the rest of the work) is highly revealing. It would be hard to imagine an abuse more certain to incur the hostility of radicals than the power of a single commercial interest over hundreds of millions of people many thousands of miles away. Yet because he and perhaps, more especially, his father had given much of their professional lives to it, he implies that it should have been sacrosanct. The unusual ill-temper is shown, too, in the phrase *Parliament, in other words Lord Palmerston.* Mill knew perfectly well that it is normal for the Government, headed by the Prime Minister, to initiate legislation, and that, since all governments as a condition of their survival have a majority in the House of Commons, it commonly happens that what governments propose becomes law. Mill shows a marvellous lack of self-knowledge here. Henry John Temple, 3rd Viscount Palmerston (1784–1865). The supersession of the East India Company came in 1858.

Representative Government. Ch. xvii. *Of the Government of Dependencies by a Free State.*

Page 132

Stanley. Edward Henry Stanley (1826–93), eldest son of 14th Earl Derby, succeeded father 1869.

Capitol. The Roman setting here recalls Gibbon's account of the genesis, also in Rome, of his history. It is not clear whether this consciously occurred to Mill.

comfort. Helen Taylor (1831–1907), the original editor of the *Autobiography.*

Page 135
Labouring Classes. Bk. IV, ch. vii.

Page 138
Pestalozzi. Johann Heinrich Pestalozzi (1746–1827), Swiss educational
theorist.
Humboldt. Wilhelm von Humboldt (1767–1835), German philologist.

Page 139
Fichte. J. G. Fichte (1762–1814), German philosopher.
Maccall. William Maccall (1812–88), published *Elements of Individualism*
1847.
Reform. Published 1859.

Page 140
Ballot. On this great issue of mid-Victorian controversy (finally enacted by
Gladstone's Liberal administration in 1872), Mill was at odds with most
radical and 'advanced' opinion, and agreed with many Tories, and
conservative-minded Whigs. All agreed that the Ballot (secret voting)
would reduce the influence of landlords, employers, and the prosperous
classes generally. Mill's view was that no-one who would not exercise
the vote fearlessly deserved to have it.
Marshall. J. G. Marshall published *Minorities and Majorities: Their Relative
Rights* in 1853.
1859. Lord Derby (1799–1869) and Benjamin Disraeli, 1st Lord
Beaconsfield (1804–81), failed to carry a Reform Bill in 1859, but were
successful in doing so in 1867.
Representation. Thomas Hare, *A Treatise on the Election of Representatives,
Parliamentary and Municipal* (1859).

Page 141
writings. 'Recent writers on Reform', *Fraser's Magazine*, April 1859.
Austin. John Austin, *A Plea for the Constitution*, 1859.
Lorimer. James Lorimer, *Political Progress Not Necessarily Democratic*, 1857.
treatise on the Mind. Alexander Bain (1818–1903) published *The Senses and
the Intellect* (1855) and *The Emotions and the Will* (1859).

Page 142
Suez Canal. Constructed 1859–69. The British Government acquired a
large interest in 1875.
Dissertations. Brougham's *Letter to the Marquess of Lansdowne* (1848),
reviewed by Mill, *Westminster*, April 1849, under title 'The French
Revolution of 1848 and Its Assailants.'

Page 144
Subjection of Women. Published 1869.
volume. Fraser's Magazine, October–December 1861, reprinted 1863.

Page 145

Slave Power. John E. Cairnes, *The Slave Power: Its Character, Career and Probable Designs* (1862).

Garrison. W. L. Garrison (1805–79).

Phillips. Wendell Phillips (1811–84).

Brown. John Brown (1800–59).

Page 146

Hughes. Thomas Hughes (1822–96), disciple of Thomas Arnold, author of *Tom Brown's Schooldays* (1857). Liberal M.P. Wrote 'Opinion on American Affairs', *Macmillan's,* September 1861.

Ludlow. John Malcolm Forbes Ludlow (1821–1911).

Bright. John Bright (1811–89), famous campaigner of the 'Anti-Corn-Law League' in the 1840s. Speech *On America* 4 December 1861.

United States. Charles Wilkes seized the Southern envoys, J. M. Mason and J. Sidell.

Page 147

America. Fraser's, February 1862.

study. 'Austin on Jurisprudence', *Edinburgh,* October 1863.

Philosophy. Sir William Hamilton (1788–1856). *Lectures on Metaphysics and Logic* published posthumously 1859–60. Mill's dating is a mistake. Mill's attack published 1865.

Notes to Reid. Works of Thomas Reid, ed. W. Hamilton, 1846.

Page 148

Discussions. Discussions on Philosophy and Literature, Education and University Reform. Published 1852.

Page 149

proofs. It would be interesting to know what these proofs are.

treatise. See note to p.141. Mill treats two works as one.

followers. H. L. Mansel (1820–71). Mill refers to *The Limits of Religious Thought* (1858).

same names. Cf. Mill's *Examination. Collected Works,* Vol. IX.

Page 151

Positivism. Published 1865. Retracts earlier more favourable view of Comte.

Lucas. Frederick Lucas (1812–55). Catholic journalist and politician. An English convert from Quakerism with a special interest in Irish questions.

Duffy. Sir Charles Gavin Duffy (1816–1903). Irish nationalist and colonial politician.

Page 152

locality. Mill proved his sincerity by contributing substantially to the expenses of like-minded candidates, while refusing to pay his own.

Page 153

publication. Mill is conflating two letters to James Beal, 7 March and 21 April 1865.

liars. Collected Works, Vol. XIX, p.338.

Page 154

responded. The meeting took place on 8 July 1865, in the Pimlico Rooms, Winchester Street.

competitor. W. H. Smith, elected in 1868, and later became a Cabinet minister, trusted by Lord Salisbury for his administrative acumen.

Reform Bill. Enacted 15 August 1867.

Bill. This bill, which did not become law, was debated in spring 1866. Mill's speech was on 13 April.

Page 155

capital punishment. Speech of 21 April 1868. Mill's view here was, as on so many issues, conservative.

neutral vessels. Speech of 5 August 1867.

suffrage. Speech of 20 May 1867.

Representation. Speech of 30 May 1867.

Ayrton. Acton Smee Ayrton (1816–86).

Ireland. Motion proposed 8 February 1866 by Daniel O'Donaghue.

McLaren. Duncan McLaren (1800–86).

Potter. T. B. Potter (1817–98).

Hadfield. George Hadfield (1787–1789).

Page 156

Ireland. Suspension was 17 February 1866. Mill's speech on the same day.

Fenianism. A brotherhood, formed in 1864, for the overthrow of English rule in Ireland.

exhausted. Speech of 17 April 1866.

stupidest party. Speech of 31 May 1866, defending remark in *Considerations on Representative Government*.

Reform Bill. Speech of 9 May 1867.

Page 157

crowd. This episode was widely regarded as very grave. See Matthew Arnold's *Culture and Anarchy* (1869).

Beales. Edmond Beales (1803–81), president of the Reform League.

Walpole. Spencer Horatio Walpole (1806–98), Home Secretary in Lord Derby's administration.

attended. Mill's speech was reported in *The Times*, 31 July 1866.

suffrage. Because of his support for female franchise.

ballot. Cf. note to *Ballot* p.140.

Page 158

talking it out. Bill of 3 May 1867, which did not become law.

Lord Derby. 14th Earl Derby (1799–1869).

Burke. General Burke (1829–78), Irish nationalist.
carried. Bill of 30 April 1866, which did not become law.
speeches. Mill's speech, 17 May 1866.
Government. Bill of 18 February 1867.
menacing aspect. Mill was not a Home Ruler, and died before this issue
 became serious at Westminster in 1886. His Irish policy might be
 described as 'killing Home Rule by kindness'.

Page 159
England and Ireland. Published 1868, reached 5th edition following year.
Land Bill. Enacted 1 August 1870.

Page 160
Resolution. J. F. Maguire (1815–72). Mill's speech 12 March 1868.
negro slavery. Not quite fair. For instance, Dickens, certainly never a
 supporter of negro slavery, was a supporter of Governor Eyre.
Buxton. Charles Buxton (1823–71).

Page 161
best of my speeches. 31 July 1866.
Bow Street. London WC2.
Cockburn. Sir Alexander Cockburn (1802–80).
Old Bailey. Central Criminal Court, London EC4.

Page 162
assassination. A note by Helen Taylor in Columbia MS states that threats
 of assassination were received at least once a week.
despotisms. Act of 26 July 1866.
political. Act of 9 August 1870.
Government. Act of 31 July 1868.
Christie. W. D. Christie (1816–74).
Pulling. Alexander Pulling (1813–95).
Chadwick. Sir Edwin Chadwick (1800–90), famous as sanitary reformer.
Fawcett. Henry Fawcett (1833–84).

Page 163
spoke. 26 March 1868.
Judges. This measure laid to rest a long history of controversy, as when
 Wilkes was excluded by earlier Houses of Commons.
General Election. Of 1868, which led to Gladstone's first administration.
Anstruther. Sir Robert Anstruther (1824–88).
remedy. Cf. note to *Ballot* p.140.
adopt. Mill's speech, 5 July 1867.

Page 164
Board. Act of 9 August 1870.
women. Among them Barbara Bodichon, Mentia Taylor and the
 educationalist Emily Davies. George Eliot refused.

Page 165

Miss Nightingale and Miss Mary Carpenter. Florence Nightingale (1820–1910) pioneer of nursing by educated ladies, and Mary Carpenter (1807–77) philanthropist and educationalist.

Page 166

Plato. 'Grote's Plato', *Edinburgh Review*, April 1866.

Rector. A prestigious post, held by direct election of the students. Among other Rectors was Carlyle.

Page 167

Analysis ... Mind. 2nd ed, J. S. Mill, Longmans, 1869 Mill seems to have been almost alone at this time in thinking the book admirable.

Findlater. Andrew Findlater (1810–85).

thrown out. Although the Liberal Party won, Mill's particular friends did badly. Lord Amberley was defeated, and Roebuck lost his seat after nearly twenty years. Some thought that Mill's action in contributing to the election expenses of Charles Bradlaugh, atheist candidate at Northampton, may have helped to cause his defeat.

Page 168

Reform Bill. Disraeli's resolution was presented 11 February 1867.

suffrage. Of course, including women.

Page 169

Bradlaugh. Charles Bradlaugh (1833–91) was the subject of prolonged controversy in the 1880s because he claimed the right to affirm at his initiation to the House of Commons, but on this occasion (1868) he was defeated at the polls. Cf. note to *thrown out* p.167.

competitor. Again, W. H. Smith.

Page 170

Fortnightly Review. Mill published two articles at this time, 'Endowments', April 1869, and 'Thornton on Labour' May–June 1869. John Morley (1838–1923) was later to become a Liberal Cabinet Minister, who resigned in 1914, because of his opposition to war with Germany.

finish them. In addition to the *Autobiography*, Helen Taylor published after Mill's death in 1873 his *Three Essays on Religion* (1874).

Speeches

Page 171

1823. Mill was 17 in May 1823. The manner of these speeches is that of the Oxford Union. So, once again, Mill was younger by several years than young men making similar speeches after formal education.

Rousseau. J.-J. Rousseau (1712–78). Mill's hostility to his primitivism is at first surprising.

Hurons and Iroquois. Indian tribes in America, here used as types of primitive civilization.

mala fide. With bad faith.

happiness. Bentham's utilitarian principle assumed as self-evident.

Page 172

with it. Ironical in view of the account in the *Autobiography* of his feelings in 1826, when he found aiming at happiness only made him unhappy.

Page 174

lost sight. It would be instructive to have a list of those (if any) who have ignored so obvious a point.

kings. This is a good example of the oblivion of actual history to which Macaulay drew attention in criticizing James Mill – and Mill was too young to have deviated very far from his father as yet. Did it not occur to him that Catholic priests were still proscribed by the monarchical and aristocratic government of England?

Page 175

priesthood. Presumably the Anglican clergy.

Page 176

Utopia. Utopia (Gk, nowhere) published by St Thomas More in 1516.

golden age. Mythical time in many cultures without sin or trouble.

Page 177

Baring. Alexander Baring, Lord Ashburton (1774–1848), banker.

Cribb. Tom Cribb (1781–1848), famous boxer.

despot … score. Napoleon defeated, various kings restored.

Chelsea hospital. Royal Hospital, Chelsea SW3, founded by Charles II for the care of disabled soldiers.

Wellesley. Sir Arthur Wellesley, Duke of Wellington (1769–1852), the victor of Waterloo.

ceteris paribus. Other things being equal.

Page 178

quartern loaf. Refers to Corn Laws, taxing imported food.

Languedoc. A characteristic preference for France.

free. Helots were Spartan slaves. The words reflect Mill's partisanship for Athens derived from excited reading of Thucydides.

Page 179

hodie mihi, cras tibi. To-day for me, to-morrow for you.

Page 180

Civil List. Royal income voted by Parliament.

999. This whole passage is in the style of Æsop, one of Mill's early Greek books.

Page 181

Game Laws. Severe laws against poaching, a particular radical grievance, since so many members of Parliament were landlords.

Six Acts. Cf. note to *Six Acts* p.55.

Massacre. The shooting in St. Peter's Square, Manchester which led to eleven deaths in an anti-Corn Law crowd on 16 August 1819. *Peterloo* was coined on analogy of *Waterloo.*

Page 182

Castlereagh. Robert Stewart, 2nd Marquis of Londonderry (1769–1822), better known as Lord Castlereagh, Foreign Secretary.

guillotine. Presumably means the hangman. An odd example of his preoccupation with France.

Page 187

education and public opinion. **An** obvious example of Mill's tendency in youth to advance a dubious opinion, and pre-empt discussion of it by saying that it was *proved.* It is hard (or impossible) to imagine how such a proposition could be 'proved'; and certain that it never has been.

Page 188

dreaded. A characteristic anti-English generalization, for which no evidence is given, or perhaps could be given.

Page 189

Combe. George Combe (1788–1858), phrenologist.

Page 191

Montesquieu. Charles de Montesquieu (1689–1755), political philosopher, most celebrated for *De l'Esprit des Lois* (1748).

Page 192

sect. Mill was unconsciously prophetic here. He was to diverge much farther from Bentham's and his father's views than he will have been aware in 1829.

Page 200

face of the earth. Mill would have been gavelled if asked how he could possibly know which nations were happiest. The persistent nineteenth century radical preference for France and the United States is, however, characteristic. See the American chapters of *Martin Chuzzlewit,* for further contrast between the philosophic and the sentimental radicals.

Page 202

Carlile. See note to p.49.

Page 203

Sheridan. R.B. Sheridan (1751–1816), comic playwright.

Vice. Unusually, the prosecution was initiated by private citizens, of whom the Duke of Wellington was one.

Clarendon. Edward Hyde, 1st Earl of Clarendon (1609–74), statesman and historian of the Civil War.

Page 204

ipso facto. By that fact alone.

Test Act. Act passed 1673, repealed 1828, requiring holders of public
offices to receive the sacrament in the Church of England.

Arbuthnot. John Arbuthnot (1667–1735), *The History of John Bull* (1712).

Page 205

Uniformity. Act of 1662, obliging holders of church livings to be ordained
by bishops, to assent to the Prayer Book, and to declare the
unlawfulness of bearing arms against the sovereign.

Occasional Conformity Act. An Act passed in 1711, but found ineffective
and soon repealed. Its aim was to prevent dissenters who held public
office from fulfilling the letter of the Test Act by receiving Holy
Communion from an Anglican clergyman.

Page 206

derision. Probably a reference to Brougham's *Society for the Diffusion of
Useful Knowledge,* parodied by T. L. Peacock as *The Steam Intellect
Society.* (See *Crotchet Castle.*) Perhaps the tone of this passage helps to
explain why Peacock, Mill's most eminent literary colleague at India
House, is not mentioned in the *Autobiography.*

Page 209

London. London University, unlike Oxford and Cambridge at this time, did
not require subscription to The 39 Articles.

Page 210

Corn Law League. Probably short for Anti-Corn Law League, founded
1838 by Richard Cobden (1804–65) and others.

The Times. Complaints about the domineering influence of *The Times* are
common in C19 literature. One of the most amusing is *The Jupiter* in
Trollope's *The Warden* (1855).

Cobden. Cf. note to *Corn Law League* above.

Select Bibliography

Manuscript Sources

The Mill-Taylor Collection. British Library of Political and Economic
    Science, London School of Economics.
The John Stuart Mill Collection. Yale University Library.
The Keynes Library. King's College, Cambridge.
The National Library of Scotland. Letters between Mill and Carlyle.
The Library of Mount Holyoake College, South Hadley, Mass. Holograph
    diary of walking tour 1832.

James Mill

James Mill: *The History of British India*. 4th ed. Ed. H. H. Wilson. 9 vols
    (1848).
W. H. Burston (Ed.): *James Mill on Education* (1969).

John Stuart Mill

Collected Works of John Stuart Mill (Toronto: from 1963).
Autobiography. Ed. Helen Taylor. (1873).
Autobiography. Ed. John Jacob Coss. (New York: 1924).
Autobiography. Ed. Harold J. Laski. (1924).
Alexander Bain: *John Stuart Mill* (1882).
Jack Stillinger: 'The Text of John Stuart Mill's *Autobiography*,' *Bulletin of
    the John Rylands Library*, XLIII, Sept 1960. pp.220–242.
    The Early Draft of John Stuart Mill's "Autobiography". (Urbana: 1961).
    John Stuart Mill's Autobiography. Ed. with introduction. (Boston: 1969).

General

Mazlish Bruce: *James and J. S. Mill* (1975).
F. A. Hayek: *John Stuart Mill and Harriet Taylor* (1951).
Josephine Mary Kamm: *John Stuart Mill in Love* (1977).
Michael St. John Packe: *The Life of John Stuart Mill* (1954).
H. O. Pappe: *John Stuart Mill and the Harriet Taylor Myth* (1960).
William Thomas: *Mill* (1985).